MONSTERS

MONSTERS

THE
1985
CHICAGO BEARS
AND THE
WILD HEART
OF
FOOTBALL

RICH COHEN

FARRAR, STRAUS AND GIROUX   NEW YORK

Farrar, Straus and Giroux
18 West 18th Street, New York 10011

Library of Congress Cataloging-in-Publication Data
Cohen, Rich.
    Monsters: the 1985 Chicago Bears and the wild heart of football / Rich Cohen.
        pages   cm
    Includes bibliographical references and index.
    ISBN 978-0-374-29868-5 (hardback) — ISBN 978-0-374-70895-5 (ebook)
    1. Chicago Bears (Football team)—History.   I. Title.

GV956.C5 C65 2013
796.332′640977311—dc23

                                                            2013021701

Designed by Abby Kagan

Farrar, Straus and Giroux books may be purchased for educational, business,
or promotional use. For information on bulk purchases, please contact
the Macmillan Corporate and Premium Sales Department at 1-800-221-7945,
extension 5442, or write to specialmarkets@macmillan.com.

www.fsgbooks.com
www.twitter.com/fsgbooks • www.facebook.com/fsgbooks

1   3   5   7   9   10   8   6   4   2

FOR MY OLD MAN,

who never told me what to love but did show me how

And none of the other men
failed to protect him; they all held their shields out in front
and lifted him up and carried him out of the fighting
to the horses waiting for him at the rear of the battle
with their charioteer and handsome, bronze-inlaid car;
and they brought him, groaning with pain, back toward the city.
But when they came to the ford of the swirling Xanthus,
they lifted him out, laid him upon the ground,
splashed water over his face, and he came to
and opened his eyes and got onto his knees
and coughed up dark blood, then sank back to earth, and night
covered his eyes, for the mighty blow still overwhelmed him.
> —Homer, *Iliad* (translated by Stephen Mitchell)

. . . but the way I got spun around and nailed in the side by a helmet
right where I was vulnerable . . . well, I knew I was in big trouble. I was
rasping, croaking when I got back to the huddle. I called an audible
designed for Willie Gault, but when I threw the ball, he wasn't there.
It got picked off. Willie had a good reason for not being where I thought
he'd be. "I couldn't hear you, Mac," he said. "Are you hurting?" Was I
ever. I told Steve Fuller to be ready. Eventually, I couldn't take it any
longer. I went in and tried to urinate. Like grape juice. I was bleeding
internally. I jumped right in the shower. I must have stayed there for an
hour, because I knew where I was going, I wouldn't shower for a week.
I was headed to the hospital for a prolonged visit.

"What's the score?" I asked the ambulance driver on the way.

"You're up 17–6 in the fourth quarter," he said.

It's the one thing that made me feel good.
> —Jim McMahon, *McMahon! The Bare Truth About
> Chicago's Brashest Bear*

CONTENTS

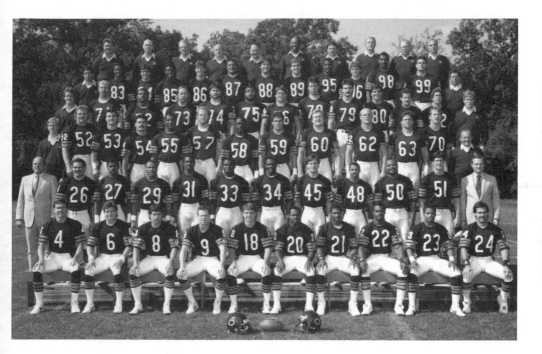

1985 BEARS ROSTER

PLAYER	POSITION	BIRTHDAY	HT	WT	COLLEGE
OFFENSE					
9 Jim McMahon	Quarterback	8/21/59	6'1"	195	Brigham Young
34 Walter Payton	Running Back	7/25/54	5'10"	200	Jackson State
26 Matt Suhey	Fullback	7/7/58	5'11"	217	Penn State
87 Emery Moorehead	Tight End	3/22/54	6'2"	218	Colorado
83 Willie Gault	Wide Receiver	9/5/60	6'0"	181	Tennessee
85 Dennis McKinnon	Wide Receiver	8/22/61	6'1"	185	Florida State
63 Jay Hilgenberg	Center	3/21/59	6'3"	259	Iowa
62 Mark Bortz	Left Guard	2/12/61	6'6"	282	Iowa
74 Jimbo Covert	Left Tackle	3/22/60	6'4"	271	Pittsburgh
57 Tom Thayer	Right Guard	8/16/61	6'4"	271	Notre Dame
78 Keith Van Horn	Right Tackle	11/6/57	6'6"	281	USC
KEY ALTERNATES					
4 Steve Fuller	Quarterback	1/5/57	6'4"	198	Clemson
80 Tim Wrightman	Tight End	3/27/60	6'3"	237	UCLA
82 Ken Margerum	Wide Receiver	10/5/58	6'0"	175	Stanford

	PLAYER	POSITION	BIRTHDAY	HT	WT	COLLEGE
	DEFENSE					
76	Steve McMichael	Defensive Tackle	10/17/57	6'2"	270	Texas
72	William Perry	Defensive Tackle	12/16/62	6'2"	325	Clemson
99	Dan Hampton	Defensive End	9/19/57	6'5"	264	Arkansas
95	Richard Dent	Defensive End	12/13/60	6'5"	265	Tennessee State
27	Mike Richardson	Cornerback	5/23/61	6'0"	187	Arizona State
21	Leslie Frazier	Cornerback	4/3/59	6'0"	189	Alcorn State
55	Otis Wilson	Linebacker	9/15/57	6'2"	227	Louisville
58	Wilber Marshall	Linebacker	4/18/62	6'1"	231	Florida
50	Mike Singletary	Middle Linebacker	10/9/58	6'0"	230	Baylor
45	Gary Fencik	Free Safety	7/25/54	6'1"	194	Yale
22	Dave Duerson	Strong Safety	11/28/60	6'1"	207	Notre Dame
	KEY ALTERNATES					
73	Mike Hartenstine	Defensive End	7/27/53	6'3"	251	Penn State
98	Tyrone Keys	Defensive End	10/24/59	6'7"	272	Mississippi State
	SPECIAL TEAMS					
6	Kevin Butler	Kicker	7/24/62	6'0"	215	Georgia
8	Maury Buford	Punter	10/24/59	6'1"	191	Texas Tech

MONSTERS

1

THE SUPER BOWL SHUFFLE

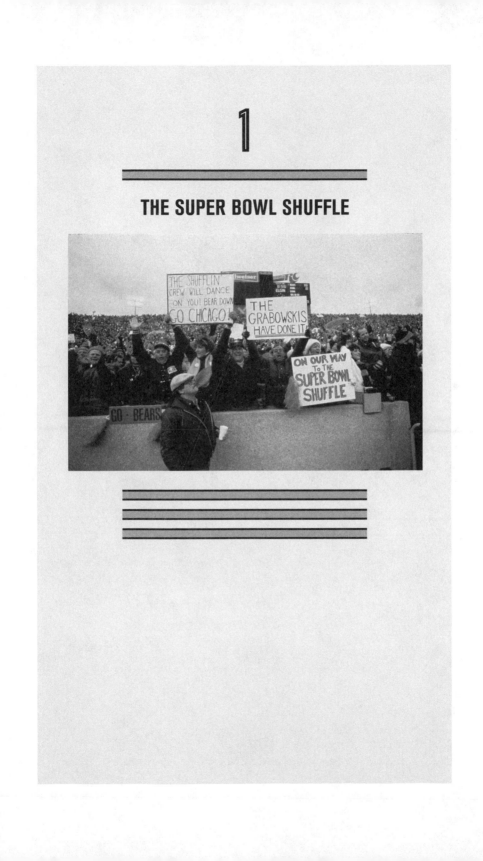

In the winter of 1986, in a manner I won't bother to go into, I came into possession of two tickets to Super Bowl XX. The Chicago Bears, the Monsters of the Midway, would play the New England Patriots in the Superdome in New Orleans. I was a senior in high school and this was my first great Chicago team, the Bears having last won a title in 1963, half a decade before I was born. The Chicago Cubs had last taken the World Series in 1908, when my Grandpa Morris was walking behind a mule in Poland.

I'd gotten permission to miss school to attend the game on the ruse that this would in fact be an informational visit to Tulane University with a side trip—"because I'll be there anyway"—to the Super Bowl. But I found it impossible to secure passage. It seemed as if half the city, experiencing the once-in-a-generation delirium of victory, was heading south. Every seat on every flight was sold, as was every seat on every train. When my parents refused to let me drive, I toyed with the idea of running away, lighting out, thumbing it. At the last moment, salvation came via a woman in my mother's office, who knew some fans who had chartered a plane—they called it "the Winged Bear"—for the trip to New Orleans. There were still a few seats in the main cabin, which is how my friend Matt Lederer and I came to leave for O'Hare airport in our Jim McMahon jerseys. I'm not sure what I expected: a Learjet with a dozen North Side business types, perhaps, or a DC-3 filled with a football-loving Boy Scout troop. We instead found ourselves seated in a tired L-1011, with a Kodiak bear painted on the tail, the rows packed with a few hundred fans of the cartoon variety: huge beer-swilling South Siders with the sort of mustaches that suggest virility. Every one of them wore either a team jersey or the type of Bears sweater-vest favored by Coach Mike Ditka. The seats were as stuffed as the knishes at Manny's deli near Maxwell Street. Beers were distributed—Mickey's, Budweiser, Schlitz—and the nasal voices rang with "We're gonna murder 'em" guarantees. It was 4:00 p.m., and some of these men had been drinking for six hours.

The flight attendants, in orange-and-blue aprons, got us seated for takeoff, but the big fat men started unbuckling soon after. They wandered in the aisles, slurring and prophesying. One made his way to the lavatory as the plane was in steep ascent. It was like watching a ball roll up Mount Everest. A stewardess ordered him back to his seat. "Lady," he said, "I'm full of sausage and beer. It's out of the way, or a big mess." Footballs were taken out of bags and spirals went zipping across the cabin. Several people were hit in the head midsentence or midbeer. A punt banged off an emergency-door handle. I envisioned the headline: BEERY BEARS FANS SUCKED TO TRAGIC DOOM.

Free-for-all gave way to pandemonium: three hundred Chicagoans blowing off decades of frustration. It was beautiful and terrifying. The pilot issued a warning. When this was ignored, he came out of his cockpit in the stern way of a parent but was driven back by a shower of empties. The rabble were led by a handful of guys from Bridgeport and Pullman. If you could morph their faces into a single face, it would be big and pink and filled with mischievous joy. They stood through the landing and sang as we touched down. Some fell in the aisles. If this were England, these would have been hooligans, but these were Chicagoans, too good-natured to plunder. As I exited the plane, I was not surprised to see the cops. A flight attendant whispered in the ear of a sergeant, pointing out the instigators, who were taken aside and cuffed.

The last image I had of these men was enormous backs, heaving with exertion, in Ditka and Butkus jerseys as they were led away. It burned into my retinas: to travel all the way to Jerusalem only to be taken into custody on the steps of the Temple. As a result, I approached the game through a veil of tears—the tears of drunken superfans arrested days before the coin toss. The arrested men never left my thoughts. I admired their commitment. They had come to express the nature of their city but never made it to baggage claim. They spent days in jail,

the poor bastards. Who were they? The unknown tailgaters and brat-
wurst eaters, the mustache combers, the last of the old-timers, the
aluminum-siding boys, the bungalow dwellers, the masses from the Back
of the Yards, the pub rats and union goons. These were the real fans.
They'd put in the years and suffered the humiliations and packed on
the pounds and cursed the fates in a way that I never could, coming
from a cozy North Shore suburb on the lake—Glencoe, if you're keeping score at home.

The '85 Bears developed a special bond with all their fans but most
powerfully with the sort I had seen taken away. It was not just that they
won—they went 15 and 1 in the regular season—but how they did it.
With personality, style. This was the team of "The Super Bowl Shuffle"—a
song released earlier that season by several of the players, it expressed
their confidence in ultimate victory—and it was made of characters.
Like the Beatles, there was a Bear for every sort of fan: Jim McMahon,
the Punky QB, for the cocky daredevils. Walter Payton, Sweetness, the
great running back, for the aficionados. William Perry, the Fridge, the
gap-toothed 325-pounder, for big tall men. Dan Hampton, Danimal,
the ferocious defensive tackle, for band geeks filled with secret violence. Mike Ditka, the coach who actually looked like a bear, for lovers
of Patton-like rhetoric and the military boot. The offense was good but
the defense was vicious: the famed 46, a concussion machine that
swarmed and confused and beat other teams bloody.

They played with a gleeful excess that seemed a perfect expression
of the city—its character, its toughness, its heartbreaks, its history. The
riots at the Democratic Convention, the El Rukn street gang, John
Belushi high on cocaine, Steve Goodman singing "A Dying Cub Fan's
Last Request," Mayor Richard J. Daley scolding reporters ("the police
are not here to create disorder, they're here to preserve disorder"), Bill
Murray playing golf on the par-three in Winnetka, the South Side blues
bars, Willie Dixon, Buddy Guy, the Checkerboard Lounge, Kup's Column, Mike Royko, Jack Brickhouse, Harry Caray, the Pump Room,
Second City, the lake in the summer and the lake when it's a sheet of
ice, Studs Terkel and Sid Luckman and George Halas's T-formation—it
was all captured in the style of that team. The '85 Bears were the revenge fantasy of suffering fans, a dream of violence, sacks, and knock-
outs. On Sunday, the object was not merely to stop the other guys but
to devour their ranks and wipe out their leaders. Now and then, when

a Bear linebacker hit a quarterback just right, you could see his eyes roll back and brain shut down and inner light dim the way the lights in the pinball machine dim when hip-checked into tilt. At night, as I tried to fall asleep, I would recite the names on the roster—Butler and Mc-Michael and Richardson and Dent—as Yeats recited the names of the heroes of the Irish Easter Uprising. Never again would I identify with a team in that way. And it was not just me. It was everyone.

Lederer and I stayed at a hotel just beyond the city limits, in Metairie. It was a dump but the best we could find. We woke late each morning, put on our jerseys, and caught a cab to the French Quarter. It was Halloween for adults, men in costume, dressed as other men, walking along Bourbon Street in packs, yammering and slugging back Hurricanes. (New Orleans is the city that turns its infrastructure-destroying nightmares into cocktails.) We stayed out from noon till 3:00 or 4:00 a.m., or, as Muddy Waters would say, "from can to can't." The drinking age was eighteen but no one checked. We waited in lines when we had to pee. When it was your turn, you stood with a crowd of grumbling men at your back. From balconies, the drifting crowds resembled schools of fish. The Bears fans in blue, the Patriots fans in red. When a school of Bears fans passed through a school of Patriots fans, there was a flurry in the water, a commotion of shoves and slugs.

At the end of each night, we went to the patio bar at Pat O'Brien's, where some Bears players hung out till the wee hours, drinking with fans who'd done themselves up as their heroes. Imagine going to a party and everyone is dressed as you. The fan dressed as Dan Hampton cedes some of his manhood in the presence of the real Dan Hampton. Defensive end Steve McMichael was there, as was guard Kurt Becker and my favorite, Jim McMahon. More than just the quarterback, Mac was the spirit of the team. He was a character, a card, a flake, completely out there, utterly unique.

Most of the players were huge, far bigger than made sense. They dressed like college freshmen on their first night off campus: khakis and penny loafers as big as snowshoes, oxford shirts straining at the chest, hair slicked back with water that never dries. We got close, tried to overhear scraps of conversation. *Did you hear what Mongo said to Danimal?* It was a peak moment in our lives and, though we did not

The author and his friend Jamie McRae shortly before Super Bowl XX.

realize it, a peak moment for them, too. These were young gods, as vivid as the astronauts in Tom Wolfe, as free as the cowboys in John Ford, gunslingers drinking rotgut and throwing dice, but it would not last. Before long, they would fall back to our world, rejoin the masses they left behind in tenth or twelfth grade.

Late one night, I found myself standing beside McMahon. He was drunk, smiling, a plug of tobacco swelling his lower lip. He wore snakeskin boots. I was wearing Vuarnet sunglasses and chewing Skoal. One of us was wearing a McMahon jersey (#9), and it wasn't him. McMahon turned me like a ballerina, read his name on my back, laughed and said, "Fuckin' A." He had a look I never fancied—pug-nosed and lazyeyed with sandy hair, like one of the ragged soldiers in the gang wars of old New York—but in those days my room was filled with pictures of McMahon. He's the reason I chewed tobacco. He's the reason I wore a headband at the gym. I wanted to carry myself with the confidence of the QB. I wanted to scamper into the end zone a step ahead of the tacklers. That morning, as I walked along Royal Street in my jersey with my half-mullet and chew, a drunk called out, "Hey, look! It's McMahon. Hey, Mac! We know it's you!" I suppose this person was mocking me, but that's not how it felt.

We got to the Superdome an hour before kickoff. We were seated at the 20-yard line. The stadium was a simulacrum of Chicago: different sections represented different city blocks or neighborhoods. We wandered through the stands, chatting with the toughs from the West Side wards and the kids from the South Shore, glad-handing like politicians, aware that, somewhere far below, the Bears were putting on tape and injecting painkillers and swallowing greenies. Ditka called his team in for a prayer. Football coaches lead their men in prayer for the same reason God is on the mind of army grunts: because no one knows when the hammer will strike steel. A great player in his own era, a hell-raiser and late-night carouser, Ditka found religion in Dallas, under the tutelage of Cowboys coach Tom Landry. Ditka was a believer, yet there was always something a little odd about his speeches and his homilies. When he went for the spiritual, he came off like a big man in a tiny coat. "All right," he said, taking a knee, "let's have the Lord's Prayer: Heavenly Father, we are grateful for the opportunity and we thank you for the talents you have given us, the chance to prove that we are the very best. Father, we ask you to give us the courage and the commitment to use these talents to the best of our ability so that we may give the glory back to you. Father, we ask that you may protect all the players in the game so they may play the game free from injury. We pray, as always, in the name of Jesus Christ your son, our Lord, Amen."

Now let's go kick ass!

In my mind, the Bears defense was dominant every play of the Super Bowl. That's memory: it takes a signature moment and makes it everything. But going back and watching the DVD, I realized it was more complicated. The defense operated in the way of a heavyweight boxer, using the first few minutes of the game to feel out the Patriots for weaknesses, setting them up for the blow that would break their will. It came halfway through the first quarter: Hampton and Dent busted through the Patriots' line, Hampton on the left, Dent on the right. These men had not been blocked: they were what Bears defensive coordinator Buddy Ryan called "free runners," meaning they hit the New England quarterback Tony Eason going full speed. He danced like an electrified wire, fell to his knees, then fell on his face. "He was a deer in the headlights," McMichael said later. "He was looking at me, Hampton, and Dent, and his eyes were saying, 'They're fixing to kill me.'"

Eason completed no passes that day; he was sacked three times and was pulled from the game. It was the worst performance by any quarterback in Super Bowl history. McMahon ran for two touchdowns, passed for another. The final score was 46–10, which makes it sound closer than it was. I stayed in the stadium long after the game. "The Super Bowl Shuffle" was being played over and over again on the scoreboard screen. When you get old, you mock the passions of your youth: you mock Peter Frampton, you mock bolo ties, you mock Arthur Fonzarelli. But I will never mock "The Super Bowl Shuffle." It was a song and a video released by several Bears, the proceeds going to charity; it opened with Payton rapping: "And we're not doin' this because we're greedy, the Bears are doin' it to feed the needy." Long after Mike Ditka and Buddy Ryan had been carried off the field, I stayed in the stands, my arms around total strangers, singing at the top of my ecstatic being. As I screamed the last verse, I had a moment of clarity. So *this* is why people suffer through mediocre season after mediocre season, I thought. So this is what's on the other side of all that losing. It's not just the victory. It's being among the winners, sinking the humdrum concerns of your life into a raucous crowd, being welcomed by the mob.

I've been an oddball all my life. I have often felt separate and alone. Standing in that crush in the Superdome was the first time I experienced total acceptance. At that moment, I knew Bears fans all over the world were feeling the exact same way. It's what the doughboys must have experienced on Armistice Day.

A friend of mine describes sports as "the most important unimportant thing in America." No one starves, no borders are redrawn, no populations are exchanged. But I disagree. I think sports have gone over the top in this country, have ascended into the stratosphere of things that really matter. Pinocchio has become a boy; the shark has entered the lagoon. Your team is a nation and on game day your nation is at war. That's what my father understood when he tried to dissuade me from following the Cubs. He believed that a Cubs fan will come to accept defeat as the inevitable end of all earthly endeavors. A Cubs fan is fatalistic: he rends his garments and cries, *Vanity of vanities, all is vanity!* The ultimate implication of my father's words was left unstated: a Cubs fan has a greater likelihood of leading an unfulfilled life. Pick your team carefully, because your team is your destiny.

In the summer of 1986, I got a job driving a van filled with mentally and physically handicapped adults. I could never get the wheelchairs properly secured. By the end of each ride, half those poor suffering souls had slid to the back, where their milky eyes peered out the rear windows. One morning, I was pulled over for racing. The cop did the slow walk. "What did you think you were doing?" he asked.

"Speeding up to avoid an accident," I told him.

He looked me over: sunglasses, chewing tobacco, football jersey—number 9.

He said, "Jim McMahon would be ashamed."

I said, "You're gonna give me a lecture or you're gonna give me a ticket, but you're not giving me both."

He said, "Who do you think you are?"

"What do you mean?" I said. "I'm a Bears fan."

2

THE WAR ROOM

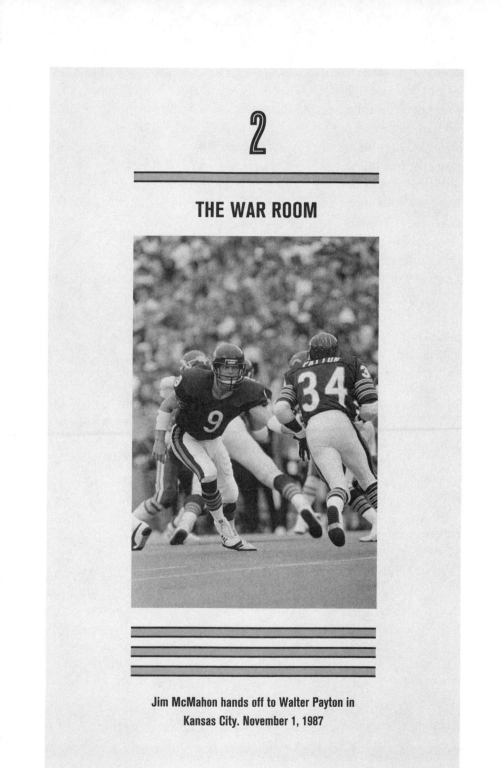

**Jim McMahon hands off to Walter Payton in
Kansas City. November 1, 1987**

As a writer, I have found the best stories tend to be those closest to me, so close that I do not even recognize them as stories until someone says, "Do you realize how much we've missed out on because of the Bears?"

These words were spoken by my wife in the fall of 2011, when, explaining why we could not go to Barbados, I told her, "I need to be home for the Packers game." She called me crazy, then left the room. I sat for a long time thinking, asking myself, "Am I crazy? Why do I give so much to a team that's done nothing but break my heart since 1986? I'm forty-five years old. Isn't there something unbecoming, even ludicrous, about my love of this team?"

I decided to explore my obsession in the only way I know: by reading and watching and interviewing and writing. This would be a book about the Bears, but also about the ecstasy of winning and what it means to be a fan. Why would a person forsake the Caribbean for an afternoon in front of a TV? What drives a fan back into the arms of his abusers again and again? I would delve into the Bears as another journalist might delve into the Amazon. I would die in the jungle or return with the answers.

I started by calling Brian McCaskey, a grandson of George Halas, who founded the Bears and helped organize the NFL. The team is still controlled by Brian's mom, Virginia Halas McCaskey, who is now in her nineties. There are eleven McCaskey siblings, and the franchise, which is worth over a billion dollars, is the family's main asset. It's therefore run with a kind of care that has struck some fans as persnick-ety. Virginia, whose husband, Ed, died in 2003, is the closest living link to Halas, whose son, George Halas, Jr., passed away in 1979, at the age of fifty-four. When a new player comes to the team, he is seated at Vir-ginia's feet while she gives a tutorial on team and league history. Brian was a perfect place to start. In addition to being a great guy, he was a fixture in the locker room in the 1980s, where he worked as an assis-tant trainer. When I asked Jim McMahon about Brian, he said, "Good taper, and the only normal McCaskey."

Brian is tall and friendly, with blue eyes and a slightly comical manner. He talked as he toured me around the team's facilities in Lake Forest, a beautiful town about thirty miles north of Chicago. We started at new Halas Hall, a training center set amid acres of gorgeous gridiron. There is a full-size indoor football field, an expanse of turf beneath a web of rafters that mimics the heavenly vault. We walked through offices and conference rooms, lingered before trophy cases and photos of great Bears of long ago. He showed me the screening room where the athletes watch and rewatch every play of every game. He showed me the weight room, the hot tubs, and the ice soaks. He showed me the locker room, where we stood before a locker decorated with a Jewish star and a menorah. "It belongs to Gabe Carimi, a line-man from the University of Wisconsin," McCaskey told me. "We call him the Bear Jew." (Carimi was traded to Tampa Bay in June 2013.) He showed me massage tables, MRI machines, and pharmaceutical closets. I ducked into the War Room, which was lined with wipe boards where information on every player in the league was written in marker. It was like the room of an intelligence agent who believes herself on the verge of a breakthrough. "I should have stopped you from doing that," McCaskey said when I came out. "The coach would have a heart attack if he knew you'd been in there."

We went across town to old Halas Hall, where the team still prac-ticed in 1985. It's now the athletic center of Lake Forest College. Run-down and dank, it's like the gym Rocky returned to when he wanted to regain the Eye of the Tiger. For players, it offered that special kind of scarcity that breeds closeness, that makes a team a team. If the Bears want to win another Super Bowl, they might think of returning to old Halas Hall. There's a practice field out back that used to flood when it rained. A larger field across a parking lot was just that—a field, choppy and sloped, the cause of innumerable injuries. In inclement weather, the team practiced in a gym, the sort best suited for dodgeball. In the 1980s, being tackled on the hardwood floor was a rite of passage.

McCaskey showed me the racquetball court where Ditka let out the beast—he was known for intensely competitive games—and the coaches' shower. "Ditka was weird about his hair," said McCaskey. "He had a special hairbrush and it had to sit outside the stall when he took a shower, with his cologne. One day, the PR guy used Ditka's hairbrush and walked out with it. So the next day, Ditka comes out of the shower, reaches for the brush, and it's not there. He went insane, totally nuts. He called a big meeting. He said only coaches were allowed to use the coaches' shower. If anyone else was caught in those showers, it was Ditka they'd be dealing with. But I liked that shower. I liked Ditka's hairbrush and cologne. So when the whole thing died down, I started using it again. And one day, as I'm spraying on Ditka's cologne, the door opens and this body fills the threshold. There was no back door, no way out, and there he is, and there I am in a towel, so I said, 'Coach, I know what I'm doing is wrong, and I'm sorry, but ever since I started using your cologne, good things have been happening in my life.' Ditka did that half smile of his and said, 'Yeah, I know what you mean.'"

The tour ended in the coach's office, which was just as I'd imagined it: a big room with a big desk looking out a big window at a football field. If the facility is the body, this is the brain. Standing there, I felt like I was inside the mind of Iron Mike, behind the optic nerve, looking through the wild man's eyes, seeing the world as he must see it. More than any other sport, football is about the coach, the general with the god complex who wants to map every sequence, prepare for every contingency. "On Fridays, after all the practices were done and the plan had been set, Ditka would sit in here and open a bottle of champagne," McCaskey told me. "He did it when the team was at its best and did it when the team was struggling. It was what he believed: it's better to win than to lose, but win or lose you should drink champagne."

I read every book and article about the '85 Bears, written both by reporters and historians. I read *Papa Bear: The Life and Legacy of George Halas* by Jeff Davis. I read Ditka's first autobiography, *Ditka*, as well as his second, *In Life, First You Kick Ass*. I read *McMahon! The Bare Truth*

About Chicago's Brashest Bear, written when the quarterback was twenty-six. It seemed as if every Bear did two things after winning Super Bowl XX: open a bar and write a book.

I sat with a pile of DVDs and watched every game the Bears played in 1985. A lot of it was boring. What makes a game exciting? The tension of anticipating the play that will bust open the piñata. Knowing the outcome kills everything.

But Ditka's postgame press conferences have lost none of their drama. Standing behind a podium, hair slicked back, he looked like a bear and behaved like a bear. His forehead was domed, and his small eyes were set close together. He shifted from side to side, taking his time, deciding which reporter to next raise up and beat down. If a question struck him as stupid, he would grunt and mutter, "next." He could make "next" sound like a nasty word. Now and then, watching on TV, you'd see a reporter raise his hand, then, fixed in the coach's glare, lower it a little, then a little more, then drop it altogether and stare into his lap. If challenged, Ditka assumed the flat-faced puzzled expression of a bear in a documentary, a grizzly that has caught an interesting smell on the wind, that has reared back on his hind legs, paws dangling, searching for prey. *Next.* He was a Kodiak rooting through trash on the edge of a national park. He was a grizzly enraged by a swarm of bees. When not kinked into a perm, his hair fell across his face. It was the color of a pelt. Some players believed he actually dyed it orange, streaked it like the ladies in Palm Beach, furthering his resemblance to the team logo.

Yet he was the most common type in the world. Every junior high school has that gym teacher who wants to be called Coach, who makes you run an extra ten laps for being a wiseass, who lines up all his students and accuses them of acting like "a bunch of ladies." Ditka was that guy for the entire city of Chicago, my own Mr. Kreutzer raised to the highest power.

If the team lost, the press conference was funereal. Ditka spoke in hushed tones. He still chewed gum, only did it slowly, in a stolid South Side, Muddy Waters beat. Da-Da-Da-Ta-Da. Nowadays NFL coaches, not wanting to crush the egos of their fragile superstars, focus on the positive: things to build on, what went right. But Ditka was from an older, harder America and preached a more ancient form of football religion. If asked, on such occasions, "What went wrong?" he might grimace and say, "You saw it. We stink." Following an especially bad loss, he said, "I'd be surprised if we won another game."

But if the team won, and they did a lot of winning in the 1980s—during a golden stretch, they went 35 and 3—the press conference was raucous. Ditka was still a bear, only now he was a happy bear shredding through picnic baskets at an ill-tended campsite in the Adirondacks. After the Super Bowl, he wore tailored suits, the big body barely contained by all that finery, but he was simpler before the win: a man in polyester coach pants and a Bears sweater-vest, a winter parka, a knit cap. The better the victory, the faster he chomped his gum, jaw working like a piston as he pointed his way through the hacks: next, next, next. Now and then, he held a press conference on the field, giving fans a chance to heckle. After one game, a fan called out, "Hey Ditkus," a combination of Ditka and Butkus. Though Dick Butkus was among the greatest Bears ever, a middle linebacker who hit with animalistic fury, Ditka seemed to take the conflation as a terrible slight. He turned on the heckler, threatening him as the reporters laughed. "I wasn't trying to be funny with the guy," Ditka said later, "because if I'd've gotten ahold of him, I wouldn't have been funny with him. It had nothing to do with fun."

After a win in Cincinnati, a fan appeared out of nowhere and intoned, in the way of a prophet, "The Bears will not return to the Super Bowl." Ditka fixed this man with a stare, then, making a zero with his index finger and thumb, spit out the words, "See that, buddy? That's your IQ."

One afternoon, as the Bears left the field in San Francisco, a woman who'd been heckling the coach leaned over the rail and shouted something vile. Ditka plucked the gum from his mouth, wheeled, and threw. It was not an ordinary wad of gum but the sort of mouthful chewed by giants. Eight or nine pieces, an entire pack of Bubblicious worked into a fist, molar marks as deep as tire tracks. For a minute, you could see it in the air. Then it vanished into the heckler's hair. Her head snapped back. She took the impact like a third-world dictator being dropped by a sniper in a town square. The police threatened to charge Ditka with assault. An officer recovered the gum, which was booked as evidence.

These press conferences were a new kind of theater in a town that had always taken its losing straight, no chaser. But Ditka neither won nor lost quietly. He was an expressive man, a fist pounder, less like the cerebral masters of the game than like his father, a union boss from western Pennsylvania. He said what he thought in the no-bullshit way of the political fixer. When I spoke to Bob Avellini, a Bears quarterback who battled with Ditka, he told me, "If the people only knew the truth about their hero Iron Mike: he called plays like a drunken fan."

Of course, they did know, and that's why they loved him. Ditka personified the town and its fans, many of whom were indeed drunk. Speaking before a big game, he expressed the pain and desire of every Bears lunatic: "In the past, we were the hit-ees. Today, we intend to be the hit-ors."

I went on the road in search of as many veterans of the '85 season as I could find. Not just players but also coaches, and not just Bears but also those who played against them, those who delivered the big hits and those who absorbed them: the subpoena servers and the subpoena receivers, the hit-ors and the hit-ees. I spoke to Ron Jaworski, Joe Theismann, Danny White—all quarterbacks pounded by the 46 defense. "Mike Hartenstein got me," said Jaworski. "He hit me on a Sunday. I woke up at Paoli Hospital in Philadelphia on Tuesday afternoon."

Brian McCaskey listed the Bears he thought I should talk to, then wrote letters of introduction. Other players I approached on my own, including my old hero, Jim McMahon. He was not hard to find. He's all over Twitter and the Internet. We were soon exchanging messages. (Here's a typical email: "rich on my way to vegas be bk on mon wont have any free time there its vegas!") I met McMahon in Scottsdale, Arizona. From there, I hopscotched from Mike Ditka to Johnny Roland, the team's running back coach, to Dick Stanfel, the offensive line coach, to Tim Wrightman, a tight end, to Tyrone Keys, a defensive end, and so on.

I met Brian Baschnagel at Walker Bros., The Original Pancake House in Wilmette, Illinois. Walker Bros. is an institution, a point of pride for locals, home of table-covering griddle cakes and silver dollar gems. One year, when my mom was sick, I used to stop there with my father every night on the way home from the hospital. It has associations for me, which was the case for everyone I met and everywhere I went with this book.

Take Baschnagel, the floppy-haired receiver known to fans as Bash: when I was a kid playing Nerf, he was the player I pretended to be. It seemed he could catch anything. He was human glue. A great player on the bad teams of the 1970s, Bash had become an afterthought by 1985. You were surprised to find his name on the roster. *My God, how old is he?* Thirty, thirty-one? He was injured that season but useful as a kind of assistant, a sporty guy in civilian clothes wearing headphones on the sideline. There's a melancholy to such players: standouts on weak teams who become relics when things change; a star in junior high who plays a bit part in high school. Some head coaches cleanse their rosters of anyone tainted by a failed regime, even the superstars— because of the inevitable mind-set, what all that losing can do to a soul. That's why God kept the Hebrews in the desert for forty years: he was waiting for the slave generation to pass away. But Ditka admired Baschnagel, whose story was not unlike his own: here was another kid who'd fought his way out of hardscrabble coal country, who took the money but played for love.

We sat in back of the restaurant, 6:00 or 7:00 a.m., where fathers, getting an early start on a day of fishing, were eating with their sons. Brian is one of the lucky few: a handsome midsized man with salt-and-pepper hair, he survived nine seasons in the NFL relatively unscathed. He showed me his hands: no busted fingers, no ruined joints. I asked about Stickum. Along with tear-away jerseys and amphetamines known as greenies, Stickum was a characteristic idiosyncrasy of pro football in my youth: a sap that receivers slathered on their hands, arms, and bodies that helped them hang on to the ball. I once saw Fred Biletnikoff, the Oakland Raiders receiver, catch a touchdown with his shin. "They got rid of it when the quarterbacks complained," Baschnagel told me. "When they tried to throw, the ball wouldn't come out of their hands." (There was a diseased elm tree in front of our house in Glencoe. The plant doctor covered the trunk with sticky chemical goop. Before heading out for a pickup game, my friends and I would press our hands in the concoction, which helped us make catches. If I die before my time, that goop will likely be the cause.)

The dining room got quiet when Bash talked. In Chicago, a Bear is royalty. Such a man, especially if he's medium sized and well put together, will be afforded special respect. He's like a war veteran, a man who went helmet to helmet in the most violent arena. In America, if you want to be physically tested, there's no better proving ground than the NFL.

Baschnagel was illuminating on the subject of quarterbacks; he made me understand the value of Jim McMahon. Retired athletes tend to be judged by their statistics, by which measure McMahon was good, not great. But what's not recorded in the numbers is the thing that matters most: his leadership, his effect on teammates. When McMahon was in a game, the Bears always believed they could win. He understood the needs of his players. "I was a receiver, and as a receiver, regardless of your other responsibilities, you wanted to catch the ball," Baschnagel told me. "That was the only statistic you'd ever have. Jim knew that. We were a conservative offense, especially early in Jim's career; our strength was our defense and our running game. We had Walter Payton. Sometimes you'd go a whole game without having a ball thrown to you. Whether it was practice or games, you wanted to touch that ball. You wanted your hands on it. We were in a practice one afternoon. It was late in the season, the last drill. We get in the huddle. A pass play is called. As we break, Jim grabs me and says, 'You haven't had the ball thrown to you—be prepared.' We get up to the line of scrimmage and I looked at the defense; they were double teaming me, inside and out. And I'm thinking, There's absolutely no way Jim's going to throw to me. I ran hard every play but I didn't even look back, at least initially. I was double covered. Jim's read would be to hit a receiver underneath. But as I'm running, I think I probably ought to look over my shoulder just to check. And there's the ball on its way, zipping between those two defenders. I go up and catch it. And I hear Mike Ditka screaming at Jim, calling him every name in the book. 'What the hell are you thinking? Brian was double-teamed, the guy underneath was wide open.' Jim completed the pass, but that didn't matter to Mike because it was a bad read. Jim just threw his hands up and said, 'Sorry, Coach, I screwed up.' And that was it. But Jim knew exactly what he was doing."

I met Kurt Becker at Harry Caray's Italian Steakhouse & Bar in Lombard, a suburb twenty miles west of the city. Though Becker is huge, six six with dark shaggy hair, he's half the size he was when he played. Asked about this, he laughed and said, "The small guys got big, and the big guys got small." Becker grew up in Aurora, Illinois, and speaks in the nasal twang of a local. He roomed with McMahon in '85, which had a downside. When McMahon got out of control, Ditka would fine him, and, when that had no effect, he'd fine Becker. "Not fair," said Becker. "Not fair." He's not a fan of the modern game: as a lineman, he's attracted to the most brutish aspects of the sport. To him, football is two big men seeing just who can push whom up against the wall. "I don't like the ball being thrown all over the place," he told me. "I like struggle, the drama of ball control. I want our offense to stay on the field. I like scoring slowly. I like eating up time on a long drive. To me, that's football: you're tired, you grind 'em, you recover, you prevail."

I met Emery Moorehead, who played tight end on the Super Bowl Bears. He grew up in Evanston. His mother worked in the post office, his father was a garbage collector. He was a high school star, then went to the University of Colorado. He played for the Giants and the Broncos before returning to Chicago. You always noticed him: square shouldered, head down, busting through the line just as he did when Evanston played New Trier. I met him in his office on the North Shore. He's a real estate broker. He's a bit of a ruin, too, a fallen-down house of a man, with all the material present but no longer distributed in the same way. I asked what it's like to play in a big game: Are you scared in the locker room before? "You're never fearful, and never ever think about what might happen," he told me. "But the year I retired, I started watching the games on TV differently. I was seeing guys get flipped upside down, landing on the back of their necks, getting up and running back to the huddle, and I suddenly found myself thinking, Dude, that's crazy! You could get killed!"

I met Gary Fencik, the team's All-Pro safety, at the Salt & Pepper Diner in Lincoln Park. He looks like he did when he played: a little guy who stayed little. He was dressed like a bond trader on his day off: faded jeans, loafers, flannel shirt. He has dark hair, a crooked smile, and a handsome face just banged up enough to be interesting. As I said, the '85 Bears had a player for every kind of fan. If you were a small white guy in Chicagoland, it was Fencik, the Yale-educated defensive back from Barrington. He was the version of us that did not peak in the tenth grade but kept getting better, until he was bathed in champagne and raising the Super Bowl trophy over his head. He still holds the team record for the most interceptions. He was an extraordinarily hard hitter. He often timed it so he reached the receiver at the same moment as the ball. To fans, he'll always be "the hit man."

As we talked, he kept an eye on the TVs showing football games. We watched as a quarterback, crushed from the blind side, was helped off the field. A few minutes later, he was back. I wondered why, knowing what we now know about the long-term effects of head injuries, a player would return after such a hit. "You will unless someone stops you," Fencik explained. "The first thing you do when the cobwebs clear is run right on the field. It's instinct. You're in the game, you get dinged, you come to on the sideline and realize your team is out there. You don't think about what it will mean when you're forty. You just think, Whoa, I'm missing it! It's panic. It's like that bad dream you have when you're a kid. It's the day of the big test and you're late for school."

After breakfast, I rode with Fencik downtown. He was looking for a place to park. When I noticed a spot, he pointed to a No Parking sign. I said I found it hard to believe that anyone in Chicago would give Gary Fencik a ticket. He said, "Yeah, well, they do," thought a moment, then added, "but not speeding tickets." He'd recently been pulled over on the highway. The cop, a young woman, took his license to the patrol car but returned in a few minutes, handed it back, and said, "My father and brothers are big Bears fans. If I give you a ticket, they'll kick my ass."

I'd long considered pro football players to be among the dumbest American celebrities. I'd interviewed more than a few over the years and always found their answers vague, bland, and thoughtless. They talked and talked but said nothing. Of course, the players had been trained to talk this way—something I understood later. A person is a person, after all, and will reflect on every situation, especially one as violently dramatic as life in the NFL, but athletes who want to stay in the league learn to answer questions without making news. The colorful players are pushed out or characterized as flakes. But talking to the '85 Bears long after retirement, I found them to be some of the smartest, most reflective people I'd ever interviewed. Something big happened to them long ago—so big it cleaved their lives into sections: during and after. And many of them have spent their middle years thinking about it: What happened? What did it mean? I found I could

Safety Doug Plank, the namesake of the 46 defense, as he was in his prime

ask them the questions I'd always wanted answered: What's it like in the locker room before a game? What does a man think as he lies broken on the field? Were you ever scared? What did you really think of the fans? When does the fake TV hate turn into the real thing? How do you go on living after the life you've always wanted is over? My notebooks were filling with more than anecdotes and stories, but with a picture of an era. This might be true if you studied any group of people carefully, but the '85 Bears offered an especially vivid sample, a collection of men who spent the peak years of their lives together before time carried them away. In the seasons that followed the Super Bowl, each went on to finish his career and live his life. Some succeeded, some failed, some died. Taken together, they experienced everything.

Of all the Bears I spent time with, my favorite was Doug Plank. He was off the roster by '85 yet remained the spirit of the team, the personification of the vicious, hard-hitting 46, the defensive scheme that defined the Bears in the 1980s. We met in Scottsdale, where Plank has lived for the last several years. In his playing days, he was a shade under six feet, a biscuit under two hundred, a quick, mean safety who roamed all over the field. His hair was surfer blond, his eyes a glazed happy blue. Every player has a Doug Plank story. He was a maniac. From first play to last, his career was defined by big hits. "I remember his final game," said Steve McMichael, a slightly crazed defensive end. "A big old behemoth pulling guard . . . came around. Here goes Doug, forcing the play. He came up, the guy didn't try to cut him, so Doug took him on high. Doug took his ass out—boom, hit him as hard as he could. It laid out the guard, but it pinched both nerves on both sides of [Doug's] neck so badly that all he could do was stand there."

"Nah, that's not what happened," Plank told me. "It was a short pass, a curl. I was coming from my safety position 'cause the pass was only ten yards. I was breaking on the ball and didn't realize that another one of our players was coming just as hard from the other side. Otis Wilson. As I was getting ready to put my helmet into the receiver, he fell down. At the last second—I don't even know if I really remember this—I saw a flash of Otis coming full speed. We went head-first. Next thing I know, I was on all fours with something dripping from my face. My helmet had come down and opened my nose. It was busted, blood pouring out. And next to me is Otis on his back, eyes wide open, staring into oblivion, out cold."

"It was in Detroit," Wilson said. "I had the receiver, and Doug—he don't see the ball. He just see the man, torpedoes himself right into people. And he got me. I'm coming this way and he's coming that way. I'm 245, he's 196—so he ain't gonna win. I was pissed off at that son of a bitch. Open your eyes! He was a great guy but he'd knock the shit out of you."

"It was a spinal concussion," Plank told me. "About the only thing I can compare it to is sticking your finger in a socket. I stuck my finger in plenty of sockets when I was a kid so I know what I'm talking about. That was happening in the lower half of my body. Numb. Pins and needles. That feeling in my left leg, it never went away."

It was Plank who gave the defense its name: the 46. Many fans assume it came from the on-field alignment of players, as with the 3–4 defense and the Cover 2. In fact, 46 means nothing more than *we're coming hard*, in the way of the man who wears that number, Doug Plank.

The defense was a puzzle, a blizzard of reads and options, but, when I spoke to Plank, he summed it up like this: "We're going to get to know your backup quarterback today."

Plank has slimmed down since his playing days but is still blond, tough, handsome, and cool. He's the sort of older kid you meet at camp and follow around all summer. He's not gotten away as clean as Baschnagel—he's had a knee replaced and has titanium shoulders. The aftereffects of life as a missile. When I asked what caused the damage, he said, "Every body has a certain amount of hits in it. Mine had 237. Unfortunately, I took 352."

Even when the Bears were bad, there was Payton on offense and Plank on defense. A late hitter? A dirty player? "Well, yeah, you'd look at it and say, 'Gosh, Plank came late and took that guy's head off.' But all I was doing was flying over the pile; what looked like a big collision was just me sailing by. One time, I remember going back and saying to the ref, 'But I didn't even hit the guy.' And he said, 'Maybe not, but you had bad intentions.' And you know what? He was right. I had bad intentions from the moment I walked on a football field."

Plank was one of the only players to ever knock the great power running back Earl Campbell out of a game. "We watched film of the Broncos' safety Steve Foley trying to tackle Earl," Plank told me. "Generally, with film, you see everyone on the line, then the action, then it cuts to the next play. In this case, we saw Earl break through the line and Foley come to make the tackle. He put his helmet into one of Earl's thighs. But his thigh pads were thirty-four inches. Mammoth. Think about it. I had a twenty-nine-inch waist. Foley got knocked back, then knocked out. Instead of cutting to the next play, the film stayed on the scene as the medics carried Foley away. Buddy [Ryan] turned off the camera and said, 'If any of you guys don't want to play this weekend, let me know.' So I sat there, thinking: You know what? I'm not going to hit Earl Campbell in the legs. He wore metal thigh pads, not the foam rubber type like in Pop Warner. When Earl hit you, it sounded like an aluminum baseball bat: *doinggg, doinggg.* So I thought, Where is Earl Campbell vulnerable? Yes, yes, between the legs. So that whole game, I was waiting for the moment I could drive my helmet into the vulnerable area. When I finally got the chance, I put him down."

Plank numbers his own concussions, from dings to who-am-I-and-why-am-I-here blasts, in double digits. He carried smelling salts in his waistband to bring himself around. After an especially big hit, he would shake his head, then look at his uniform. "If it was the dark one, I'd tell myself, 'Go stand with the guys in the dark jerseys.'" He knew the protocol, how to keep himself in a game. "You'd run to the sideline and the doctor would hold up his fingers, how many, how many? It was always two."

Judged by today's standards, Plank told me his entire career would be considered a penalty, an endless whistle blowing in the canyons of hell. "What's football?" he asked. "It's chess. Tackle chess. And what's the quarterback? He's the king. Take him out, you win the game. So that was our philosophy. We're going to hit that quarterback ten times. We do that, he's gone. I hit him late? Fine. Penalize me. But it's like in those courtroom movies, when the lawyer says the wrong thing and the judge tells the jury to disregard it, but you can't unhear and the quarterback can't be unhit."

Plank wishes every fan could cover an opening kickoff in the NFL, just for the excitement, the rush of running downfield with the noise and the color and the scoreboard and the big hit waiting as a beer waits at the end of a long day. Doug Plank represented the regular man, which is why he was so beloved by fans. He was a good high school player, but neither big nor fast enough to attract Division I scouts. So he scouted himself, writing up his games at his desk in Pennsylvania, sending these reports to Joe Paterno, the coach of Penn State, where Plank had always dreamed of playing.

The day after his last high school game, Doug was shooting baskets in the gym when Paterno walked in: glasses, blue windbreaker. He called Doug over, then turned to the gym teacher and said, "Coach, okay if we use your office?" Paterno sat Doug down, then broke his heart, returning the letters, complimenting his spirit but telling him he was too small to play big-time college football. He offered to write letters of introduction to Division III schools.

A few weeks later, Doug was called to the principal's office, where Woody Hayes, the Ohio State coach, was waiting. He said, "Doug, how'd you like a full scholarship to play football for me?"

"It's what I've dreamed of all my life," Plank told him.

Sophomore year, an assistant coach asked Plank, who rarely started at Ohio State, if he ever wondered why he'd gotten that scholarship.

"Yeah, sort of."

"'Cause Woody heard Paterno had been to see you and wanted to screw him up." After Plank's rookie NFL season, in which he led the Bears in tackles, Paterno began invoking the story as a cautionary tale.

"Keep an open mind," he'd tell his scouts. "One of the little guys might be another Doug Plank."

It was a fluke that brought Plank to the Bears, who took him, for sentimental reasons, in the twelfth round, which is like not being drafted. "That's why I played the way I did," he told me. "The good players, the guys with talent, they have an A game, a B game, a C game. They don't feel perfect, it's practice, okay, go with the B game. I didn't have that option. There was only the A game for me—as hard as I could every time or I would not be on the field; that's what gave me such intensity."

"He used to take guys out in practice like you do in games," Mc-Michael wrote. "I guess that's why our offense stunk back then, nobody was going to catch a pass over the middle. [Doug] used to hit guys so hard he'd knock himself out."

"He coldcocked me in practice," said Baschnagel. "We were just in helmets, no pads. Inside. On a gym floor. I went across the middle, and he nailed me. As he helped me up, he said, 'Oh, Brian, I'm sorry. I didn't know that was you.' Then, ten minutes later, he does the same thing. This time, as he helps me up, he says, 'That time I did know it was you, Brian.'"

When I asked Plank what makes someone a hitter, he thought a moment, then said, "Try running into a wall. A normal person will slow down at the last moment—a hitter will accelerate. When people say I was great in my day, I say, No, I was just able to control my mind for those few seconds before impact. I never slowed down. I sped up. That's what makes a hitter. Not size, not speed. It's the ability to suppress your survival instincts. We've all known big physical players that just don't want to hit. We've seen people that you look at and go, no way, but they put a uniform on and become a terror. If you can convince yourself that what you're doing on that field is not going to hurt you, you'll be capable of anything. It takes practice. You have to develop the mental capacity to keep moving those legs even when you know pain is coming.

"When I played, I played angry," he added. "It sounds childish, but I would trick my mind into believing that the person on the other side had done something to me or my family and now it was time to deliver justice. It sounds shallow, but you have to work yourself up into a fury. I never went to the Super Bowl. I never played in a Pro Bowl. But here's one thing I did do: hit as hard as I possibly could every time I possibly could."

To me, Doug Plank was a revelation. Not only because he was smart and funny but also because he has considered and reconsidered every moment of his career. He's thoughtful. What's more, he typifies the Bears mentality. "You get to Chicago and you look around and see all the incredible history," he told me. "Halas, Butkus, the defenses, the Hall of Famers, and you feel like you have an obligation. When I first got there, people told me, 'Doug, win or lose, you'd better be tough and physical, you better play like a Bear.' I remember my mind-set going out onto the fields in those first years: If we were not going to beat the other team, we were at least going to beat them up." He was a throwback, a perfect example of an old-time player; in him, you recognized the energy and gleeful anger that made football the national game. What is baseball when you can watch Doug Plank seek frontier justice on a Sunday afternoon? He could have played with Jim Thorpe, or Red Grange, or Bronko Nagurski—he could still be playing today. He's the foot soldier, the cannon fodder, the grunt, the sort of player who has lit the boards from the beginning. It was hard hitters from the grim coal towns that made the game worth watching. In Doug Plank, you see the spirit and history of the Chicago Bears, and of the game itself.

3

THE OLD ZIPPEROO

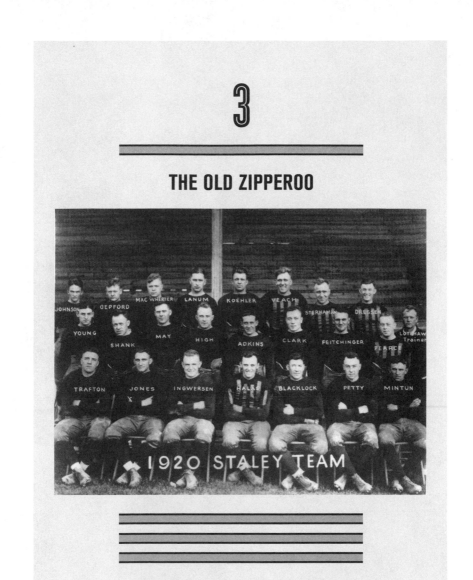

The Chicago Bears played their first season as the Staleys, the pride of
A. E. Staley, a starch manufacturer in Decatur, Illinois, one of many
industrial teams that characterized early pro football.

When I was growing up in Chicago in the 1970s, George Halas was a kind of god. His face seemed to hover over the city. The lantern jaw and steely skull, eyes blazing. Fury burned like a fire in the old man, flames seen through the window of a dilapidated mansion. Halas was an Old Testament god. In his years as coach of the Bears, he would race up and down the sidelines, screaming at referees and opposing players. The air around him turned blue. A lot's in dispute about his legacy, but one thing seems settled: his favorite word was "cocksucker." After a loss in Minnesota, he got on the plane's PA system and said, "You're all a bunch of fucking cunts." End of speech. On one occasion, when a ref threw a flag, Halas shouted, "You stink, you lousy cocksucker!" The ref threw another flag, marked off fifteen more penalty yards, then said, "How do I smell from here, Halas?" He said that he retired from coaching only because his bad hip didn't let him make it up and down the sidelines fast enough to keep up with the referees. He was known for being stingy, angry, and mean. Years before, when he docked Ditka's salary, the young tight end said, "The old man is so cheap, he throws around nickels like they're manhole covers." It was a nasty thing to say, and it stuck. By the 1980s, it was the main impression fans had of Halas. Of course, like almost everything else said about old people, it was half considered, unfair, shallow, and wrong.

The bones sat close to the surface of Halas's face. He looked like sculpture. Even when he was alive, he resembled a bust in the Hall of Fame. The high cheekbones, sharp nose, and exaggerated jaw that gave him a wicked underbite—it made the old man look like he was forever grinding his teeth or girding for a blow. His chin was dimpled in the axe-wound way of Kirk Douglas, a recognizable feature from his first schoolboy photo to the last shots snapped by local paparazzi. It was an iconic Chicago face, a West Side face, the face of a boss or alderman, as familiar as the silhouette of the Sears Tower.

Halas was born in 1895 and grew up in that part of the city once known as Pilsen, many of its early inhabitants having emigrated from the area around Pilsen, Bohemia, which is now part of the Czech Republic. Back then, Chicago was a quilt of immigrant neighborhoods, communities of outcasts, each more despised than the next. You lived with everyone from everywhere. Jews, Poles, Ukrainians, Italians,

Coach Halas working the sideline. When he disputed a referee's call, the air around him turned blue. October 25, 1959

Greeks. It gave Halas a broad-mindedness that distinguished him from other players in the early years of the NFL. Halas could get along with anyone as long as he could play.

Pilsen was one of those redbrick neighborhoods you see from the window of the elevated train, broad streets rushing toward the vanishing point, narrow houses, shades drawn in the upper stories, neon in the saloon windows, church spires, hardware stores, stoops, iron, ruin, and rain. The fire escapes were complicated weaves of rotting wood. Halas's father was a brewer, a barkeep, and a tailor. He owned a grocery on 18th Place and Wood Street, three miles west of the Loop. George and his siblings lived in rooms above the store. In the summer, George shoveled coal for 50 cents a week, money he saved for college. Later reminiscences of his youthful striving had the comical ring of the miser telling you how he walked three miles to school, uphill both ways: "It was sometimes said of me that I threw dollars as though they were manhole covers," he wrote in *Halas by Halas*. "That is correct. It is precisely what I did do. By being careful with money, I have been able to accomplish things I consider important."

Halas was a Cubs fan, a member of the last generation of Chicagoans who did not have their hearts broken by the team, then a dominant franchise. The Cubs played in West Side Park, a jewel box with curtained opera seats, brownstones looming. The stadium was demolished in 1920, lost in the way of Atlantis, sunk to the subconscious of the city. Baseball was the only pro team sport, and Halas watched with the fascination of the fan who recognizes a possibility: maybe, if I keep getting better. Though scrawny, he was a natural athlete, a master of every variety of stoop- and stickball game, the flea you make the mistake of underestimating. To get to West Side Park, he had to cross 14th Street, which meant fording the territory of the 14th Street Boys, a gang of jacket-wearing, punch-throwing gutter rats. "I would take a sock at the nearest punk and run," Halas wrote later. "I believe that's how I developed the speed that later was to be helpful in all sports."

Running from thugs was football in its primal state, with the object not scoring but surviving. In the early years of the pro game, scouts looked for players with the toughest childhoods: those who had to fight would have the instincts. The street games that preceded high school, games we all played, were football stripped to its essence—a run from the 14th Street Boys confined to a playground. Mob ball, gang ball.

Anything can be done to you as long as you hold the rock. Those who give it up too soon will be considered cowards; those who hang on as the blows rain down will be esteemed. Halas came to favor a half dozen phrases, but the highest was reserved for players who kept the ball a moment longer than seemed reasonable. Such men had "the old zipperoo."

Halas excelled in every sport, but football was his favorite. The game itself was still relatively new; it had appeared in New England only after the Civil War. Here and there, it was banned as too violent. In Boston, where it was played at the beginning of the week, it was called Bloody Monday. It eventually was picked up by students. The first official college game was played between Rutgers and Princeton in November 1869. There really was no professional football, though there were a few independent teams, perhaps, fielded by factory owners who, caught in a rivalry, might pay ringers. For its first forty years, football meant college, where it became a sensation. By the time Halas was old enough to read the sports summaries in the *Chicago Tribune*, sixty thousand fans were filling the stadium in Champaign-Urbana to watch the University of Illinois play Michigan or Wisconsin or Northwestern, or any of the other Big Ten teams.

Halas subscribed to *Tip Top* magazine, which was filled with garish illustrations of football as war. Like millions of other boys, he lived and died with Owen Johnson's football hero Frank Merriwell, whose adventures were chronicled in *Frank Merriwell at Yale*. These stories captured the appeal of the game: violence and injury; being wounded but persisting. People are currently trying to find ways to tame the game, but it will be difficult: football is violence, hitting and being hit, delivering one swift blow to the worst of the 14th Street Boys before escaping. "Frank felt himself clutched, but he refused to be dragged down," Johnson wrote in a story Halas would have read when he was eleven. "He felt hands clinging to him, and, with all the fierceness he could summon, he strove to break away and go on. His lips were covered with bloody foam, and there was a frightful glare in his eyes. He strained and strove to get a little farther, and actually dragged Hollender along the ground till he broke the fellow's hold. Then he reeled across Harvard's line and fell. It was a touch-down in the last seconds of the game."

Halas entered Crane Tech in 1909, long a powerhouse high school in Chicago, known for sports. Take the best suburban team, run them through an undefeated season, then send them to Crane Tech for a playoff—they return on a stone-quiet bus, as if they've been through a chipper. Halas was 110 pounds his freshman year—too small. He would take the ball, duck behind a blocker, then—BAM! He'd be sent sprawling. But he'd always pop back up, surface like a cork. Get to your feet one more time than you've been knocked down: that's the old zipperoo.

He took a year off before college, hoping to grow. He worked at Western Electric in Cicero, hauling cable. He played for the company baseball team and now and then took $10 to play in the backfield in a semipro football game on the South Side. In this era, the semipros were monsters, the grizzled products of factories, the sort of men you'd find in the shipyards of Danzig. Halas showed up for college in Champaign in 1914 with $30 in his pocket and a suitcase in his hand, like the guitar player in the rock-and-roll song. He joined a fraternity, waited tables for money. He studied civil engineering but dreamed of football. He played on the freshman team coached by Ralph Jones, whom he'd later hire to coach for the Bears, but was still ridiculously small when he went out for varsity. On the first play, Coach Robert Zuppke shouted through a megaphone, "Get that kid out of there before he gets killed!"

Zuppke was legendary, one of the innovators of the game. Halas credited him with inventing the huddle and the spiral, though Zuppke probably learned these tricks and much else from University of Chicago coach Alonzo Stagg—the Ben Franklin of football, the man who said and did everything first: first to send a man in motion, first to lateral pass, first to put numbers on jerseys. Football is patriarchal: the secret wisdom is passed from coach to player. Ditka learned it from Halas, who learned it from Zuppke, who learned it from Stagg. When asked where he got his plays, Notre Dame's Knute Rockne said, "I took them from Stagg, and Stagg took them from God."

Halas reached six feet his junior year. Meat and potatoes brought him to 170 pounds. He had speed and was nasty on defense, finishing plays with that extra dig that became a Bears trademark. As Ditka said, "Victory is a matter of imposing your will." Halas broke his jaw on the field, and his leg. He was the kid on the sidelines, waiting stoically as a trainer stitches his lip, piercing and pulling, breaking the string. Illinois won the Big Ten his senior year. For Halas, this team became the model for all the others. It was not just the excellence but also the closeness of the squad: the hours on trains and buses, the locker room talk, the society of boys. As the season came to an end, players began to make career plans. Though Halas earned a degree in civil engineering, he did not want to be cooped up in an office. He wanted to kick and tackle in the snow, bust his jaw and run free. Once you get the taste of the sport, you never want to do anything else.

There was a senior banquet following the season. Everyone got drunk, Zuppke said a few words. He was intelligent, less dictator than tactician. He was born in Berlin. They called him "the German." He reminded the boys that they'd never play the game again. Pro football was still crude and rudimentary, a sandlot game, the provenance of working-class thugs. Zuppke congratulated his men, then spoke that bit of doggerel that every coach speaks at the end of the season: "You're the best bunch I've ever had." You smile and tear up but never believe it. "It's a shame," Zuppke went on, "just when I teach you fellows how to play, you graduate and I lose you. Football's the only sport that ends just as a man's career should be beginning." But George Halas was special: he was the kid who actually took the coach seriously. Remembering Zuppke's speech years later, he said, "Those words were to govern the rest of my life."

America had entered World War I before the football season. Halas had waited until the last game, then enlisted in the navy. In honor of his service, the school awarded him the credits he still needed to graduate. He wanted to go overseas, fire guns and fight for freedom, but was instead sent to the Great Lakes Naval Training Center near Lake Bluff, Illinois, where he was added to the roster of the football team the navy brass was assembling from its bounty of conscripts. Halas was ranked an ensign, but all he did was play. In this way, he got to know the other football standouts of his time: Paddy Driscoll from Northwestern; Hugh Blacklock from Michigan State; Jimmy Conzelman from Washington University. If you look at the first busts in the NFL Hall of Fame, you'll be looking at much of the navy's World War I team.

The players were assigned to Navy Special Services, fitted with dress whites and travel sacks, then sent on the road. They whistle-stopped from college town to college town, where they whipped just about every football power in the nation. The games were meant to boost morale and serve as a recruiting tool. Halas soon took over as coach, his first experience in a job that would define him. They beat Michigan and Illinois, and battled Notre Dame to a tie. The season ended in Pasadena, California, where the navy played a team of All-Star marines in the Rose Bowl, then called the Tournament East–West football game. This game stands at the peak of Halas's amateur career. It's the moment he realized how good he'd become. The stadium was packed; the nation's best players were out there in smocks. Halas carried the ball on offense, covered the speedsters on defense. If you came across the middle, you were going to get hurt. For Halas, it was one of those perfect days when the sun shines and the dirt flies and everything is revealed: He could read each play before it had been called, knew where the ball was going before it got there. He did not follow nor anticipate. He knew. He caught a pass from Paddy Driscoll, turned upfield, and ran for a touchdown. In the second half, when the outcome was still in doubt, he read "pass" in the eyes of an opposing halfback, drifted back, jumped. He was up there a long time before the ball found him, nestled in his arms, went to sleep. He hit the grass running: seventy-seven yards through a tunnel of lunatics. They dragged him down at the 3. He was named Rose Bowl MVP, then smiled all the way back to Illinois. He got drunk with the boys, laughed, told stories. Then it was over. The war, the team. Everything. He was back in Chicago shortly after Armistice Day, the delirium of Clark Street, the el rattling past. Confetti, banners, the celebratory howl of a town drunk on promise, and meanwhile the sharp-jawed athlete stands like a boy in a Sherwood Anderson story, asking himself, "What the hell am I supposed to do now?"

A few years earlier, when Halas was playing baseball for the University of Illinois, he had been scouted by the New York Yankees. He was a right fielder, a switch-hitter with a knack for getting on base. The scout invited him to tryouts, but the war intervened. He decided to head to spring training after he was demobilized. His mother objected. Halas had a degree in civil engineering, and she wanted him to use it. To her, he must have seemed like the college graduate who refuses to assume the responsibilities of adulthood. But if he was going to spend the rest of his life in an office, why hurry to get started?

He arrived in Jacksonville, Florida, in the winter of 1919, carrying a glove and a letter from the scout. They put him in right field and told him to shag flies. It was the dead ball era. Babe Ruth was still in Boston, where he spent most of his time on the pitcher's mound, a left-handed ace who, now and then, when he came to the plate—big powerful man that he was—drove a pitch into the deepest recesses of Fenway Park. George Halas was the exact sort of player that prospered in that ancient dispensation: the dead ball was all about bunting for singles, stealing bases, coming into second spikes high. He looked like Ty Cobb, the foul-tempered star of the major leagues—something the scout had probably noticed. And played like Cobb, too, without the talent. Halas was a fighter, a battler, a hustler, a go-getter, but despite the occasionally inspired play, he was not an artist on any field, baseball or football, which is why he is remembered less as a player than as a founder, an innovator, and a coach.

The Yankees already had some of the players who would be part of their great teams of the 1920s. Lefty O'Doul was pitching, as were Bob Shawkey and Carl Mays, but for the most part the roster was a grab bag of the old and infirm, leftovers, has-beens, spare parts. Frank "Home Run" Baker, Ping Bodie, Duffy Lewis. The most famous player on the team is remembered less for what he did on the field than as a warning to workingmen who want to go skylarking: Wally Pipp, the first baseman, who, in 1925, decided to sit out a game—because the season is long, the body weary—opening a spot for Lou Gehrig, who occupied it for 2,130 consecutive games. Not long ago, during a preseason Patriots game, when wide receiver Wes Welker was out with injury, his replacement returned a kick for a touchdown. Pulling Welker aside, Patriots coach Bill Belichick asked, "What's the name of that guy who played first base for the Yankees before Gehrig?"

Halas was a switch-hitter, unusual for the time. He was a fine fielder, too, able to break on the ball with the crack of the bat and cover vast swaths of outfield. He was speedy, mean and, if he knew a fastball was coming, he could hit. One afternoon that spring, he faced the Brooklyn Robins' Rube Marquard, who threw a fastball as Halas was thinking fastball. He swung from the heels, the bat whipping across the plate. *Crack.* The sort of contact that vibrates through your entire body. The hands know it's gone before the brain—the flash of lightning that precedes the thunder. The Yankees were on their feet, hooting as Marquard kicked the dirt and the ball vanished. That night, Yankees manager Miller Huggins took Halas aside: *Pack your bags, son. We're taking you to New York.* Halas was given a standard rookie contract: $400 a month, plus a $500 signing bonus.

Halas's single season of pro baseball reads in the record book as a joke, the answer to a trivia question. In the course of twelve games, he came to the plate twenty-two times and got two hits. His career batting average was .091. In later years, friends would speak of the day he faced Walter Johnson of the Washington Senators, one of the game's great pitchers. Halas hit two long flies off Johnson, which, had they been fair, would've been home runs. Harry Caray, the Cubs' announcer, had a term for such near misses: "long strikes." Halas struck out in eight of twenty-two plate appearances. Because of his fastball prowess, he was soon facing nothing but spitters, changeups, and curves. By June, he was dreaming of a foul tip, a taste of the ball. He was valued for the fire he brought to the cause. He was a respected bench jockey, the name given to players who excelled in the art of heckling.

One afternoon at the Polo Grounds, in New York, Halas went after Ty Cobb. Halas considered Cobb a model, a man with a surfeit of zipperoo. (To become an adult, you must kill your parents.) Every time Cobb came to the plate, Halas moved to the top dugout step. He stood there, calling Cobb a dog, a cocksucker, a cheap piece of nothing, a motherfucker. Cobb finally flung down his bat and stormed over. Halas froze. There stood his hero, eyes wild. "Punk, I'll see you after the game. Don't forget, punk!"

Halas stayed in the locker room after all the other players had left. He lingered in his street clothes, waiting for the trainer to turn off the lights. He hoped Cobb would be gone, but there he was, fists at his side, standing in the tunnel. He made a motion like he was going to crack Halas, but held out his hand instead, saying, "I like your spirit kid, but don't overdo it." Halas walked Cobb back to his hotel, a jaunt down Broadway in the fading gloom of old Manhattan, talking all the way. "Direct your energy positively," said Cobb. "Don't waste yourself being negative." They remained friends the rest of their lives. I have a picture of them taken years later, old men in Bermuda shorts, in the sun, the entire history of American sports.

Halas hurt his hip in June, jammed it sliding into third. On an off day, he went to see a doctor known as Bonesetter Reese. The ensuing treatment bothered Halas for the rest of his life; he would eventually need to have that hip replaced. The injury did not improve his chances of staying in the majors. He had a crushing plate appearance against the Chicago White Sox. This was the team later known as the Black Sox; with the participation of Shoeless Joe Jackson, Happy Felsch, Chick Gandil, Lefty Williams, and four others, they would throw the 1919 World Series. Halas faced them at Comiskey Park, a few miles from the apartment where he grew up. It was a homecoming—his friends and family were in the stands. Halas badly wanted to perform, get some wood on the ball. But Eddie Cicotte, who would post an astounding 1.82 ERA that season, was on the mound for the Sox. Halas had determination and hustle, but Cicotte had a wicked knuckleball. In football, hustling can make all the difference, but when you're hitting a baseball, all the effort in the world won't help. In baseball, effort is the enemy of contact. On one pitch, Halas watched as the knuckler dipped and dived in for a strike. On another, he looked like a man trying to kill a bee with a Louisville Slugger. Sweat soaked his jersey. Halas struck out on three pitches as his family watched. He called it the worst day of his life.

Shortly after the game, Miller Huggins told Halas he would be sent to the minor league club in St. Paul, Minnesota, where he'd get the at bats he needed. He was on a train a few hours later. Cornfields and forest. The Night Ride of George Halas, nothing behind him, nothing ahead. He worked like a dog in Minnesota, but word soon arrived from New York: the Yankees had acquired a pitcher they intended to play in right field. When they got Babe Ruth, Halas knew he'd never play for the team again.

By the end of the summer, Halas had his own drafting table on the design floor of the Chicago, Burlington & Quincy Railroad, known as the CB&Q. The company had rail lines across the Midwest and West; its tracks serviced Illinois, Iowa, Nebraska, Missouri, Colorado, Texas, and New Mexico; its gondolas were filled with Pennsylvania coal; its flatcars were heavy with Wisconsin lumber; its boxcars were loaded with Montana beef—seemingly endless trains on endless tracks, delivering the raw products of the continent to factories where they were processed and returned as ingredients. The CB&Q boomed after the

First World War, which meant new routes and new trunk lines, the spurs running across factory yards where the men on break played football. Halas designed cast-iron bridges that crossed gullies and ditches, the waste places of industrial life. It was a good job: $55 a week, with the prospect of advancement. He might spend a month designing a span meant to carry a heavy train over a slag heap. An elegant sketch. Blue pencil on drafting paper. He was given the designs of fellow engineers to check for stresses. Geometry and algebra, like back in college, only without the release of a game on Saturday.

On some weekends, he played sandlot football. It was the age of the factory team. Every refinery put together its squad of eleven. They played before mean local crowds, a gridiron chalked behind the mill, brick buildings, black windows, a hundred yards of dirt on a desiccated stretch of lakefront. Pushed by rivalries, the best teams broke away to become independents, free to recruit, bring in ringers, college stars gone to ruin—a shade too old, a step too slow, but in need of cash. The first professional leagues formed in western Pennsylvania and Ohio, the names of its defunct teams recalling an America that's gone the way of Carthage: the Massillon Tigers, the Youngstown Patricians. The first pro player was William "Pudge" Heffelfinger, a Yale all-American, who in 1892 took $500 to play for the Alleghany Athletic Association. The first great pro team was the Pittsburgh Stars, which dominated something called the National Football League in 1902. The Stars were led by Bucknell graduate Christy Mathewson, who would become one of the storied pitchers in baseball history. There were no written rules in these leagues, or schedules, or playoffs, or champions. Everything was agreed to before the game. By 1920, there were a handful of independents that operated in a near professional way. Chief among them was the Canton Bulldogs, which featured Jim Thorpe, the first star of American football.

Halas was recruited by his former navy teammate Paddy Driscoll, who had been playing for the Hammond Pros, an Indiana team that competed in the factory belt. He was paid $100 a game, nearly double his weekly railroad salary. He faced Thorpe on a sepia-toned afternoon in Canton. On one play, as Halas crawled away from the pile, Thorpe threw a leg over his back and said, "All right, if you are a horse, I'll ride you."

Halas's bridge-building career ended with a phone call. It came from George Chamberlin, an executive at the A. E. Staley Manufacturing Company of Decatur, Illinois. *What do we make? We make starch, son.* He asked Halas to meet him at the Sherman House hotel on the North Side. February 1920, the gray days of winter, when the lid that covers Chicago every autumn is still firmly in place. Chamberlin said his boss, Mr. Staley, wanted to field a company football team that could compete with the best factory squads and independents. He'd already done it with baseball, building a roster around "Iron Man" Joe McGinnity, who'd pitched ten seasons in the major leagues. The Staleys were a sensation in southern Illinois, the bleachers of the factory stadium packed with boosters. It proved a boon for the company: good for morale, good for name recognition, good for starch. He wanted to do the same with football. Halas was approached for his pedigree: a student of Zuppke, a star at the University of Illinois, the MVP of the Rose Bowl, a season with the Yankees. He'd be given a job at the factory but be expected to do only a nominal amount of work.

When the offer was made, Halas must have realized how bored he'd been at the CB&Q. He told Chamberlin he had to think it over, but that wasn't true. It was time he needed—to prepare his mother, who considered it a terrible idea. Here was Halas, forsaking a good job at a big company, for what? Decatur? A blister of a town 172 miles south of the only city that mattered. The boondocks, the sticks, a stain in the cornfields where Illinois bleeds into Dixie. And why? So he could make another run at his old dream, which was a life dedicated to a game. America has become endless childhood, where any passion can take you pro. Halas played a part in creating this world. Before him, football was a boys' game. You played it because you loved it. If you took money, you were a whore. After him, football was everything.

Halas told Chamberlin he would take the job on the following conditions: that he be allowed to recruit, bring in ringers from around the region; that he be given power to hire these men, offer them jobs at the factory that paid at least as much as they'd make on the best independents—$100 a game; that these men be allowed to practice two hours a day, regardless of their Staley chores. Chamberlin got in touch with the boss, who agreed. Halas gave the railroad notice and put his blue pencils away. From now on, his drawing would be confined to X's and O's.

George Halas arrived in Decatur on March 20, 1920. He was surprised by the bustle of the place, a manufacturing hub surrounded by soybeans and corn, the fields as flat as the sea. When you stand on a berm, you can almost see the curvature of the earth. At night, stars cover the sky from the peak of heaven to the bank of the river, which unwinds toward the Mississippi.

He rented a room in a boardinghouse on El Dorado Street, across from the Staley factory. There isn't a plaque yet, but there should be. He met with Augustus Eugene Staley, the president and founder of the company, who would later remember the young Halas for "his drive, energy, pep and ambition." The old zipperoo. The factory is still there, a maze of buildings and breezeways, warehouses and processing floors, burners, cookers, conveyors, and spinning machines churning out high-fructose corn syrup and starch.

Halas was given what mobsters call a no-show job, a title to explain his place on the payroll. No one expected him to master the trade. According to Halas's grandson Patrick McCaskey, George worked in the yard, unloading freight cars. He was later moved to the glucose department, then to starch.

He spent most of his energy on the team. In addition to the power to hire players, Staley had given Halas $1,000 for supplies, travel expenses, etc. He began that summer by chasing down standouts he'd known in college or the navy. He signed six former Big Ten players, including Paddy Driscoll, Jimmy Conzelman, and Dutch Sternaman, an Illinois teammate who would become a part owner of the Bears. He brought in George Trafton, who'd played for Zuppke at Oak Park High School before becoming a Notre Dame star; Trafton was the first center to snap with one hand. Halas kept just one player from the team Staley had fielded before his arrival: Chuck Dressen, a gifted local who was technically the first quarterback of the franchise. Dressen played a single game for Halas, then went on to a good pro baseball career with the Cincinnati Reds. He later managed half a dozen major league baseball teams, including the Brooklyn Dodgers and the Detroit Tigers.

People think of the men who played in the early days of pro football as a distinct species, prehistoric, as tiny as pygmies. By the standards of today they were small and slow, yes—but not that small and not that slow. The average player on the Staley line was over two hundred pounds and over six feet tall. These were not scrubs; most of them had played at universities where football was big business. They practiced two hours a day, working themselves to exhaustion. They played their first game Sunday, October 3, 1920, at Staley Field. Two thousand people watched the Decatur Staleys roll over the Moline Tractors 20–0. Dutch Sternaman scored three touchdowns. Halas set up in the back-field, hands on knees, coaching as he waited for the snap. The team played thirteen games that season, the Illinois Central carrying them from factory town to factory town. They faced the Rock Island Inde-pendents, the Kewanee Walworths, the Hammond Pros. You would hardly recognize some of these games as football: it was a street fight, a contest to see who'd submit. They played the Chicago Tigers in Cubs Park, later named Wrigley Field—the team's first appearance in what would become their home stadium. They hosted the Canton Bulldogs, a game in which Halas once again grappled with Jim Thorpe. Thorpe did not use his arms to tackle. He simply ran you over. It was said he wrapped his pads in sheet metal, suiting himself in armor.

After the game, Thorpe said, "Pretty nice crowd here."

"Yes, maybe we ought to have a get-together, and form some kind of league," said Halas. "We could really build this into something."

The Staleys finished with ten wins, one loss, and a tie. Despite the record, the camaraderie, and the thrill of the games, Halas was disap-pointed. This was a million miles from the glory of college. There were just not enough quality clubs to play, and, even if good teams could be found, the games were put together in such an on-the-fly manner, the record seemed pointless. There was no way to compare, to identify the best. Halas's motto was "Never go to bed a loser," but who could tell the winners from the losers after such a slapdash season?

In the summer of 1920, Halas wrote Ralph Hay, the owner of the Can-ton Bulldogs. Hay had tried to set up a pro league the year before, but it fell apart. Halas suggested they try again. Ralph Hay is like one of the unfamiliar names on the Declaration of Independence: a big deal then, a footnote today. Short and stocky with meaty hands, he was an ener-getic bald man who sold cars. An exchange of letters followed: Halas to Hay, Hay to the owners of a handful of quality football clubs. A meeting was scheduled for September 17. Halas went by train, a trim man in a dark suit, a skinny tie, a newspaper in his fist. He rapped it on his knee when he had an idea, grinned, looked out the window. It was already in his head, the league, the teams, the stadiums. Halas was traveling with Morgan O'Brien, a Staley engineer and a football fan, the first of those innumerable guy Fridays who would do anything for the coach just to be close to the game.

They reached Canton in the afternoon. The streets were shaded by awnings. The awnings snapped in the wind. Twenty or so men turned up, the owners of a dozen clubs who crammed into Hay's auto show-room. As there were not enough chairs, many of them sat on the running boards of Hay's Hupmobiles. Halas did a lot of talking. He wanted a schedule, he wanted standings and rules, he wanted a commissioner, and he wanted a winner. In this way, the league was born. For the first two seasons, it was called the American Professional Football Association, a name later changed to the National Football League. Jim Thorpe was named commissioner, as he was the game's only star. A terrible administrator, he was soon replaced by Joe Carr. The charter members were required to pay a $100 fee, forked over in greasy bills or check or IOU. *The tickets getting here cleaned me out.* Over the next ninety years, the $100 Halas used to purchase his franchise doubled in value, was raised to the tenth power, and multiplied by a gazillion. In September 2012, the *Chicago Tribune* estimated the team's worth at $1.19 billion.

The list of NFL charter teams reads like a roll call of nineteenth-century street gangs: Canton Bulldogs, Decatur Staleys, Cleveland Indians, Dayton Triangles, Akron Pros, Rochester Jeffersons, Rock Island Independents, Muncie Flyers, Racine Cardinals, Hammond Pros. Industrial towns—that's where the league started, where its personality formed. It's a ruggedness that still lingers in the mentality of the coach who distinguishes between hurt and injured: injured is broken, meaning *you're done*; hurt is pain, meaning *get back out there, you fuckin' pussy.* Only two original franchises survive: the Chicago Bears and the Arizona Cardinals, who previously played as the St. Louis Cardinals, the Chicago Cardinals, and the Racine Cardinals, not because they were based in Racine, Wisconsin, but because the roster was made up of guys who hung out on Racine Street on Chicago's South Side.

4

LEATHER HEADS

Red Grange, the Galloping Ghost, played seven seasons for
the Bears and put the NFL on the map.

The early years of the NFL recall a lost chapter in the leisure life of America. It was a time of over-the-hill quarterbacks and asthmatic runners, men traded for equipment, fans deputized to play. It was fun in the way of a fad or an enterprise everyone expects to fail: enjoy it while you can, soon you'll take your place on the factory floor. The league was considered disreputable, the Wild West of professional sports. Each year, the names of the teams changed as old powers faded and factory squads ascended. Thirty-five franchises folded in the first decade, including the Milwaukee Badgers, which featured Paul Robeson, the great African American bass-baritone, who played one season in the NFL while attending Columbia Law School; the Providence Steam Rollers; the Akron Pros; and the strangest team in sports history, the Oorang Indians. The passion project of Walter Lingo, who made a fortune in dog kennels, the Oorang Indians were based in LaRue, Ohio, the smallest town to ever boast a professional anything. Lingo, a digger of arrowheads and builder of tepees, loved all things Native American and staffed his team entirely with Indians. He recruited from the Carlisle and Haskell Indian schools as well as Chippewa reservations in Wisconsin and Minnesota. The names on the starting roster included Big Bear, Red Fang, Little Twig, Deer Slayer. He signed Jim Thorpe when he was so broken-down no other pro team would have him.

Halas made the great play of his career against Oorang. It happened in Chicago, on a rainy afternoon. Thorpe was carrying the ball, plunging into the pile. Halas put his head into the big man's stomach. You could hear the wind leave his lungs: *oof!* The dark face scowled as the ball came loose and bounded across the field. Halas picked it up, made one cut, and was gone, with Thorpe behind him. "I ran faster and faster but I sensed he was gaining," Halas wrote. "I could hear the squishing of his shoes in the mud. When I could almost feel his breath, I dug in a cleat and did a sharp zig. Thorpe's momentum carried him on and gave me a few feet of running room. He narrowed the gap. I zagged. Just short of the goal, Thorpe threw himself at me and down I went, into a pool of water. But I slid over the goal. No professional had run 98 yards for a touchdown. None did so again until 1972." The Green Bay Packers entered the league in its second season; the New York Giants came a few years later. Tim Mara, a bookmaker who knew Halas from the smoky back rooms where ballplayers and gamblers mingled, paid $2,500 for the franchise. He was no football fan but figured anything in New York was worth $2,500. The Steelers started as the Pittsburgh Pirates in 1933, the hobby of former prizefighter Art Rooney, who knew everyone because he basically grew up in a saloon. The Redskins began in Boston but were moved to D.C. by George Preston Marshall, a Southerner who made a fortune in laundry. Marshall, the premier racist of the NFL—because of him, African Americans were kept off rosters for years—had his wife write the league's first fight song:

> Hail to the Redskins!
> Hail victory!
> Braves on the warpath!
> Fight for old DIXIE! . . .
> Scalp 'em, swamp 'em
> We will take 'em big score . . .

When I think about those early days, I imagine black-and-white photos, moments of football time frozen in the phosphorous stink of a cameraman's flash. Bloody faces beneath leather headgear, busted teeth, bloody hands, a ball wobbling in the cold air. The league was filled with characters: Shipwreck Kelly, Benny Friedman, Johnny Blood. Its great early star was Thorpe. By making him the first commissioner, Halas and Hay seemed to connect their game to the original inhabitants of the land, distinguishing football from fey sports like baseball and golf, which stunk faintly of Europe. Football was American, its first star a big gamboling red man, who, a generation before, you might have faced in more dire circumstances at the Little Bighorn. The presence of Thorpe, who was a myth when he was still alive, seemed to prove what the champions of the game claimed from the beginning: though the West had been won and the Indian Wars had ended and the cowboy had faded away, the spirit of the frontier lived on, on the football field.

Thorpe was a perfect symbol of the frontier because he was actually born there, in Indian Territory in 1887 or 1888. His parents were of mixed heritage, part Irish, part Sac, Fox, and Potawatomi Indian. Thorpe grew up on reservations all over the Midwest. The skills Thorpe developed while rambling in the open country were just the ones he'd need for football: speed, endurance, stealth. His Indian name was Wa-Tho-Huk, "Bright Path." He was as fast and strong as anyone who ever lived. His career in organized sports began at the Carlisle Indian Industrial School, where, according to lore, he walked onto the field one day and did a just-for-the-fun-of-it high jump in street clothes that set a record: five feet nine inches. He was nineteen. He played every sport at Carlisle

Jim Thorpe, the first great star of professional football

but excelled in football, where he was coached by Pop Warner. It was Warner who convinced Thorpe to go out for the U.S. Olympic Team. In 1912, Thorpe won the decathlon and pentathlon in Stockholm. He was covered in gold. At the medal ceremony, he was given gifts by Czar Nicholas II and King Gustav V of Sweden, who shook the Indian's hand and said, "Sir, you are the greatest athlete in the world."

Thorpe's response—"Thanks, King!"—was said to demonstrate the casualness of the new American character. He returned a hero, marched in parades, and was showered in honor. He called it the peak of his life. That's the way of the world: you are shown everything, the entire hand, fanned out with kings and one-eyed jacks, a moment before it's taken away and shuffled back into the deck. A few months after Thorpe's return, a newspaper scared up an old minor league box score, which proved Thorpe had been paid a few dollars to play a handful of baseball games for the Rocky Mount Railroaders of the Carolina League. College athletes earning food money in the summer leagues was a common practice. Thorpe stood apart only for his naïveté: he didn't know enough to invent an alias. In a letter to the Olympic Committee, he begged for forgiveness. "I hope I would be partly excused because of the fact that I was simply an Indian school boy and did not know all about such things." His records were stripped from the books. He was asked to return his medals as well as the gifts that had been given to him by the czar and the king.

For Thorpe, it was the trauma that confirmed his sense of the world: its prejudice, its hypocrisy. From there, his story is desultory, an opera of decline shot through with occasional moments of triumph. He bumped from town to town, sport to sport, playing 289 games in major league baseball, mostly for the New York Giants, where his name was still a draw. Like Halas, he could not hit the curve. He married, drank, lost a son, and eventually reached Canton, where he would put the NFL in the news. According to Grantland Rice, a prominent sportswriter of the time, "Thorpe was the cornerstone, badly used, but nevertheless a cornerstone of professional football."

He played for a half dozen teams, valuable as a name long after his body began to fail. He spent less and less time practicing, more and more time drinking. He was a barroom brawler. By 1926, he embodied everything the game does to a man: strong and skinny at the start, he was beefy and broken at the end, alcoholic, in constant pain, bitter and confused. His boyish face had become a mask. His body wasted, the world-class speed gone. It was with melancholy that Rice wrote, "I can still see Thorpe as Pop Warner described him when he first came to Carlisle from the plain country of Oklahoma: a skinny Indian youngster weighing around 130 pounds . . . but moving like a breeze."

Thorpe was the subject of perhaps the first great football movie, *Jim Thorpe—All American*, starring Burt Lancaster. You see him tackle, hit, break free; you see him robbed of everything, humiliated—all in hallucinatory close-ups that anticipate modern sports coverage. Near the end, Thorpe sits alone in L.A. Coliseum, the empty seats rising high above him like a grave. He's nothing but self-pity, rage, regret. Of course, there's a happy ending. But in real life, Thorpe continued to struggle, working construction, digging ditches. He appeared in B movies, often playing the Indian who gets killed. In 1950, diagnosed with cancer, he went to a charity hospital. He was destitute. His wife begged donations. "We're broke," she told reporters. "Jim has nothing but his name and his memories." He died in 1953. He was sixty-four, just a belly and a dollar or two.

Football is an angry game, played with punishing violence. People get destroyed on the field, lives end. It makes sense that its first star was someone who'd already lost everything, a ruined man, ill-treated, stripped to his essential qualities: speed, strength, power. Jim Thorpe is the spirit of the game. Every NFL hit still carries the fury of the disgraced Indian, prowling the field, seeking justice.

5

THE EYE IN THE SKY

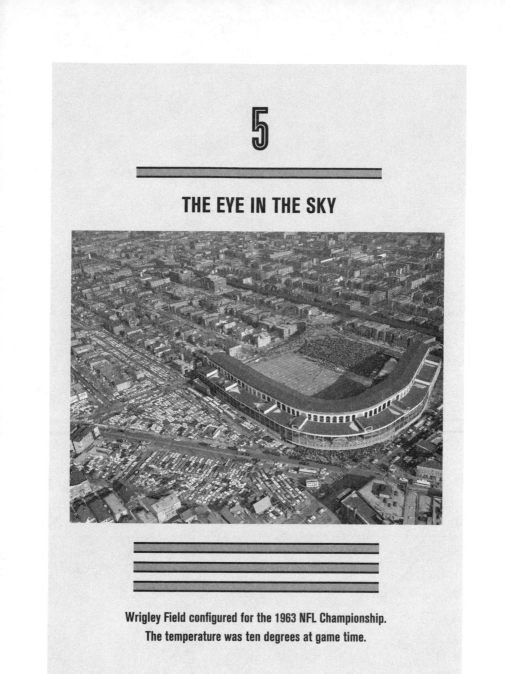

Wrigley Field configured for the 1963 NFL Championship.
The temperature was ten degrees at game time.

My first job after college was at *The New Yorker.* **I was a** messenger and a receptionist. I was supposed to deliver packages, sort mail, and answer the phone, but I spent a lot of time working on stories. On one occasion, a valuable piece of art entrusted to my care was destroyed. It was not my fault but I was blamed. On another, a panic button was accidentally pressed and the authorities were summoned. Finally, one day, the managing editor called me into her office, sat me down, and said, "It's clear to everyone that you care more about writing than about answering the phone." I mention this only to explain my sympathy for George Halas, who, in the summer of 1921, when he was twenty-seven, was called into Eugene Staley's office. Staley sat him down and said, "George, I know you like football better than starch."

Staley did not blame his employee. After all, Staley brought Halas to Decatur to do exactly what he'd done: build a team. But he hadn't counted on the cost. It turned out Staley couldn't afford to employ sixteen men to play football. He'd already lost $14,000 on the team. He felt guilty about the situation: he'd made promises, and a young man had quit his job and moved to a strange town on the basis of those promises. With this in mind, Mr. Staley made Halas an offer, the deal that would bring the Bears to Chicago. Staley would give Halas $5,000 to take the team independent, get them up and running in a new home, a business like any other, with payroll covered by ticket sales. Staley's only condition was that the team keep his name for another season. This explains the first line in the Bears record book, which lists the Decatur Staleys.

A few weeks later, Halas worked out a deal with Bill Veeck Sr., the president of the Chicago Cubs. The Bears would play in Wrigley Field from 1921 to 1970. In their first home game, they beat the Rochester Jeffersons. Wrigley Field was particularly ill suited for football. The end zones, which are normally ten yards deep, were foreshortened by a dugout on one side, an outfield wall on the other. A wide receiver might make a catch, then fall into the dugout. On one occasion, Bronko Nagurski, the great power runner of the 1930s, took the ball, put his head down, bulled through every defender—and straight into a brick wall. He got up slowly. When he made it to the bench, Halas was concerned:

"You okay, Bronk?"

Nagurski said he was fine, but added, "That last guy gave me a pretty good lick, coach."

In the early years, most NFL teams played in baseball stadiums, and many took the name of the host team. Hence the Pittsburgh Pirates, who played in Forbes Field, and the New York Football Giants, who played in the Polo Grounds. Halas considered naming his team the Cubs, but in the end, believing that football players were much tougher than baseball players, he called them the Bears.

Chicago was booming in 1922. It was the Jazz Age, the city of the gangster, the great metropolis taking in and spitting out the raw produce of the nation via freight yards and slaughterhouses and lakefront factories. The first skyscraper had been designed in Chicago, and the city was being remade in its image, a line of towers rising and falling along South Michigan Avenue like notes on a musical score. There are certain times when everything is in the right place, when all the players are at their instruments—you want to slow the spinning world and let the moment linger. Big Bill Thompson was serving as mayor in 1922, Al Capone was at his club in Cicero, Louis Armstrong was on the South Side playing his horn, and Carl Sandburg, who was at his house in Evanston, had turned it all into verse:

They tell me you are wicked and I believe them, for I
    have seen your painted women under the gas lamps
    luring the farm boys.
And they tell me you are crooked and I answer: Yes, it
    is true I have seen the gunman kill and go free to
    kill again.
And they tell me you are brutal and my reply is: On the
    faces of women and children I have seen the marks
    of wanton hunger.
And having answered so I turn once more to those who
    sneer at this my city, and I give them back the sneer
    and say to them:
Come and show me another city with lifted head singing
    so proud to be alive and coarse and strong and cunning.
Flinging magnetic curses amid the toil of piling job on
    job, here is a tall bold slugger set vivid against the
    little soft cities;
Fierce as a dog with tongue lapping for action, cunning
    as a savage pitted against the wilderness,
    Bareheaded,
    Shoveling,
    Wrecking,
    Planning,
    Building, breaking, rebuilding . . .

Halas was living in Oak Park with his wife. Her name was Wilhelmina Bushing but everyone called her Min. They'd met in high school. She'd been in the stands at one of his indoor baseball games, rooting for the other team. She heckled whenever Halas came to the plate; she was beautiful. The combination was irresistible. Halas kept after her until she said yes.

Their daughter, Virginia, was born on January 5, 1923. Their son, George Jr., known as Mugs, or Mugsy, was born November 4, 1925. In the first years after Decatur, the Bears had a co-owner in Dutch Sternaman, but Halas eventually bought him out for $38,000 and would never share ownership again. He took odd jobs and started businesses instead, anything to make the money he needed to hang on to the team (football would not be a going concern until the 1940s). For a time, he worked at his brother-in-law's ice plant, the huge blocks clattering down steel chutes, trucks waiting to make the early morning deliveries. In charge of the night shift, he'd get to the plant at around midnight, spend hours checking orders and deploying men, go home for five or six hours' sleep, have a breakfast of cornflakes and banana, then head to practice. He would eventually quit the icehouse, but he always approached football with the glee of a man who has snuck away from his real job.

Halas played his last game in 1928. He appeared just four times that season. His body had begun to fail. Hips and knees, his poor head, which, in the course of twenty seasons, had been slugged, crunched, dinged. His reflexes, too, the internal mechanism, which causes everything to speed up as you age . . . you see the ball, reach for it, but your hand arrives a moment too late. You shake your head and think, Two years ago, I had that.

At first, Halas retired altogether, bringing in his freshman college coach, Ralph Jones, to run the team. But he couldn't stay away. The Bears were his life. He'd never really let go. By 1930, he was back on the sideline—only the uniform had changed: from jersey, helmet, and cleats to jacket, loafers, and fedora, a program curled into a megaphone, carrying the West Side growl: *Hey, O'Brien, why don't you shut up, ya fuckin' pop-off artist!* Despite the occasional profession of exhaustion, followed by a brief retirement, George Halas would remain on the sidelines for the next thirty-five seasons. He's among the most winning coaches in NFL history, with a career record of 324–151–31.

He tends to be depicted as the personification of the old-time coach, the grandfather with the iron fist. Even his own players regarded him this way: "As a tactician, he was simple," said the Bears linebacker Doug Buffone. "They're either gonna knock you down, or you're gonna knock them down." But the opposite is closer to true. Halas was one of the great intellectuals of the game, a brainiac, a football genius. As a thinker, he stands in a line that starts with Alonzo Stagg and includes 49ers coach Bill Walsh and Patriots coach Bill Belichick. It was Halas, as much as anyone, who invented the modern NFL offense and lifted the game from the ground into the air.

His innovations, various and brilliant, were driven by the oldest of playground motivations: he wanted to kick ass. "I play to win," he said. "I always will play to win. I speak no praise for the good loser, the man who says, 'Well, I did my best.' I have learned to live with defeat but each loss is an agony which remains with me for several days and is dissipated only by the growing prospect of victory."

Halas was probably the first coach to use game film—to shoot every practice and play, then huddle in a screening room with players, watching and rewatching, searching for the weak point or hidden detail. It's become an NFL cliché: the head coach gathered with his men, breaking down each failure but passing over moments of excellence in silence; you don't get praised for doing what's expected. But Halas was among the earliest to identify film as a way to glean hidden information. It's what the old man had always been after: the fresh vantage point or unnoticed angle, a perspective from which the game could be seen as if for the first time. *Jesus, no wonder we're getting killed on third down. That cocksucker is missing the block.*

He was probably the first to employ an "eye in the sky," a coach hidden in the bleachers from where he could see enemy formations as clearly as a general studying drawings in the book by Clausewitz. Like just about every meaningful breakthrough, it came about by accident. One afternoon, when the Bears were playing the Yankees, Halas sent his assistant Luke Johnsos into the stands with a note for Mrs. Halas. While awaiting Min's response, Johnsos looked at the field. He had been a good football player but had never seen the game from this high. He suddenly recognized it as something other than big men in a scrum: from here, it was patterns, the arrangement of pieces. Things that had been hidden—What's happening in the secondary, that area behind the linebackers where defensive backs guard against the pass? Where's the safety, the player who functions as a last line of defense?— were revealed. "I must have been standing in the fortieth row," Johnsos said later. "And I could really see what the defense was doing from up there. It looked crazy. The way they were aligned. There was a big hole in the middle of the field. I ran down to the sideline and I told the coach, 'Hey, the middle is wide open. I could see it from the stands.'" Halas looked at Johnsos, then looked at Min. He called over his players, issued a few curt instructions. "Coach ordered a receiver to circle back behind the defense line," Johnsos said. "The quarterback threw him a pass and he went all the way for a touchdown."

Halas sent Johnsos back into the stands with a pad of paper. He was to study the defense. If he spotted a hole, he would write a note and hand it to a runner, who'd carry it to Halas. But half the time, the note did not arrive until the play was over. Before the next game, Halas had a phone installed in the press box. Johnsos would sit up there with binoculars. When he spotted something, he would call Halas, who had another phone installed by the bench. When Halas wanted to know what the linebackers were doing or how the flanker kept getting free on the deep pattern, he would call the "eye in the sky." It was a logical innovation, perhaps inevitable, but it changed the conception of the game. A coach was now able to operate from a position of omniscience, the position of a god, where he could linger over each move the way a chess master lingers, his hand resting on the rook, considering each consequence before committing. "If you go to the Folies Bergère in Paris, sit in the front row," Johnsos said, "but at a football game, sit high so you can see the teams deploy."

When other coaches figured out what Halas had done, they demanded their own eye in the sky at Wrigley. Halas bitched—it's not an advantage if everyone's got it—but complied. He then positioned the Bears marching band behind the visitors' bench. Every time a visiting coach picked up the phone, the band launched into the fight song—just one tactic in Halas's war of discomfort and deprivation. "Teams visiting Wrigley Field constantly complained about lack of soap, towels, programs," Halas wrote. "They put it down to my stinginess. But why not deprive visitors, if doing so upsets them? What better location for the band than directly behind George Preston Marshall, tootling in his ears? And if Curly Lambeau had trouble seeing the play from his specially allocated bench in a far corner, so much the better for the Bears."

In the 1930s, NFL offenses still operated in the preindustrial spirit of mob ball. The quarterback might call for the snap, but the action was controlled by a halfback who pitched out as he raced along the line, ran it himself, or tossed downfield. Known as the option or the single wing, this offense was easy to learn but offered a limited number of ways to score. It was often three yards and a cloud of dust. But the league changed the rules in the 1930s to make the game friendlier to the pass—the ball itself was redesigned—and it meant terrific opportunity for the coach who could capitalize.

Halas's greatest innovation came in the 1930s, with the introduction and refinement of the modern T-formation, bastard sons of which still dominate pro football. In this way, Halas and his assistants invented the look of the modern game.

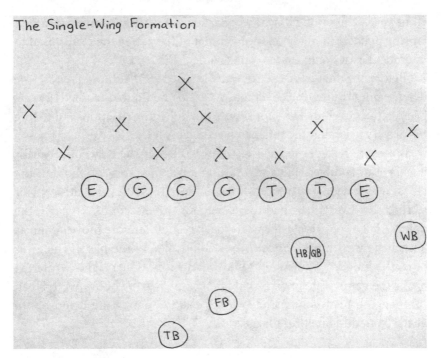

The Single-Wing Formation

Invented by Pop Warner in 1907, the single wing dominated early professional football. It usually featured a halfback or fullback who took the snap, then raced across the field, cycling through options: he could run, pass, or pitch out. The formation, with its tailback (TB) and wingback (WB), recalls an earlier era of football.

The new alignment was called the T-formation because that's what it looks like from above: first the center, then the quarterback, then two halfbacks and a fullback in a line behind—the arms of the T. Halas played it at the University of Illinois and used it with the Bears, but those were antique versions. In the 1930s, working with Ralph Jones, he rebuilt the T around the forward pass. The scheme was centered on the quarterback, who was raised onto a kind of pedestal. He would be the master of the new offense, the first among equals. Instead of plunging into the line, he would take the ball from center and drop back, positioning himself amid a circle of guards, who would keep rushing defenders at bay. This is the pocket. It's like a diving bell, a bubble of air in a violent sea. It was revolutionary: after all, the object of the game is to push the ball forward, advance it down the field. But here was Halas deploying an offense in which the first move was *backward*! Five or eight yards the wrong way, the quarterback setting himself in a collapsing pocket from where, in the midst of the action, he's supposed to operate like an eye in the sky, make a decision, execute.

Before the snap, the quarterback looks downfield and "reads" the defense, identifying the coverage. Who's being double-teamed? Who's been left uncovered? He then shouts out coded instructions, adjusting his players to exploit the mismatches or gaps. If the quarterback spots a weakness in the defense, he is also free to change the play entirely: this is called an audible. Halas was taking advantage of a loophole in the rules, which seemed to picture the offense in static formation prior to the snap. Every man had to be "set" for three seconds. To catch the defense out of position, the quarterback could therefore move a man as long as he was in his stance three seconds before the play. "Thus was born the modern T-formation with man-in-motion," Halas wrote. "It broke the game wide open. Football became a game of brains. Instead of knocking men down, Coach Jones tried to entice the defense into doing something helpful for us."

The Modern T-Formation

With the modern T-formation, the Chicago Bears elevated the quarterback to a position of supreme importance and invented the NFL offense as we still know it today.

The Bears tried to install the modern T in 1935 and again in 1936, but failed. It was too complicated for the quarterback. What a task! He had three seconds to decide, maybe five. After that, the walls cave in. Three hundred plays, each with its contingencies, but how many would he remember after he'd been concussed? In the past, the quarterback had been just another player; Halas made him paramount. "Physically, he'd have to possess a ballet dancer's footwork in designed pivots, step-overs and spins and the ability to throw with accuracy and precision from a drop-back set or on the run, and he had to be able to withstand punishment from onrushing linemen. Since the rules at the time forbade a coach from shuttling in plays, the quarterback . . . also had to be a 'field general.'" Looking over the playbook, Halas turned to his assistant, Clark Shaughnessy, and said, Jesus Christ, Clark, the quarterback has to be a coach on the field.

Clark Shaughnessy came into George Halas's office carrying a tin of film.

"Coach, I've got something to show you."

Shaughnessy was brilliant, a tactician. Tall and angular, a football academic, he'd coached under Stagg at the University of Chicago and would later take over at Stanford. He sat with Halas in the Bears' screening room watching black-and-white footage of college boys racing around in the gloom. It was not the game that interested the coaches. It was number 42, the Columbia halfback. He seemed to be involved in every play, every point. The great players, the naturals . . . you just can't stop seeing them.

"What's his name?"

"Sid Luckman."

He played halfback at Columbia, punted, returned kicks. On most plays, he ran, but what got Halas's attention were the occasions when he lingered in the backfield, hung back, then let the pigskin fly. He was a hybrid, a big kid with the body of a running back—a shade over six feet, he played at two hundred pounds—who had the eyes, the arm, and the sense to find the open man deep downfield, drop a ball over his shoulder on a dead run. Luckman's ball, a tight spiral, was famously easy to catch. Halas was most impressed by his accuracy, how each throw threaded its way through the outstretched hands of defensive backs. And the way he moved! The way he looked! Dark and hand-some, the tough, brooding kind of handsome, the don't-fuck-with-me kind, with a fighter's worn features; he'd break his nose a dozen times before it was over. And the poise, the grace under pressure. Here was a kid who'd had a mediocore Columbia team competing with Fordham, Navy, Pitt. Now and then, you see something in larval form and know what it will become. In Sid Luckman, Halas recognized the modern quarterback before that position existed.

It was not just Luckman's athletic skills, it was his background. In a game populated by coal-town toughs, Sid was an oddity: an over-educated Brooklyn kid who excelled in math. It was grades that got him into Columbia, a school that did not offer sports scholarships. And he was a Jew. Halas was the least prejudiced man I've ever studied—his only question was, "Can he help the Bears?"—but he was enough a product of his time to believe something like the following: when it comes to running this new, hypercomplicated offense, you could do worse than get yourself an Ivy league–educated Jew who's built like a bruiser. Or, to resort to the West Side vernacular, "You'd need a Jew to run this fucking thing."

Halas went to see Luckman in person: because there's the film, then there's the stadium, with its weather and the sound of the hits. This was at Baker Field in upper Manhattan in 1938. Columbia was hosting Syracuse. Halas took Luke Johnsos along; who better to judge than the eye in the sky? Tickets had been left at the front gate by Grantland Rice. Sid did everything that afternoon: returned kicks, made tackles, completed passes. "They played in the mud and his pants didn't even get dirty," Halas wrote. "He ran backwards faster than he ran forward. Just think of what he could do if we gave him protection." It snowed in the fourth quarter, big flakes. Luckman was stepped on, the cleats of a Syracuse player driven into his face, blood in the snow. Columbia won 13–12. Luckman changed into street clothes and was heading to the hospital to have his nose fixed when his coach, Lou Little (aka Luigi Piccolo), took him aside and said George Halas of the Bears had been at the game. "He wanted to get a look at you."

Luckman was used to strangers coming to get a look—older men lin-gering outside the fence, taking notes as he played. He'd been a legend in New York, the talk of those fathers who paid too much attention to the neighborhood games.

He dated his interest in the sport to his eleventh birthday, when his father gave him a football. Even this object of fun was presented as a tool for advancement. "Dad said owning a football in our hurly-burly neighborhood was like owning real estate," Luckman wrote. "It set a boy apart, because not many could afford a football with a star's name stamped on it." Luckman went everywhere with the ball. He was the kid you see throwing passes to himself under the streetlight. He became a standout on the vacant lots, the player who can't be brought down. When his mother complained about the game's violence—even when he was All-Pro, she refused to watch—his father admonished her, saying, "If a squirt isn't knocked around now and again, Ethel, how'll he ever grow into a tough fellow?"

Sid's hero was Benny Friedman, the top quarterback of the time. His father took him to the Polo Grounds to watch Friedman play for the Giants. They waited outside the locker room. Benny came out in a suit, hair wet from the shower. Sid's father waved. "Hey Benny, Mr. Friedman, I have a prospective pro for you." Benny got down on a knee. Sid asked the best way to throw. Benny went to the locker room and returned with a football. He put his fingers on the laces, then had Sid place his own fingers on top. Sid wanted to know the secret. *How do you get the ball to really fly?* Benny couldn't tell him. Even the wizard does not understand the magic behind his most astounding trick.

Luckman became a star at Erasmus Hall, a storied high school in Flatbush, Brooklyn. His victories were chronicled in the newspapers: Erasmus 26, Lincoln 6; Erasmus 27, New Utrecht 0. In many games, he scored every point. He was heavily recruited by colleges but turned down several scholarships to play for Lou Little at Columbia, an inspirational coach who told parents, "I'm out to make men first, then football players." At Columbia, Sid Luckman is remembered for a few defining afternoons: the defeat of a powerful Army team at West Point; the game against Yale, in which Sid completed ten of seventeen passes, two of them for over 50 yards, and ran for another 103. At twenty, he already looked the way he will always look in the minds of a certain generation of fans: big and rugged but not pretty, eyes carrying that mischievous twinkle.

The Bears traded up in the draft to get Luckman, but when Halas called with the news, Sid told him he wasn't interested in playing pro football. The NFL was still somewhat disreputable, a league of hooligans and thugs.

"Well, what the hell do you plan to do?" asked Halas.

"I'm going into the trucking business."

"The trucking business? Since when does a fine prospect for pro ball take up trucking?"

Thus began what Halas called Operation Luckman, the all-out campaign to secure the services of the player he believed capable of running the modern T. There were phone calls, discussions, drop-bys. One evening, Luckman got a surprise visit from Benny Friedman. He said his biggest regret was not being young enough to play for Halas. "Have you taken a look at what he plans to do out there? This modern T-formation? It's the coming thing! The ideal system for a quarterback! You don't have to run, or buck the line, or make fancy dives!"

Halas visited a few days later, sharp blue eyes taking in the Luckmans' Brooklyn apartment. The moon sat low on the river. The foghorns moaned. By the end of the night, Sid had agreed to play for the Bears, having been enticed by what Halas claimed to be the largest bonus in team history. "Five thousand dollars. No one since Jesus Christ got so much." Not true—Bronko Nagurski got the same, and the great Red Grange made a lot more. But it was big money for Halas—a billion manhole covers.

Luckman went to his first practice at the end of the summer. He stood to the side in his pads, the bonus baby getting a look at the offense that had blanked every previous passer's brain. "My first glimpse showed a quarterback crouching behind center, and three mates five yards back of him, crosswise, like the crossing of a letter T, but ready to shift into any number of alignments," Luckman wrote later. "On a signal, the men seemed to run in different directions, and the quarterback would take the ball, and fake it to two or three men and fade back for a pass. The whole system was based on split-second timing. When it worked, there was no better system. When it failed, you saw a mob of puzzled athletes running harum-scarum."

By the 1980s, the modern T had evolved into the typical formation of my youth, with Walter Payton set up behind the fullback, who, on

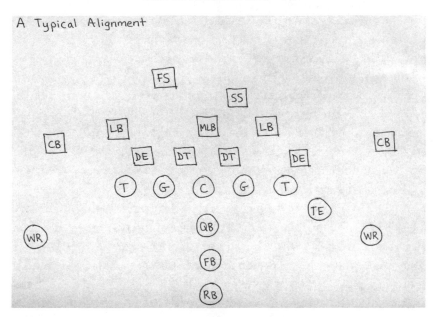

A Typical Alignment

A typical alignment: Here are an offense and defense arranged in generic formations, circa 1985. The offense looks as the Bears' did in the 1980s, with fullback Matt Suhey and running back Walter Payton, quarterback Jim McMahon, wide receivers Willie Gault and Dennis McKinnon, and Emery Moorehead at tight end. Guards and tackles are arrayed on the offensive line, protecting the QB on passing plays and opening holes or clearing paths on the run. The defense is arranged in a loose "4-3," a popular formation probably pioneered by Tom Landry when he coached for the New York Giants in the 1950s. On defense, the big men on the line, defensive ends and defensive tackles, rush the passer; the middle of the field, the secondary, is patrolled by the linebackers, with a middle linebacker serving as a field commander. The cornerbacks cover the wide receivers. Downfield, they are helped by the last line of defense, the safeties, here a strong safety and a free safety.

many plays, ran clearance for Sweetness the way a secret service agent is supposed to run clearance for the president when things get hairy.

Luckman struggled that first season. There were too many plays, too many variables. He spent his nights poring over the playbook, but the drills were never like the games. He would take the snap, turn the wrong way, run into his own man; trip over a pulling guard; get tangled in his own feet; miss a read and get plastered by his own tackle; confuse a signal and send a receiver to the wrong spot, resulting in an interception that, to a fan, would look like nothing more complicated than an errant throw.

One afternoon, the backfield coach Carl Brumbaugh said, "Sid, do you realize the job expected of a Bear quarterback?"

"Realize it?" Luckman answered. "I'm worried sick over it."

"I sat in my room trying to unravel the potpourri of plays, which were given such names as crack-back, running-swing-switch, cross buck, and so forth," Luckman wrote. "In Chicago, the quarterback handled the ball on almost every play. The responsibility of his position frightened the newcomer. He might never run a yard forward but he was the key man, flipping, faking, spinning."

No matter how hard Luckman tried, there was always something he missed. What's more, he had to master the position while also playing defense. Like most quarterbacks, he played safety on the other side. This meant no sitting with a coach and a clipboard, trying to figure out what went wrong—it was right back out there, where at least you could vent your spleen by taking off a few heads.

He was also having trouble adjusting to the culture of the game—the East Coaster, the Ivy Leaguer, the Jew. He never mentioned his situation, but it's implied in the part of his autobiography where he goes to Coach Shaughnessy for advice: *I'm the quarterback. I'm supposed to lead. But how can I lead when they won't accept me?* Shaughnessy thought a moment, then said, "About the players, and your squabbles, time will tell. You'll find it worthwhile to get along with them, because they're a good bunch. Oh, a few natural prejudices are bound to show. They may be pros, but they're still boys at heart with the ordinary tendencies of boys. I think when they get to know you, they'll feel different. Yes, I'm almost sure of it."

By midseason, Luckman was depressed. He couldn't sleep. "Make use of those extra hours," Shaughnessy told him. "Go through the playbook instead of counting sheep!" On some nights, Sid played an entire game in his imagination, then woke up and did it all over again for real. Halas never gave up on the rookie but did let him return to the single wing. It would restore his confidence until he mastered the T.

In other words, Sid Luckman failed before he succeeded, proving what I always tell my piano-lesson-avoiding son: You've got to be bad before you can be good at anything.

———

In Chicago, they're still waiting for the next Sid Luckman. Here he is in 1942, shortly before World War II upended everything.

Then, one afternoon, it clicked. What had been fuzzy became clear. What had been chaos became order. It was the fall of 1940, the Bears were playing Green Bay. They had returned to the T. Crouching under center, Luckman looked up and suddenly the defense opened like a book. *There are the answers, all of them, right there! You can read them!* He shouts a few coded words. His players shift. He takes the snap.

Everything slows, he knows where to turn, when to look. Receiver one is covered? Okay, what about number two? There he is, open. I'll throw him the ball. Oh, look, he's got it. And he's running. We've scored a touchdown.

The team got better and better. At times, they seemed unstoppable. The other boys loved Sid now, this kid racking up unheard-of numbers. Three hundred yards in the air. Four touchdown passes, five, six. The 1940 roster boasted several stars: George Wilson, George McAfee, Bill Osmanksi. It's considered one of the best clubs in history, the equivalent of the 1927 Yankees or the 1976–77 Montreal Canadiens. There've been only a few teams worth remembering by fans in other cities. This is when the Bears became known as the Monsters of the Midway, a nickname lifted from the University of Chicago Maroons, who played on what had been the Midway of the 1893 World's Fair and excelled in the Big Ten till the university president ended the football program. Halas took the name, as he took everything else he thought would help his team.

After finishing 8 and 3, the Bears faced the Washington Redskins in the NFL Championship. The Skins were favored by 10. Whereas Chicago was led by an untested Ivy Leaguer, the Redskins had Slinging Sammy Baugh, a lanky Texan once considered the best quarterback ever. If a writer wanted to praise Luckman, he'd call him "Halas's answer to Sammy Baugh."

George Preston Marshall, the owner of the Redskins, needled Halas all that week. At issue was a game the teams had played earlier in the season. The Bears were down 17–14 with less than a minute. They had the ball near the Redskins' goal but no time-outs. Halas told George McAfee to fake an injury to stop the clock. The refs saw through the ruse and penalized Chicago, assuring a Redskins victory. Halas, who insisted the injury had been real, bitched about it to anyone who would listen. "I probably used all the words I had used on the Chicago streets and in ballparks and training camps and maybe even made up a few new ones," he said. Marshall called Halas and his team "a bunch of crybabies." He sent Halas a telegram when the Bears clinched their spot in the championship: "Congratulations. I hope I have the pleasure of beating your ears off next Sunday and every year to come. Justice is triumphant."

In the locker room, Halas gave a speech organized around the hideousness of being called a crybaby: *Are we just gonna take it? Are we gonna let that cocksucker get away with that bullshit? Or are we gonna go out and show that pop-off artist who the real crybabies are?*

As the team ran onto the field, Halas held Luckman back, put his arm around him. He told Sid the first three plays to call: How they react, that's going to show us everything we need to know. He squeezed Sid's shoulder, said he was proud of him, and wished him luck. The relationship between these two men was the coach/player relationship in platonic form. Years later, shortly before he died, Halas wrote Luckman a letter. They were both old men, with their glory days a million years behind; the letter ended, "My devoted friend, you have a spot in my heart that NO ONE else can claim. I love you with all my heart."

Sammy Baugh marched his team downfield on the first drive. There was something romantic about him . . . the slow walk, the laconic way. He never got flustered. He was relaxed when he threw. Whereas Luckman released from his shoulder, Baugh extended his arm to its apex, releasing at twelve o'clock, a premonition of the over-the-top style of the moderns. He got his team into Bears territory. On one play, he eluded the rush and found a receiver in the end zone. He hit him in the chest, a beautiful West Texas spiral, but the receiver dropped it. A groan went up from the stands. It would be Washington's best chance of the day.

Two plays later, the Bears had taken over and Luckman was thinking through Halas's plays as he walked to the line. For a quarterback, a lot of any game is played in his head, a stream of consciousness: first I do this, which will make him do that, but if he does that, I'll go here, which will make him go there and do that, in which case I will do this, unless, of course, they do that, in which case I'll come back with this, then look for McAfee, and if he's covered . . .

The early break came on the ground. One of the innovations of the modern T was trickery, fakes and feints that disguised the most basic play; half the time, the defense didn't know who had the ball. Sid called it in the huddle: "Spread left-0-scissors 46." He hiked, faked right, then tossed to Osmanski, who got tangled up in the line, broke free, then made it to the outside, where a hole opened. He went the length of the field, a perfect run, but it's the block that opened the hole that people remembered. For years, it was the most famous block in NFL history. It was made by George Wilson, who, according to Luckman, "coming from his right end position, dashed at an angle toward [Osmanski's] line of flight. Around mid-field . . . he hurled his body, at full speed, into Malone of Washington, who bounced back into his partner, Justice, and the two of them somersaulted helplessly over the sideline." In other words, one guard took out two tacklers—in bowling, they call this picking up the 7–10 split. "Watching it," Luckman wrote, "I assured myself that I'd seen the most wicked block perpetuated by man or beast. When Osmanski returned from his sixty-eight-yard touchdown gallop, he found us slapping Wilson on the back and frolicking around. He couldn't understand it, of course, because he was the only man on the field who missed the spectacle."

Football is Nietzschean. It's a question of finding a play or a sequence of plays that breaks the enemy. In the 1940 Championship, it happened during that run by Osmanski. "Washington's hopes began to dampen," wrote Luckman. "The whole business had happened in 58 seconds."

Luckman passed for more than three hundred yards, completing touchdown after touchdown. Fans, who'd come to see a battle, found themselves at a clinic instead, a public demonstration of the modern T-formation. "Everything seemed to click. Even a boner was good for ten yards," Luckman wrote. Coming back to the bench, the quarterback "found Halas delirious with joy . . . After we'd rung up our fiftieth point or so, he began to murmur: 'Wonder what Mr. George Preston Marshall is doin' at this stage?'"

"With Luckman calling the plays with the genius of a clairvoyant, the Bears were a perfect football machine," *Time* reported. "By the end of the third quarter, the game had become an undignified rout."

In the fourth, Halas told his kick holder to kill the play instead of going for the extra point. Nine footballs had already been booted into the stands and he didn't want to lose any more: *Who do you think pays for those balls, smartass?*

Seventy-three to zero—it remains the most lopsided championship game in NFL history. The next morning, *New York Times* sportswriter Arthur Daley began his column, "The weather was perfect. So were the Bears."

In the locker room, a reporter asked Sammy Baugh what might have happened if his receiver had made that catch on the first drive. A shift in momentum can mean everything. "We would've lost 73 to 7," said Baugh.

In the following seasons, most teams in the league adopted some version of the modern T-formation. Halas taught it to anyone who was interested; this might seem like giving away company secrets, but he was generous with ideas. He believed the Bears had come up with a better kind of football that would benefit the league. He wanted to win, but he also wanted to produce a superior product. In the off-season, he wrote a book with Clark Shaughnessy and Ralph Jones, *The Modern "T" Formation with Man-in-Motion*. He sent Luckman to Columbia and Notre Dame to teach the offense to college quarterbacks. It was complicated, with a steep learning curve. If Halas could get colleges to run it, he would secure a supply of game-ready athletes.

Within a few years, the only team running the old offense was the Steelers, and they stunk. The single wing had gone the way of the Spanish caravel. In this way, Halas remade not just the Bears but also the game, joining the ranks of Knute Rockne, Alonzo Stagg, and Walter Camp, innovators whose inventions now seem inevitable. In 1941, Halas hired a writer to pen a new fight song, tasking him to take special notice of the team's recent accomplishments.

> Bear down, Chicago Bears, make every play clear the way to victory.
> Bear down, Chicago Bears, put up a fight with a might so fearlessly.
> We'll never forget the way you thrilled the nation, with your T-formation!

Thus began the great dynastic run of the Bears. For Chicagoans, it would never be as good again. A modern fan, especially if born after 1950, is akin to a modern Roman: deep down we know, no matter how we prosper, that our achievements will always pale in comparison to those of antiquity. Early in the 1940s, the Bears played twenty-four games without a loss. They won their second championship in 1941 and did not lose again until December 1942, when the Redskins got revenge in the championship. Luckman had his best game in 1942 in the Polo Grounds in New York. It was Sid Luckman Day. He threw for close to five hundred yards and completed seven touchdown passes, which remains a record. The Bears got even with the Skins in the 1943 Championship, but it was a different world by then. America had entered World War II. As the nation's young men went overseas— Luckman joined the merchant marine; Halas spent three years in the navy—NFL rosters were increasingly filled by old-timers, has-beens, never-coulds. Bronko Nagurski rejoined the Bears. He was in his mid-thirties, a kind of Methuselah. He had not played in five years. He had been working as a professional wrestler, a circus performer, a gas station owner, and a tiller of the land. When handed the ball, he'd head upfield, yelling, "Let the farmer through."

The Monsters reassembled for one more championship run in 1946, older, slower, thicker, but determined to execute once more. Luckman was like old Picasso, subsisting on savvy. He threw seventeen touchdown passes, which led the NFL. The Bears finished 8–2–1, then played the Giants in the title game. Chicago clinched it in an unlikely way: Sid, kneeling in the huddle, covered in grime, called his own number: *Trust me, I see something.* He had to repeat himself before the boys agreed: "Bingo, keep it." He went to the line, looked here, looked there, took the snap, faked a handoff, a beautiful fake, jogged toward the sideline as if to say, The old man needs a rest, then took off, the ball hidden beneath his arm. It was a long moment before the Giants realized what was happening, that it was Luckman, the ancient, who had the dingus. He ran nineteen yards for a touchdown, his feet getting heavier with each step. The Bears won 24–14. If the war had not intervened, that team might have won seven titles. As it is, they won four and must be considered among the best in history.

Luckman returned for 1947, but he was a beat too slow, a season past prime. I once met a pro baseball player who, pontificating on the fate that awaits every athlete, said, "Some guys go on and on, but others just fall off the table." Sid Luckman was a fall-off-the-table type. He was a leading quarterback right up to the moment he could no longer convert a single play. During one of his last days on the field, he took a whack to the head that knocked him insensible. That was December 14, 1947, the worst game of his career. The magic was gone. He took himself out with twelve minutes left. After that, he was old and done, just as confused as he'd been at the beginning. "It's strange how many top-flight stars lose their championship urge almost overnight," he wrote. "One season you'll find them hustling like young colts, and the next they'll appear listless and off the pace."

He stuck around a few more years, the coach's confidant, a monarch emeritus. When a hero gets old, he takes your youth with him. Luckman retired in 1950 but remained a figure in Chicago for decades. He was the best that had ever been, Sid the Great, who still holds just about every important team passing record. If you follow the Bears, you're familiar with the phrases "not since Luckman," "maybe the next Luckman." He was part of Halas's crew, one of the knock-around guys—Kup, Brickhouse, Sid—sitting at a round table at the Palmer House. He had all kinds of jobs in the years that followed, but the remainder of his life was mostly spent being Sid Luckman. That's why it's so hard for a star athlete to move on. No one wants you to, nor will they let you; they need you to be what you were when you were the polestar, on one knee, calling your own number: "Bingo, keep it." Sid Luckman played football a million years ago but died in 1998, which seems like yesterday. His ghost went out in Aventura, Florida, where the pinochle is high-stakes and the pools reek of country club chlorine.

6

THE QUARTERBACK

Joe Namath preparing for Super Bowl III. Florida, 1967

Gary Fencik heard this story from Virginia Halas McCaskey, who, as of this writing, is in her nineties and controls the Bears. She began attending games in the 1930s when she was eight or nine, watching from the wooden seats at Wrigley. Her favorite player was a receiver from Vanderbilt named Dick Plasman. He had huge hands. You see it in team photos in which he extends his fingers in the way of a magician about to demonstrate an illusion. If you were a kid, he would be your favorite, too. He was the last professional to play without a helmet. For several years, he was the only bare-headed nut out there, dodging defensive backs, his curly blond hair waving. In a game where everyone else was clothed in leather, he was like a man among machines. The action shots are especially jarring: all those helmeted figures moving in the muck, this lone bare-head among them like the fool without a coat on the coldest day of the year.

"Virginia Halas used to go see him play in Wrigley Field," Fencik told me. "The end zone at Wrigley, on one side, was cut short by the outfield wall. On the other side was the dugout. Well, Virginia was there, a little girl cheering for Dick Plasman," who streaks across the secondary, throws up his hands, catches the ball, then is carried by his momentum into the dugout. Someone screams. Coaches come running. A man pops his head out, waving frantically. A doctor hurries down from the stands. There's a long delay. It feels endless. Finally, they come out with Plasman on a stretcher. His eyes are closed, his body motionless. His head is wrapped in a bandage and the bandage is soaked in blood. For Virginia Halas McCaskey, well, it was one of those things you experience when you are young, and you're never quite the same. "She thought she'd seen her favorite player die," Fencik said. "She thought she'd seen Dick Plasman die."

I mention Dick Plasman because you will not see his like again: he was the last of a species, the last of the free-spirited wild men who played the game in the beginning. The war changed everything. The NFL became more professional, better suited to the big market corporate culture that emerged in the fifties and sixties. Football became a different game because America became a different country.

The crucial shift came as a result of a tweak in the rules. The military draft that began before Pearl Harbor hurt all pro sports, but football more. After all, who was being drafted? Able-bodied men in their early twenties—the exact sort that filled NFL rosters. A football player was usually washed up by thirty. Many gained twenty pounds in their first year of retirement. It's the same today. Players work like dogs and eat like sharks; then, when they quit, they continue to eat like sharks but don't work at all. The freshman fifteen? How about the post-NFL forty? Baseball might get by with out-of-shape old-timers but, on a football field, such men were in danger. Back then, the rules required a player to play offense and defense. But few of the old-timers who returned when military conscription devastated the league were in the kind of shape required. Take Bob Snyder, a retired Bears quarterback—he was thirty—whom Halas asked to coach. The invitation was a ruse. Once Snyder was on the field, a football was shoved into his hands. "No way," said Snyder, "I'm up to about 240 pounds—50 pounds over my playing weight. I'm full of beer."

In 1943, after a sorry season in which out-of-shape athletes stood doubled over between plays, huffing and puffing, the NFL decided to change the rules. For the first time "free substitution" would be allowed, meaning players could go in and out of games without restriction. This was done to give the old-timers a chance to recover, but the unintended consequences were dramatic. Now a player could specialize, appearing in a game just long enough to perform a single task. A fullback might be brought in only in short-yardage situations; a runner might play only on kickoff and punt returns. Eventually, football rosters became divided into two teams: offense and defense. "What the rule has accomplished for tactical football is something Halas always hoped for but had not found feasible," Luckman wrote. "The creation of defensive and offensive units which are switched constantly as the ball changes hands on the field." Over time, football became strangely regimented, a game of specialists.

The coaches loved it. Not only did free substitution let them field superior teams, it also gave them control. They'd been banned from shuttling in instructions or calling plays from the sideline. Once a possession started, it was up to the quarterback. But with the rule change, a coach could send in a new play before every down, as long as it was carried by a substituting player. Football became a coach's game as a result, men with clipboards, men in gray suits and fedoras. The war ended but the new rule stayed on the books.

The game changed in organic ways as well, evolving with the spirit of the time. It was just different after the war. For one thing, a certain brand of racism became harder to excuse. If 418,500 Americans died fighting for Roosevelt's Four Freedoms, how do you tell the owner of the Rams he can't sign Kenny Washington because he's African American? The unspoken agreement that barred blacks from the NFL fell away. Halas denied any such agreement had ever existed—there were black players on the early NFL teams—but in fact a black player had not suited up in twenty years. Some blamed it on George Preston Marshall, who would not integrate the Redskins until he was forced to by members of the Kennedy administration, in an effort led by Interior Secretary Stewart Udall. For an owner like Halas, who cared less about race than about winning, access to such a huge pool of untapped talent was a boon. The Bears' first black player was Eddie Macon, taken in the second round in 1952. The Bears fielded the first black quarterback in the NFL, the perfectly named Willie Thrower, who completed just three passes in 1953.

But the war's most astonishing effects on the game were stylistic. This is a theory of mine—I can't prove it—but it seems to me that football, which has been thematically linked to warfare from its beginning, is especially sensitive to innovations on the battlefield. Within a decade of World War II, football playbooks were filled with lessons seemingly learned at Calais, Dunkirk, Normandy. The NFL was founded after World War I, and the sport, in its early years, was a game of trenches, big men, and mud, a test of wills, a war of attrition. In the 1920s, scores often lingered in single digits. Halas broke the stalemate with the modern T-formation, which came into its own in 1940, shortly after the start of World War II, in which the Wehrmacht pioneered the blitzkrieg, a term retrofitted for use in the NFL. By the 1950s, football had followed the air force's F-80 jets into the skies. For Halas, the reasoning was probably the same as it had been for Curtis LeMay: Why crawl, when you can rain terror from above?

Some of this influence was probably conscious, as coaches who read newspapers and watched newsreels borrowed the language and tactics of war; some of it was unconscious, as coaches were affected by the culture, which in the 1940s and 1950s was dominated by the military. Over a thousand NFL players had been in the service, some of them in positions of authority (Halas, a lieutenant commander in the navy, spent three years in the South Pacific). For many, it was the defining event of their lives: it's no wonder they absorbed its lessons. Tom Landry, the Cowboys coach and an architect of the modern NFL defense, was a pilot in the Army Air Force's 493rd Bombardment Group. He flew thirty missions over Germany and crashed his B-17 in a Flemish field when he ran out of fuel. Vince Lombardi, the dominant NFL coach of the era, perfected his craft at West Point, as an assistant under Army coach Red Blaik. Most weeks, Lombardi carried game film to an apartment in the Waldorf Astoria, which he screened for General Douglas MacArthur, a football nut who plied Lombardi with theories.

Luckman wrote of playing against Mario Tonelli of the Chicago Cardinals, who survived the Bataan Death March. "I shrunk from 200 pounds down to a 109-pound weasel of a man," Tonelli told Luckman. "It's crazy and impossible to picture myself as the same fullback who once ran 50 yards against Minnesota . . . Fact was, I couldn't think much about the game at all, watching nine out of ten of my buddies die of starvation and beatings."

The war's influence was especially clear in the emergence of the celebrity coach, a mirror of the celebrity general. D-day gave us Eisenhower and Bradley; the Ice Bowl gave us Landry and Lombardi. Preseason training camp was remade as a kind of boot camp, with barracks, curfews, and ordeals of deprivation meant to break individuals and build teams: a man does not risk his life for an abstraction such as victory, but he will kill for his teammates. Lombardi did not let his players drink water during practice, as such luxuries weaken men. "Football requires spartan qualities," he explained. "Sacrifice, self-denial—they're cliché words—but I believe in them with every fiber of my body . . . Men want to follow. It gives them security to know there is someone who cares enough to chew them out a little bit or to correct their mistakes." Lombardi perfected the football aphorism, which echoed the slogans of war. Patton said, "Courage is fear holding on a minute longer." MacArthur said, "In war there can be no substitute for victory." Lombardi said, "Winning isn't everything, it's the only thing." Ditka emulated this aphoristic style, but, Ditka being Ditka, always overshot the mark. Urging his players to shake off a loss, he told them "The past is for cowards and losers."

Pro football looked different after the war, and it would have a different focus. It had been the team, the scrum. It would become the individual. Lombardi denied it, but he was among the biggest individuals of all. As was MacArthur. As was Patton. That's the meaning of celebrity general. *I'm in front. Follow me.*

Of course, Lombardi meant for himself to be *the* individual, the general in charge of the division, but once that genie was out of the bottle . . .

If you want to understand what happened to the NFL, don't look at Jim Brown or Tom Brady. Look at Homer Jones, a Giants receiver who, attempting to distinguish himself in the 1960s, became the first man to "spike" the ball. In the past, a player handed the ball to the referee after scoring, or he might toss it into the stands. Jones heaved the ball into the turf instead, driving it into the end zone like a coup stick. You go from there to Billy White Shoes Johnson's touchdown dance, to the Ickey Woods shuffle, to Terrell Owens's Sharpie.

As the modern game emerged, here was the big question: Who will represent the league? The coach or the quarterback? Who will determine its style? Lombardi, with his coach pants and short sleeves and wire frames and buzz cut? Or Joe Namath, with his white shoes and fur coat and Lincoln Continental and Fu Manchu mustache, which, in 1968, he shaved on live TV for $10,000? (Namath was on Richard Nixon's enemies list, apparently on general principle.) According to David Maraniss, the author of *When Pride Still Mattered*, Lombardi's last words, spoken in a delirium on his deathbed, were: "Joe Namath! You're not bigger than football! Remember that!"

But Joe Namath was bigger than football—or, more dangerous, Joe Namath and those who rode the tails of his fur coat would become football. It had been the muck and the mire of a team in the pile, but it would be the quarterback. As Louis B. Mayer knew, every picture needs a star. In this inhumanly violent game, where players are armored and often indistinguishable, the quarterback is the standout, the figure onto whom we project our fantasies. More than just another player, he's an archetype, like the cowboy or gangster. He stands for certain national characteristics. He represents us. His career is our life compressed to a handful of seasons. If you pick one to follow and he prospers, you will ultimately see a man when he's young and green, and when he's so old only knowledge and desire remain.

You can have a quarterback as a Catholic has a patron saint, a figure to focus on amid the chaos. Sid Luckman was the first to lead a modern offense. Johnny Unitas was the first to become a pop star—this had everything to do with television. Joe Namath was the first to become a trendsetter and revolutionary, a flash of color in a black-and-white world, "a real ring-ding-a-ding finger-snapper," *Sports Illustrated* reported in 1965, "a girl ogler, a swingin' cat with dark good looks who sleeps till noon." But my favorite was Jim McMahon, who served as a kind of avatar. His struggles seemed to replicate and amplify my own, what I faced and how I wanted to react. The way he responded in crucial moments, how he seemed to get even better after he'd been hurt, the way, in the midst of the crowd, he always seemed in some fundamental sense to be all alone—it was everything I wanted to be.

How does the quarterback represent us?

The quarterback is man in pain. Via his suffering, we witness our own suffering at a safe remove. We eat chips and drink beer as he's lacerated, stepped on, stomped, taunted, concussed. It's the sort of physical torment that certain Christian sects fixate on, a Jesus-on-the-road-to-Calvary spectacle that is liberating because it shows you're not alone. *The Passion of the Quarterback.* When I asked McMahon what sort of injuries he had in the course of his fifteen-year career, he gripped his shoulder and said, "Well, I destroyed my shoulder. You maybe know about that; it was bad. Then there was the Charles Martin thing"—the dirtiest play I've ever seen. "I wrecked my hands and knees, my head, lots of dings and concussions, go into a room now, can't remember why I'm there, like, *Who are you and why are we talking?* Haha, just kidding—*or am I?* In '91, I broke five ribs off my sternum in New York and bruised my heart. I could've punctured it, but it just bruised. That was an unusual injury: How many other guys have broken all those ribs off the sternum? Some guys get a cracked rib here or there, but to break them off your sternum? And then to hurt your kidney the way I hurt mine . . . ?"

The kidney was a defining injury for McMahon. It happened in 1984, when the Bears hosted the Los Angeles Raiders, the reigning Super Bowl champs. The Raiders were considered the meanest team in the NFL, so for the Bears this was a nasty version of *King of the Hill.* Some consider it the most violent game ever played. Los Angeles lost two quarterbacks that afternoon. Their third-stringer, thirty-eight-year-old punter Ray Guy, refused to go in. There was a fifteen-minute delay while the first-stringer, Marc Wilson, was medicated, taped up, and sent back out.

In the third quarter, Mac, seeing no open receivers, tucked the ball under his arm and took off. "As I was running, I got jerked from behind," he said, "and when I got jerked, my kidney was exposed and that's when the guy hit me. And his helmet, it just sliced it in half."

Sliced what in half?

"My kidney."

Mac took two more snaps: it's what the offensive lineman loved about him—he played the game like Doug Plank, a human missile living in the right fucking now.

"There was clearly something wrong with him," Kurt Becker said. "He was barking out plays but we couldn't hear him. His voice was gone and he was white like a ghost but would not leave. We had to basically carry him off the field."

"I went down to the locker room—this was in the middle of the game—and I found Jim there, standing at the toilet, in his pads, pissing blood," McMahon's agent, Steve Zucker, told me. "He was really hurt. He was streaming blood, dark red blood."

"I was in the ICU at the hospital for ten, eleven days," said McMahon, "fighting with the doctors, who wanted to take it out—it wouldn't stop bleeding. But if I had just one kidney, they'd never let me play again. So I refused, and after about three days, it closed up."

I asked if he still suffered any effects from that injury, thirty years later. "If I drink hard liquor, it hurts like hell," he said. "I can drink beer all day, but there's something about hard liquor. I'll wake up the next day and it kills. It still functions, but it kills."

When the quarterback is injured, we get to see how he deals with pain. In this, he is an example for the common fan. How he reacts shows us how we should and should not behave. We're all going to get hurt and die. The only freedom is the freedom to choose how we respond. Nature gets the first move and the last, but if you concentrate, you can work in a few moves of your own between. Some quarterbacks stay and play through the pain, while others cry as they are carried away on an electric cart. A few years ago, when Bears quarterback Jay Cutler injured his knee and took himself out of a playoff game, fans, the media, even a few former players denounced him. What sort of message does it send the team and the city? In this game, if you can walk, you play.

There is nothing more thrilling in sports than a wounded player who overcomes the pain to win; it's the closest the game comes to a religious moment. This is why fans reacted so fiercely to Cutler; he seemed to be robbing them of a shot at transcendence. When I asked Rob Ryan, a producer at NFL Films, why football became more popular than baseball, he said, "It's a word we're not allowed to use because of the concussions, but it's violence. Fans love to see the player wounded and even more to see that player get off the turf and stay in the game and strike back. Ben Roethlisberger limping across the end zone, Jack Youngblood playing on a broken leg in the playoffs, Emmitt Smith going on with his busted ribs and bruised lungs to carry the ball thirty times for almost two hundred yards in a big game against the Giants. He's dying, but he's playing. People can connect with that. It's how they want to be."

Season after season, the injuries build up and the interest is compounded—how does a player deal with it? To my mind, there are two ways, hence two basic kinds of quarterbacks. There are those who turn to religion. The randomness of the career-ending disaster seems to demand professions of faith. God can give even a torn ACL meaning: it's how He wants it, all part of the plan. That's why football seems so much more religious than other sports. God is in the pregame prayer and the postgame invocation, with the priest on one knee and in the circle of big men at midfield. He's there with Tebow Tebowing and with every wide receiver who points to the sky when he gets into the end zone. ("I had my own feelings about praying before a game," Bernie Parrish wrote in *They Call It a Game*. "If God would just stay out of it, I would win by myself. As Phil Harris used to sing in the thirties and forties, 'Lord don't help me, but please don't help that bear.'") Every time a player stays down too long, athletes on both sidelines take off their helmets and whisper in the heavenly ear, because it's a violent world and the worst can happen and there but for the grace of God go I.

The other type of quarterback is hard-bitten, Bogartian. He seeks a worldly solace, which partly explains the long relationship between professional football and every variety of painkiller and stimulant. Novocaine, Xylocaine, Vicodin, amphetamine. Halas took whiskey from a flask—because, years later, he could still feel the place where Jim Thorpe took him out at the end of that glorious run. Johnny Blood, who started his career with the Duluth Eskimos, was the first player to use the pep pills known as greenies. "Doctors say that drugs like Dexedrine or Benzedrine do not have an effect on one's performance," wrote Parrish. "Perhaps not, but after that day [when we took them before] practice, we were convinced they were great. I never played another game in my college or professional career without taking Dexedrine or Benzedrine. The last season of my career with Cleveland I was taking ten or fifteen 5-milligram tablets of Dexedrine."

"When I first got in the league there'd be bowls of different-colored pills in the locker room," McMahon told me. "Take two of these, take two of those. You'd figure out which ones you liked, which ones you didn't. They definitely get you ready to go. Then you didn't sleep for two days. I took what they called 'Up Times.' It was like drinking a pot of coffee. I'd take a couple of those and a couple of painkillers to even it out. I didn't want to feel anything until the game was over."

"The intimacy of our doping ritual had begun with codeine and Demerol," Peter Gent wrote in *North Dallas Forty*. "At first, the pills were used just to bear the pain of shredded and smashed muscles and ligaments. Then later we combined them with alcohol to shorten the long, anxious return trips to Dallas. We would sit, strapped in our seats, packed in ice or wrapped in elastic, in lengthy discussion of the sounds and feelings of excruciating injuries . . . I was high on something all the time—codeine, booze, grass, speed, fear; in fact, I doubt that during a season I was ever in a normal state of mind, if there is such a thing as normal."

For quarterbacks, the drugs are often the only way to stay on the field. I believe I once saw a photo of McMahon, taken from above, surrounded by coaches and players shielding him as a doctor plunged a hypodermic into his fist. "When I broke my hand, they'd shoot it five or six times around the bone and they always hit a nerve," McMahon told me. "I'd go numb, couldn't feel the ball. Nothing to the elbow. It first happened in '84. I came off the field 'cause I'd landed on my back and busted my hand. I couldn't feel it. I went to reach for some water and I couldn't hold the cup. It just fell out. My hand was already about *that* big. I said, 'Doc, look.' He said, 'It's just a bruise.' Everything was just a bruise. I cut my kidney in half, and it was just a bruise. That night it was killing me. I go to the hospital on my own, get it X-rayed. They said, 'You've broken a bone.' They casted it. I go to work the next morning and they're all freaking out. The trainer said, 'What are you doing with a cast?' I said, 'My hand's broke.' 'Well, you can't let the press see that.' 'Well fuck, they're going to figure it out sooner or later. I can't throw a spiral 'cause I can't feel the ball.' But they didn't want anybody to ever know you were hurt."

It was a rap on McMahon: great competitor but can't throw a spiral.

"You know why?" he asked me. " 'Cause I was being shot up. When you can't feel the ball, you have no idea where it's going. It wasn't my fault. It was Novocaine or Xylocaine . . . one of the 'caine brothers."

How else does the quarterback represent us?

He replicates our predicament in the world, known as the human condition. Life is a game and we're in it but also removed, which is exactly the position of the QB. He leads the team but is separate, a freak, part player, part coach, potential hero, possible goat, but never really one of the boys. A football field is about duplication. There are multiples of every sort of player in most alignments: four linemen, two running backs, three linebackers. But there's only one quarterback. He carries the weight of the endeavor on his back. He's critical and he's alone. As such, he understands the mercenary truth of the world better than the rest: there's no sentimentality; regardless of the past, the minute he falters, he's gone. It's the same for everyone, of course. Each success only brings you closer to inevitable failure. There is no team, as there is no nation; it's only you, in your helmet, in your head. "When an athlete, no matter what color jersey he wears, finally realizes that opponents and teammates alike are his adversaries, and he must deal and dispense with them all, he is on his way to understanding the spirit that underlies the business of competitive sport," writes Peter Gent. "There is no team, no loyalty, no camaraderie; there is only him, alone."

How else does the quarterback represent us?

He shows us how to deal with old age and death, for the pro athlete must get old when he is young, must lose all he has trained for and dreamed about for years and then lose everything else. In other words, the quarterback dies twice. I could never hear too many last-season, end-of-career stories: How did you finish? How did you walk away? It's a model you apply to your own life. Do you go out like John Elway, whose last game was a Super Bowl? Or do you stick around till they make you leave, like Johnny Unitas, who was broken when he played his last game in San Diego? Or Brett Favre, who went from team to team in those final seasons, selling his services like a hired gun?

Here's a question I've long asked myself: What, if anything, redeems the game? What justifies the physical pain and mental anguish and bad endings and dings and morning fog and ultimate failure suffered in the course of every career?

It's the joy of the sport, of course, the way you feel when everything works, when every defender is fooled and every tackle is broken and even the boners are good for ten yards. It's the thrill of fear and the pride you take in overcoming that fear. It's finding a way to win even though you're past your prime, the knees gone, the arm gone. For a fan, nothing beats the satisfaction of watching an ancient mariner of a QB find a way to get it done.

I remember seeing a Redskins game with my father when I was small. It must have been 1977 or 1978. The starter had been knocked out, forcing the coach to bring in Billy Kilmer, who, at that moment, was as old as anyone who'd ever lived. He was out of condition, pear-shaped, slow. My father told me that Kilmer had missed the entire '63 season after falling asleep at the wheel of his '57 Chevy and driving into San Francisco Bay—it was part of a colorful past, the storied career of the man who'd been around forever. He had played his first NFL game in 1961, when Chuck Bednarik was still going both ways for the

Philadelphia Eagles. Bednarik had played his first game in 1948, when Luckman was still out there. And Luckman played with Nagurski, who played with Grange, who played with Halas, who played with Thorpe. In other words, via this one player, you could trace a path back to the dawn of football. And meanwhile, there was Kilmer, marching down the field. His passes were knuckleballs, but they kept finding their target. "Look at that son of a bitch," my father said. "Can't run, can't throw, but he still finds a way!"

7

MIKE DISCO

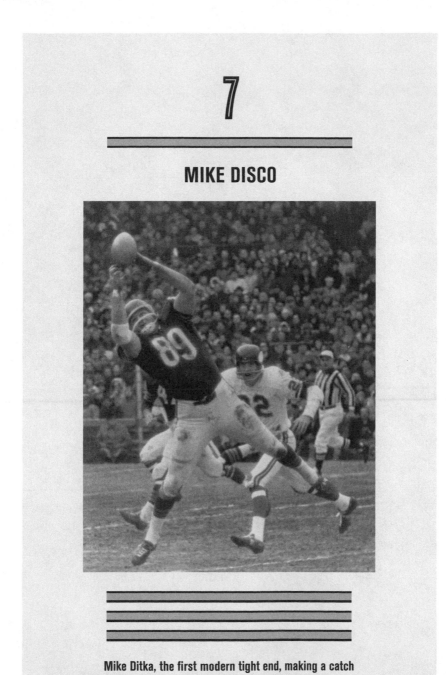

Mike Ditka, the first modern tight end, making a catch in Wrigley Field on November 24, 1963

The pieces of the 1985 Bears began to come together in 1939, when Mike Ditka was born in Carnegie, Pennsylvania. His parents had emigrated from the Ukraine, where the family name was Dyczko, which each uncle Americanized in his own way, Disco being the least fortunate variation. It's hard to imagine Mike Disco becoming anything but a dancing machine; Ditka was more appropriate for a son of Aliquippa, the tough west Pennsylvania factory town where he spent his formative years. His father was a welder in a steel mill, "a burner" on a train that ran through the factory that employed just about everyone in town. The old man would come home with blisters on his hands, wounds of a working life. He'd been a marine and was a strict disciplinarian. "What he said, he said, that was it," Ditka wrote. "He didn't spare the rod." Ditka's autobiography is filled with phrases like "worst beating of my life." "If I didn't [do what he said]," wrote Ditka, "he gave me a hard time. By a hard time, I mean he simply whipped my ass." Such poundings usually came in response to some bit of mischief. A neighbor once described young Mike Ditka as "a high-intensity boy." On one occasion, experimenting with cigarettes, he burned down a stand of trees behind the family house. When Ditka's father came home, he wondered what had happened "to the forest."

"Ask your son," his wife told him.

"I got nailed," Ditka wrote. "He had an old leather Marine belt. It was probably the hardest whipping I ever got."

Some people, you see a picture of them taken in third or fourth grade, you have no idea who it is. Of course, when you're told, the features reassemble themselves in a familiar way and you think, Oh yeah, now I see my friend. But with Ditka, you know right away: the chipmunk cheeks and broad forehead, the mouth turned fiercely down, the amused glint, the peaked, bearlike hairline—it was all there from the start. And the smile. Mike Ditka has a great smile. It wrinkles his cheeks and makes his eyes vanish. It's a cute smile, surprisingly adorable in an otherwise fierce face. In fact, it's so cute it's scary. If a bear smiled at you, that would be scary, too. You see a thing like that in the woods, you think, I'm done.

Ditka grew up in the 1940s and 1950s, a boom time for Aliquippa and places like it, hardscrabble towns in Appalachia, where refineries churned out steel for the battleships and fighter planes to defeat the Communists. Main Street was filled with life—candy stores, the men's shop, the five-and-dime, the union hall, the saloon, parades and banners, excited talk about the high school football game against Beaver Falls. The slums were at the bottom of the valley, in the shadow of the mill, tin roofs, sagging porches, old men in undershirts, smoking cigarettes and drinking beer. "It was a very ethnic area," Ditka wrote, "which was also very prejudiced. Whether you were a Polack or a Hunky or a Jew or a Dago or a Wop or a Cake-eater or Colored—we didn't use the other slang word for blacks—it was prejudiced."

The rich people lived up the hill—the more you had, the higher you got, until you reached the mansions built into the ridgeline, from where you could see other valleys where other factories spewed smoke, prejudice, and gridiron heroes. It was the kingdom of football, the breeding ground of so many of the players who defined the game: Bednarik, Unitas, Montana, Marino, Namath—the list is ridiculous. When I asked Ditka why so many great players came from western Pennsylvania, he said, "It's the work ethic, the way people were brought up. The parents came from the old country and worked in the mills and the mines. People didn't have anything but didn't need anything. They were tough. Were they tougher than they were in Nebraska? I don't know. But they were tough."

Ditka spent his free time playing games in the lots between the houses. Basketball, baseball, mob ball. He was a bad loser from the beginning. If things went wrong, he went nuts, stormed off, stormed

Jones and Laughlin Steel Company. Aliquippa by night

back, threw a bat, chucked a ball, hit a guy, stormed off again, came back again, hit someone else. He was made for football. It became increasingly obvious as he got older. He was a late bloomer, small his first years at Aliquippa High School, but this just added intensity to size when he finally grew in his junior year. He credits everything to his high school coach, Carl Aschman, whom he ranks with the other great coaches of his life: George Halas and Tom Landry. Ditka played every position in high school—offensive line, running back, linebacker, punter—but mostly he was just out there kicking ass. Later, explaining why he loved football, he wrote, "When you step onto the football field, everybody's equal. And when you step off, everybody's not equal anymore. Somebody's won and somebody's lost. Somebody's dominated and somebody's been dominated. Somebody's taught and somebody's learned."

Aliquippa won the Pennsylvania State Championship in 1955, with Ditka playing both ways, a mill town all-star. He was recruited by Jim Finks at Notre Dame—Finks was the Bears general manager when Ditka took over as coach—and Joe Paterno at Penn State, but chose Pitt for its premed program. Ditka planned on being a dentist after football—imagine those giant fingers rooting around your mouth. By 1959, he'd become one of the best college players in the nation. He played linebacker on defense and fullback on offense. He was quick, hard-hitting, and mean, but his hands were what made him special. It was rare for a big man to have such soft hands. Pitt did not throw often, but when they did go to Ditka, he almost always made the catch. And after he made it, he was nearly impossible to bring down. A player that size running in the open was a new development, so new most pro scouts hardly took notice. It was assumed that Ditka would play defense in the NFL, where his soft hands would help him make interceptions.

When the Bears drafted Ditka first in 1961, it was with another idea in mind. Halas and his assistant, George Allen, wanted to put Ditka on the offensive line. He would block on most plays but now and then skirt away from the trenches, head downfield ten or fifteen yards, turn around, and catch a pass. Winning football games is not about pitting strength against strength, speed against speed. It's about finding a mismatch, a situation in which their little guy has to tackle your monster, or their monster has to chase your sprinter. If Ditka got downfield, he'd be covered by defensive backs half his size. It was a strategy made possible only by Ditka's special gift: big guys almost never had such soft hands. In this way, Halas created what has since become a dominant weapon in the NFL: Mike Ditka was the first modern tight end. "Nobody threw to the tight end back then," he told me. "He was just another guy on the line of scrimmage, next to the tackle. Then Halas had this idea to throw me the ball. He realized it was hard for me to get off the line when I was next to the tackle, so he moved me three or four yards down. I was the first tight end to flex out."

Ditka was twenty-one when he arrived at training camp. He had also been drafted by the Houston Oilers of the new American Football League, but his dream had always been to play in the NFL. His first contract paid him $12,000 plus a $6,000 signing bonus, which George Allen said was the "biggest contract we've paid anyone since Red Grange." When Ditka brought the agreement home to Aliquippa, his father looked it over, frowned in a slightly disapproving way, and said, "Most men have to work a long time to get that kind of money."

Ditka had the hands but caught the ball in the untutored way of the sandlot. Turning what you've always done by instinct into a practice, a

trade—that's what makes you a professional. Halas brought Sid Luckman back to work with Ditka, teach him the proper way to catch. Sid
was forty-four years old, faded, soft, ancient, a figure of lore. He had a
method, a way to concentrate the rookie. He gathered a pile of footballs
and wrote a number on each: 27, 61, 33. Ditka ran pattern after pattern.
As soon as he made a catch, he had to call out the number on the ball.
This would teach him the art of high focus: just you and the ball, watching it all the way into your hands. In 1961, Ditka caught fifty-six passes
for 1,076 yards. He scored twelve touchdowns. No tight end had ever
done anything like it. He was named Rookie of the Year and made the
Pro Bowl, an honor he would secure in each of his first four seasons.

It was not just the statistics that earned Ditka respect—it was how
he played, the fierceness of his game. He answered every challenge,
returned every insult. He tore it up. In his fifth game, the Bears played
the Baltimore Colts, where Ditka faced Bill Pellington, one of the
toughest linebackers in football. He'd knocked out the Lions' tight end
Jim Gibbons not long before. "So all week all I heard was how tough
Bill Pellington was and how he was going to knock the crap out of me,"
Ditka wrote later. "Well, I lined up on the first play from scrimmage
and by God they were right. He punched me right in the mouth. I wore
that little, thin bar [on my helmet] that didn't protect anything. He
punched me right in the mouth and I said, 'Oh, Boy.' On the next play—
I don't know what the play was—didn't matter. I didn't even care. I don't
know if it was a pass play or a run. I just gave him a head fake, drew back
and punched him as hard as I could."

In Green Bay, Ditka battled Packers Hall of Fame linebacker Ray
Nitschke on the field and off. One night, after a rough game, they ran
into each other in a restaurant. They started jawing back and forth.
Then Nitschke pointed a big finger in Ditka's face and said, "I'm going
to get you."

"If you get me, you better get me good," Ditka said. "One thing in
life you've got to remember is if you're trying to get somebody, you
don't get got."

Ditka was guided by a code, a slightly demented sense of football
right and wrong. In the third quarter of a game in Los Angeles, a
drunken fan dashed onto the field. The cops pursued. The crowd roared.
It used to happen a lot: a drunk running higgledy-piggledy as police fell
all over themselves. As he crossed midfield, Ditka stepped out of the

huddle and ended it with a single blow. The guy went up, turned over in the air, then dropped lifelessly to the ground. He looked dead. It was sickening—a butterfly meets a tank. Explaining why he did it after the game, Ditka could have been summing up his entire philosophy: "Because that guy's got no fucking right to be on the field! The field is for players!"

Ditka played his first NFL game in Minneapolis against the expansion Vikings. He earned notice from the veterans right away. A rookie is supposed to be quiet in the huddle, but Ditka cursed everyone out for letting the game slip away. Losing to an expansion team is a particular kind of ignominy. The plane was quiet going home, the Convair 320 rumbling through the dark. Halas came on the PA: "I want to say just one thing to you guys. You're nothing but a bunch of cunts!"

Halas taught Ditka the game: how to play, how to coach, when to praise, when to call the boys a bunch of cunts. Watching him operate was better than ten years in school. He was a wizard, a pioneer, but it was his attention to detail that really impressed. I mean, here was this guy, a founder of the NFL, a standout for Coach Zuppke, a man who stripped the ball from Jim Thorpe, and what's he doing at age sixty-six? Weighing every kid on the roster, standing by with a clipboard, stopwatch, and pen. "Nobody weighed anybody except him," Ditka said. "He didn't trust anyone. We had to do it twice a week." It was a $23 fine for every pound over. "The most fun anybody ever had was the weigh-in. They used to trick the scales. The old man would go crazy. One guy would get on and another guy would put his finger under the cheek of his ass. Another guy would get on the scale with weights in his jockstrap."

Halas personally negotiated every contract. No lawyers, no agents, just you and the old man, eyeball to eyeball across the desk. "Halas embarrassed you," said Ditka. "Ripped you apart. After I signed my first contract for $12,000 plus that $6,000 bonus, I made Rookie of the Year and All-Pro. I came back and he offered me $14,000. I said, 'Coach, you're making a mistake. I made $18,000 last year. You're giving me a $4,000 cut.'"

"How do you figure you made $18,000?"

"Twelve plus six is eighteen."

"Well," he said, "The six was a bonus, remember? The bonus doesn't count."

Ditka begged and pleaded until Halas agreed to bump him up to $18,000, then reached into his desk and brought out a contract already made out in that amount.

The Bears had floundered in the seasons since Sid Luckman retired. That's what happens when a dynasty collapses: the palace falls to ruins, the countryside is plunged into darkness. When Ditka was drafted, it had been fifteen years since the team won a championship. His arrival marked a crucial step on the road back. He gave the Bears a new spirit. They were better in 1961 than they'd been in 1960, and still better in 1962. By 1963, they were ready to make a title run. In addition to Ditka, there was linebacker Bill George, quarterback Bill Wade, running back Willie Galimore, defensive tackle Doug Atkins. Mike Pyle played center, a nasty position: you start the play with the snap, then get hit in the head. In the old days, before it was banned, the defensive player lined up across from the center—the noseguard—often reared back and slapped the center on the ear, knocking him silly.

Mike Pyle was unusual. Most pros come from waste places, mill cities and industrial towns. But Pyle grew up in Winnetka, on Chicago's North Shore. His father was an executive at Kraft Foods. Mike went to Yale, where he was tapped by Skull & Bones. (Yalies of that era still speak of the Pyle brothers with awe.) I took a special interest in Pyle because we went to the same high school, New Trier, which has turned out lots of bankers, doctors, actors, and politicians—Charlton Heston, Rock Hudson, Donald Rumsfeld—but few professional athletes. We are the candy-asses by the lake. It made Pyle seem a kind of wonder, a New Trier Indian who'd gone all the way. He spoke at a pep rally my senior year. There is a picture of it in my yearbook. He was still a big man, straining the stitches of his suit, bearded, with thick wrists. He was forty-seven, forty-eight, the age that I am now, but I feel the same age as always, whereas he seemed so much older. I can't recall a word he said, but I do remember how he looked, the way he carried himself. He pounded the lectern as the high school football coach nodded at his side. He was like Hemingway returning to Oak Park High in a cape, unbuttoning his tunic to show the seniors his scars. I asked Ditka about Pyle: What's he up to now? The coach crossed his arms, looked at me. "I love Mike, but he's not doing well," he said. "You know, in my day, the helmets were not the best, just a piece of plastic, and the center got pounded, slapped in the head all game. I used to talk to Mike every week but it's been a long time since he's called."

The '63 Bears opened with a string of victories. By late November, the fate of the season hung on a game against the Steelers. That Friday, as the players were packing, word came over the radio: President Kennedy had been shot in Dallas. A few hours later, when the first reports were followed by news of the president's death, the country was plunged into black sorrow. Everyone assumed the game would be canceled. The American Football League canceled everything, but NFL commissioner Pete Rozelle said the games would go on, a decision he later regretted. The Bears did not want to play: How do you gin up the fury? How do you convince yourself it matters? "We wanted no part of it," Ditka told me. "We're Americans first and we were destroyed, but we're soldiers, too. They tell us to play, we play. Then, of course, you get out there and get popped in the mouth, and the world disappears and there is only the game."

November 24, 1963: the emperor lay dead in the capital but the gladiators carried on at the Forum. The game was played at Forbes Field in Pittsburgh in front of a glowering crowd of drunks who should have been somewhere else. Before the coin toss, Halas got his team in a circle and said, "We're going to play this game to get people's minds off the assassination." Late in the fourth quarter, the Bears were down 17–14. If they lost, no championship. Clouds rolled in from the west. Billy Wade took the snap. Ditka went upfield, hit a linebacker, turned, looked the ball all the way in, caught it, tucked it, and headed for the end zone, the burner's son running under an inky sky. He had about seventy yards to go. Every time a Steeler came up to make the stop, Ditka would bring his big forearm around. He broke tackle after tackle, leaving the wounded in his wake. He was finally brought down by defensive back Clendon Thomas deep in Pittsburgh territory. He'd gone fifty yards after the catch. He lay on the field spent, a burned-out engine. In Chicago, they called it "the run." "That was the luckiest run in the world," Ditka said. "It was a combination of me being tired, them being tireder, and poor tackling. It was terrible."

The Bears kicker Roger Leclerc hit an eighteen-yard field goal to tie the game. Pittsburgh got the ball back with seconds left, ran a play, then another, then before anyone realized what was happening, a Steelers receiver was going downfield for a touchdown. He crossed the goal line and raised his arms, but at some point, way back there, impossible to hear above the din, a whistle had been blown. The play was no good though no one was sure why. In the meantime, the last second had run off the clock. It was over. A murmur went through the crowd: *Halas paid off the refs! He bought the fuckin' thing!* The drunkest fans came over the wall. It was a mob. The refs blew their whistles but were quickly overwhelmed. The Bears grabbed their coach and raced through a storm of beer cans. They got to the locker room and shut the door only to realize a Pittsburgh reporter had followed them inside. He was waving his notebook in the old man's face, cursing, *You bought it, you evil bastard, you bought it, didn't you?* For a long moment, Halas stared into the face of the reporter as you stare into a garbage compactor that will not turn, wondering, *What the hell is down there?* His eyes flashed, but before he could move, Ditka had the reporter and was carrying him through the locker room and dumping him in the hall. He slammed the door. It got quiet. They stared at each other. Someone turned on a TV. Cronkite or Brinkley. What he was saying made no sense: the man who'd shot the president had himself been shot in a garage in Dallas.

The NFL Title Game was played in the Polo Grounds in New York. The Giants were led by the Hall of Fame quarterback Y. A. Tittle. One of those ancients who seemed to play forever—he was thirty-seven when he faced the Bears in the championship—Tittle was the subject of perhaps the greatest sports photo ever taken. It shows him on his knees on the turf. His helmet has been knocked off, blood trickles from his head. Beaten and old, the gladiator suffers stoically. The final score was Bears 14, Giants 10. "I guess today's game proves that if you live long enough, everything you want to happen will happen," Halas said. He was named Coach of the Year. He was sixty-eight. It was the last time he'd see the Bears win a championship.

"Why didn't you repeat?"

"What's that?"

"Why didn't your championship team repeat?"

This was me talking to Ditka over dinner one night. He sat back in his chair, his eyes glittering as he said, "Well, you see, right there, you've put your finger on the big question. Why's it so hard for a team that's won to win again? Maybe winning is the greatest thing that can happen to a team and also the biggest disaster. It's never the same after you win."

8

SUCKING IN THE SEVENTIES

Chicago in the funkadelic summer of '76

I grew up in the 1970s. It was a sad time in my country, my city, and my house. Everything sucked. In my earliest memory, I'm wearing a T-shirt that says IMPEACH DICK NIXON. I have no idea who that is. There are always hearings on TV. It seems as if everything good is over, the best of life consumed—my generation has been left the rind, the husk of a city. Do I blame Jimmy Carter? Of course I do. And Mayor Daley, and Rick Reuschel, and the rock band Chicago. On short autumn days in my town, you could see melancholy rising from the ground. Like sand from the beach, the sadness was in your shoes in the morning and in your bed at night. Chicago, which boomed for a hundred years, had, by the time of my childhood, fallen into gray dissolution, a seemingly endless decline. As Ray Liotta says in *GoodFellas*, "This was the bad time."

Start with the crime—that fantastic run of infamy. It had been glamorous in the '20s and '30s, Al Capone and Bugs Moran and downtown turf wars. John Dillinger was shot coming out of the Biograph movie theater. Leopold and Loeb, whatever else you might say about them, at least put some thought into it. After Nails Morton was bucked and trampled to death by a horse in Lincoln Park, his friends brought the animal back to the ill-fated spot and whacked it. But by my first year in grade school, this magnificent underworld panoply had broken into a mash-up of nihilistic tribes: Latin Kings, El Rukns. In the newspapers, they were depicted as shapeless mobs creeping out of the slums. Like the ancient hordes, they were coming.

And the housing projects, those carefully arranged monstrosities. The Robert Taylor Homes—bleak beyond bleak. You'd see them from the highway, blank towers and black windows, weedy yards, a man skulking in an alley. In the summer, on game days, the elevated train did not make local stops between the North Side and Comiskey Park but just rattled on through the South Side like a closed coach carrying Russian aristocrats through territory that has fallen to the Reds. What I'm describing could probably be characterized as white anxiety in the wake of white flight, a suburban fear of the city. But for me it was just the world as seen from the backseat of a Buick station wagon. I mean, what does a kid really know?

Mayor Richard J. Daley died in 1976. For several days, his face was seen, in the way of a religious miracle, floating above the slaughter yards. While sitting on a storm-grounded plane at O'Hare one October, the man seated next to my father said, "It never snowed this early when Daley was mayor." When the plane, having finally gotten clearance, broke through the clouds into the sunshine, the passengers cheered. That's how it was in Chicago when I was small. The sun went away in October and stayed away until mid-April. A lid closed over the city. You had to remind yourself not to panic.

Jane Byrne was elected mayor in 1979. She had short blond hair and the clipped officious manner of someone else's mom—she wants to punish you but has been forced to acknowledge you're outside her jurisdiction. She was beyond her depth. She made the city feel ungovernable, doomed. In response to a crime wave sweeping the North Side, she moved into Cabrini-Green. I'm not sure what it was supposed to accomplish: bring attention to the plight of people trapped in that housing project; show the rest of the city, "Look, it's not so bad!" It backfired when a journalist, having tailed the mayor, reported that she almost never stayed there, and, when she did, was protected by armed guards.

Superrats were said to have taken over entire blocks—slum raised, monstrous. The most impressive, descendants of the Norway brown, were smaller than a husky, bigger than a beagle, with needle teeth, yellow eyes, and graspy claws. They were on the move, colonizing in the way of the ancient Phoenicians, advancing from neighborhood to neighborhood, destroying stuff and grossing people out. News anchors showed maps: where they'd been, where they were, when they'd get to you. And they were coming, as sure as the turning of the earth. I don't know if superrats were real or if they were a nightmare conjured by the city's subconscious. I only know that I did worry about them, as did my friends and siblings. At times, it verged on hysteria. One afternoon, my sister, returning from town in our parents' car, slammed on the brakes, pointed at our dog, Fluffy, a terrier mix who had grown a little paunchy, and screamed, "Superrat!"

We first heard about John Wayne Gacy in 1978. He was a contractor, a serial killer, a clown. He performed at parties and painted clown pictures in his spare time. A body was found in the crawl space beneath his house that summer. Then another. Then another. And so on. The victims were boys around my age, hired for odd jobs. He gives you ten bucks to mow his lawn and no one ever sees you again. I remember watching the news as bodies were exhumed from beneath his house at 8213 West Summerdale near Des Plaines, a town not far from my own. I used to go there to play hockey. (A girl spit on me after one of those games.) Seeing the house was terrifying because it was so ordinary. If you can't tell the house of the serial killer from the other houses, what chance do you have?

The White Sox played baseball on the South Side. And though I grew up north of the city, in an area populated by Cubs fans, there was no small number of Sox fans. For the most part, these were the fathers of my friends, men who'd grown up near Comiskey Park. Meatpackers, record producers, traders—they spoke with a nasal twang. Now and then, they took us to a game at Comiskey. One afternoon, as my friend Danny's father was locking his Cadillac in the parking lot, we were surrounded by young men, one of them carrying a crowbar, which he flipped hand to hand. He said, "Give me twenty bucks, and I'll make sure no one throws a crowbar through your window."

As part of a promotion, fans were invited to bring disco records to a doubleheader in July 1979, where radio shock jock Steve Dahl piled and detonated them in center field between games, blowing a hole in the grass and inciting a riot. Fans tore up the place. It was called Disco Demolition. The second game could not be played and the Sox lost in a forfeit. For part of the 1976 season, the Sox played in what are considered the worst uniforms ever: shorts. Even on a bang-bang play, players refused to slide. Jimmy Piersall, the team's color commentator, went on a Mike Royko television special, filmed at the Billy Goat Tavern, where, in the course of discussing the wives of White Sox players and why they were always on him, Piersall called the wives "horny broads." He was suspended. Harry Caray, the play-by-play man, quit in protest and was then hired by the Cubs. Ah, the Cubs! My Cubs! They're always bad, but they were worse in the '70s. That's when they acquired Dave Kingman, a gangly slugger who one season struck out 131 times. At a game in '75 or '76, in Los Angeles, two deranged fans ran onto the grass and attempted to light an American flag on fire. The match flickered, but Rick Monday, the Cubs center fielder, scooped up Old Glory before it ignited, and carried it lovingly to safety. Then what do the Cubs do? Trade Monday for Bill Buckner.

In Chicago, it all added to a sense that every season was doomed before it began. We had lost, and lost, and would lose again. That's why my father begged me to root for the Dodgers. He believed a Cubs fan will have a bad life because a Cubs fan will accept losing as inevitable. "And it's not just the Cubs," he told me, "but all the teams around here"—my father grew up in Brooklyn. The Sox had not won the World Series since 1917. The Black Hawks had not hoisted the Stanley Cup since 1961. The Bulls had never been champions of the NBA. I once saw a kid with a T-shirt that said, in giant letters, CHICAGO CUBS, WORLD CHAMPS, then, in little numbers, 1908. The Bears had last won in 1963, but that was before I was born, before the Super Bowl, and before football had overtaken baseball in popularity. By the end of that sad decade, many of us had come to believe that winning was reserved for other people in other towns.

I had just missed the last of the great Bears, the last players who belonged in the pantheon with Luckman and Grange. These men, whom you could almost see in the distance, disappearing like the caboose of a train, had been driven from the field by injury. That's football—the average running back lasts just over two years in the league.

For starters, there was that personification of football grace, Gale Sayers, a running back who made his Wrigley Field debut in 1965. He came from Kansas—the Kansas Comet, a fleet flash of lightning who could switch direction without losing speed. Deceptively quick, Sayers could wrong-foot a defensive back with his eyes or the shift of his hips. He made the professionals on the other side look clumsy. His best runs unfolded like Coltrane solos. You never knew where he was going, but, once he found a line, it seemed like it had to be that way. It was as if he could see the field from above, knew just when to cut, where to find a path. ("Give me eighteen inches of daylight, that's all I need.") He scored twenty-two touchdowns in 1965 and 132 points, rookie records. The films made of him that year probably give the best sense of what Red Grange might've looked like in his prime. There have been only a handful of runners like that.

On December 12, 1965, in the mud at Wrigley, in an otherwise inconsequential game against the 49ers, Sayers put on maybe the greatest running performance ever. What was it like? One winter, I played pickup football with friends in a park in my town. It had rained the night before, the rain turned to ice. I was in cleats; everyone else wore sneakers. Whenever I turned, the kid coming at me was carried away by his momentum, gone. I weaved through defenders as if they were highway cones. It remains an outstanding afternoon of my life. I figure it was like that for Sayers times a billion. Halas pulled him after his fifth touchdown, but the crowd kept chanting his name. He went out for a punt return—just so the fans could get another look. You can watch the film: Sayers camped under the ball, hauling it in, sizing up the field, making a move, accelerating—his sixth touchdown. He gained 332 yards, a record. But it was never numbers that defined Sayers—it was the surfeit of grace, the cool of his game. In sports, it's style we remember. Not Mickey Mantle's home runs but how he tossed away his helmet when he failed; not Michael Jordan's dunks but how he slowed at the decisive moment, as if savoring it. Gale Sayers is remembered because he was beautiful.

A few years ago, speeding along Route 35 in Connecticut, I almost ran into a deer, a big buck with a full rack at the peak of autumn. The road was black, the trees were gold. I slammed on the brakes, locked 'em up, skidded. The deer stopped and stared, hesitated, then took off. As the buck got clear of the road, it stutter-stepped before bounding away—it was a kind of end zone dance, an animal telling itself, *I did not die today.* It was one of those naturally occurring outbreaks of style that the Darwinists could never explain. What's the advantage in this? The deer running was survival; the deer stutter-stepping was God.

Sayers was banged and twisted from his first day in the pros. It's human nature: if, in the midst of a brutal world, you see a high-flying thing, you want to crush it. The first serious injury came in his third season. His foot went this way, his leg went that way. Ever tune a guitar one turn too many? The ligaments in his knee snapped. The doctors said he wouldn't play again, but he worked and worked and came back to lead the league in rushing once more—he'd become a different kind of runner, more ordinary. People know this story from *Brian's Song*, a movie about Sayers and Brian Piccolo, who shared the backfield in Chicago. Piccolo died of cancer in 1970. That movie—a story of rivalry, friendship, disease—is etched in the memory of a generation of fans. Billy Dee Williams as Sayers; James Caan as Piccolo; Jack Warden as Halas. It's a tearjerker. The first notes of the theme song can turn me into a puddle of goo. When I asked members of the '85 Bears what they knew about the team before being drafted, many of them said, *"Brian's Song."*

"Did you cry when you watched it?" I asked McMahon.

"Fuck yeah, I cried. Do you think I'm some kind of monster?"

Sayers's second injury came in 1970. It was the other knee. He never could make it back. He retired in 1971. He'd spent less than three full seasons on the field. Sayers was elected to the Hall of Fame in 1977. He was the youngest player to ever receive the honor. In case you're wondering, that's not good.

Dick Butkus was drafted in 1965, the same year as Sayers. Two picks, two Hall of Famers. He was the flip side of the coin, the other face of the NFL. Sayers was the rainbow, Butkus the thunderstorm. Sayers was the horn solo, Butkus the cymbal crash. It's this mix of sugar and salt that gives football its tremendous vitality.

In many ways, Butkus was the model for the '85 Bears, the template the team was in search of whenever it went looking for another hard hitter to fill out the roster. McMichael and Singletary have each spoken of reading Butkus's book *Stop-Action* in high school, memorizing passages, wanting to intimidate in the way of Butkus. Whenever a new defender showed up in Lake Forest, he knew he had to play to the level of the original madman. At its best, the '85 defense operated in the spirit of Butkus, the brutal middle linebacker. He twisted heads, bit people in the pile. Now and then, you'd see a running back raised off the ground, then driven back, feet still moving like the legs of a flipped cockroach. He last suited up a million years ago, but I still hear him barking like a dog, bloody fingers wrapped in gauze, steam jetting from his mouth, monster of monsters. "I didn't just want to end a play," he said. "I wanted to rip their fucking heads off." He was a South Side legend long before he was famous, a man among boys at the Chicago Vocational High School. The lunchroom turned quiet when he entered, the stillness that tells you a shark is gliding over the reef. Even the greasers avoided eye contact. He was dynamite on the field, big and fast with a lust for contact. Loving to hit is not enough. You have to love getting hit, too.

He was all-American at the University of Illinois in 1963 and 1964. He came within a few votes of winning the Heisman Trophy. Halas always paid attention to local products. He wanted to give fans a hero and also thought, all things being equal, a Chicagoan was going to be superior. (When I was a kid, I had a T-shirt that said CHICAGO: YOU GOTTA BE TOUGH.) The Bears took him in the first round. He made All-Pro his first eight seasons. In 1970, he was on the cover of *Sports Illustrated* under the headline THE MOST FEARED MAN IN THE GAME. He carried nastiness like a torch, preserving Bears tradition in a dark age.

He had terrible knees and often seemed to be playing on one leg. By 1973, he was like a jellyfish in a puddle: dangerous but only if you step on it. He did not suit up for the 1974 season. According to the AP, Butkus claimed that surgeons as well as a team physician had looked at his knee and basically called it a day. The Bears refused to pay off the remainder of the linebacker's contract. Butkus said the team was at fault—its doctors and trainers had not warned him of the long-term effects of the cortisone shots he was given every time they wanted to wheel the mad dog back onto the field. Butkus announced his retirement and sued the Bears for $1.6 million. Halas was infuriated but eventually settled for $600,000. Butkus's number was not retired until 1994, which seemed like an intentional slight.

And yet when Butkus was elected to the Hall of Fame, he asked Halas to induct him. If you can explain this, perhaps you'll understand the love and hate that drew and repelled players and fans with George Halas. He was cheap, shortsighted, and mean but also genuine, brilliant, and loyal. He was the coach of your youth, the flask-carrying miser who stands for all coaches and all fathers, for authority everywhere. You hated and cursed him but found yourself craving his approval. You don't want to want it, but you do. When Halas did an event for his autobiography, Butkus stood in line, then handed the book over for an autograph. "To Dick Butkus," Halas wrote, "the greatest player in the history of the Bears. You had that old zipperoo!"

Halas retired in 1968. He'd been in and out of the game a half dozen times. He would leave, but he could never stay away. A season or two after a big press conference—*So, this is it, boys, you won't have Halas to kick around anymore*—he'd be back on the sideline, fedora low, cursing through a rolled-up program. But this time was different. This time he was truly and irredeemably old, seventy-three, shrunken, hobbled. He had a bad hip, which made it painful to walk. On game days, after the players had gotten their injections, the doctor shot up Halas, too, deadening the joint so he could function. "Dr. Jim Stack provided some relief at critical periods by inserting a five-inch-long needle through the groin into the hip," Halas wrote. "He felt around to find where the head of the femur fitted into the socket and injected painkiller directly into the joint. The injection would see me through the game." But the shots were increasingly ineffective, and by 1967 Halas could not get around quick enough to curse out the referees. "I had to give up running along the sidelines, instructing officials, encouraging Bears, and taunting our opponents," said Halas, "all activities which were part of the game and appreciated by our fans."

He spent much of his last season on one knee; at practice, he traveled by golf cart. By then, the consensus was that Halas had stayed too long. He was out of touch with the modern game. In the *Chicago Daily News*, Mike Royko described him as "a tight-fisted, stubborn, willful, mean old man." According to Royko, Halas conducted a postgame interview "in his long underwear on a bench in front of his locker sipping from a pint of whiskey." Halas was outraged: *That cocksucker, everyone knows I don't take whiskey from the bottle. I drink it out of a can.* When the criticism became intolerable, Halas finally stepped aside, turning the keys of the machine over to his assistant, Jim Dooley, the first of a generation of pretenders who, in retrospect, seem like nothing but stepping-stones to Ditka.

Halas had been a good coach right up to the end. The team went 7–6–1 his final season. He retired with a 324–151–31 career record. He'd won eight NFL titles. But the roster was a mess, and the team fell to pieces not long after he moved to the owner's box. The year 1969 was the worst season in franchise history. After they lost the first seven games, there was nothing left to play for but the number-one draft pick. If the Bears wanted to improve, the best thing they could do was lose. But on November 9, they defeated the Steelers, the only team as bad as the Bears. Chicago was not even best at being worst. They finished the year in a 1–13 tie with Pittsburgh.

The number-one pick would go to the winner of a coin toss. This was done in New Orleans during Super Bowl week. Halas tapped his son-in-law to call it for the Bears, Virginia's husband, Ed McCaskey, a tall man who was as nice and handsome as could be—perhaps too nice and too handsome as far as Halas was concerned.

Virginia Halas met Ed McCaskey in Philadelphia. She was enrolled at the Drexel Institute of Technology, studying to be a secretary; he was a student at the University of Pennsylvania. Ed grew up in Lancaster. He was a naturally elegant man who was immediately liked by just about everyone. He did not have a lot, but he was hardworking and decent. On paper, he was perfect. He said grace before each meal, adding, "Oh, God, please convert the Russians."

In spite of this, or maybe because of it, Halas did not trust Ed McCaskey at first. Halas was the sort of father who examined his daughter's suitors through hooded eyes, trying to figure the angle. He asked two Pennsylvania friends to do some snooping on McCaskey. The "agents" in question were Bert Bell and Art Rooney, the owners of the Philadelphia Eagles and Pittsburgh Steelers. They gave the young man the okay—Rooney supposedly protested, "Whoever said Halas was such an angel?"—but the old man was not convinced. His worst fears were realized when he found out how McCaskey made a living: he's not a crook, he's a goddamn singer, a nightclub dandy! According to family lore, McCaskey would have been the front man of the Harry James band had he not been aced out by Frank Sinatra. There is a beautiful symmetry in this: Halas was replaced by the Sultan of Swat, McCaskey by the Chairman of the Board.

Years later, McCaskey actually recorded a crooney version of "Bear Down, Chicago Bears." (It was played at his funeral in 2003.) But when McCaskey showed up in Chicago with a ring to ask for permission to marry Virginia, Halas said, *Gimme that.* This was at Halas's apartment before World War II. It was summer. The old man had stripped to his underwear. "Don't you know I own a jewelry store," he said. "You'd have done much better than this. You can give her the ring, but you can't get married."

Like protagonists in a Billy Joel song, Virginia and Ed eloped shortly before Ed went off to war. He saw action in France and Belgium. When he returned, Halas gave him a job at May & Halas, the old man's sporting goods company. (Their slogan was, "A Bear for Quality.") Conditioned by the marginal early days of the NFL, Halas had invested in half a dozen side businesses: laundries, oil wells, athletic equipment. In 1967, McCaskey went to work for the Bears, where, according to biographer Jeff Davis, he was given an out-of-the-way job. It's like that scene in *The Godfather*, when Don Corleone, speaking of his son-in-law Carlo, says, "Give him a living, but never discuss the family business with him." By then, the team's daily operations had been turned over to Halas's son George Jr., known as Mugs, who'd been designated to run the club when the old man died.

Ed McCaskey picked heads in that coin toss. It was tails. A reporter shouted out, "McCaskey, you bum, you can't even win a coin flip!" Pittsburgh used the first pick to take Terry Bradshaw from Louisiana Tech. The Bears traded their number-two pick to Green Bay for veterans—all of whom were soon out of the game. The Steelers would become one of the great dynasties, winning four Super Bowls with Bradshaw at quarterback. The Bears? Well, the Bears kept on being the Bears.

I first watched the Bears in 1974 on the black-and-white TV in the kitchen. I went to my first game a year later. I went with friends; every third parent had tickets. When I asked my father if I could go, he would say, "You know what you're doing," or, even more damningly, "We can't tell our children what to love."

The Bears left Wrigley Field after the 1970 season. It was by league order, which required each team to play in a stadium with at least fifty thousand seats. They moved to Soldier Field, a coliseum just off South Lake Shore Drive. Low and white, it went forever. At one point, it seated one hundred thousand people. From the cheap seats, the game looked like a dispute in the distance, something that was none of your goddamn business. The façade is ornamented by columns, which gives everything a gladiatorial feel. The first teams I remember seeing there were quarterbacked by Bob Avellini, whose name makes a certain generation of Chicagoans wince. I also remember Roland Harper, Gary Huff, and Doug Buffone. Gary Fencik said Buffone smoked cigarettes during halftime, the butt shoved between the tips of his taped fingers. "I'd watch him puffing and be like, 'Guys, I might know why we're getting winded in the fourth quarter.'"

I sometimes wondered why anyone would attend a pro game. It's never as good as watching at home. Football is the ideal television sport—yet another reason it superseded baseball. The field is actually shaped like a screen, and the action divided as if designed for replays and commercials. At the stadium, you spend most of your time waiting, or trying to figure out what just happened. Yet there is something irreplaceable about going to a game, especially in Chicago. It's the weather of the world experienced in the extreme: heckling and cursing, intoxication, brawls. The colder and the more miserable, the more authentic the experience. We usually sat in the upper deck, covered in blankets, hot-water bottles in our laps, our teeth chattering, our eyelashes freezing. The skyscrapers loomed, the lake taunted us with fantasies of summer. In my memory, it's always fourth quarter and the Bears are always down. Behind us, defeats. Before us, a January of Sundays. But it was at just such moments that you finally understood Chicago, its resilience, its patience, and its humor. One year, after an especially brutal loss to the Redskins, I was crossing Lake Shore Drive amid a sea of depressed fans. Our heads were down, our eyes wet with tears. Nothing awaited us but despair. Just then, a Polish cop with a big cop mustache saved us all. "Get your heads up," he said. "Tomorrow is another fucking day."

Was there a consolation? Was there a salve, a relief for all this suffering? Indeed, there was.

His name was Walter Payton, and he was the man who carried us through that long dark night of losing. For many, Payton was the only reason to remain a Bears fan. As my friend Mark said, "There is only Walter, but that's enough."

They called him Sweetness, a nickname meant to suggest the greatness of his best moves, but it more perfectly captured his personality. He cried when he was drafted in 1975. He did not want to go to cold

Chicago. He did not want to play on that terrible team. Who could blame him? He had grown up in the South, where a cold day was 55° and a bad season was 7 and 3. But the fans loved Walter from the first. It was not just his talent, or the contours of his fireplug body, or the high-kicking, heads-up way he ran, or how, at the moment of contact, when most backs brace or run out-of-bounds, he would instead deliver a blow. It was his incredible sweetness. Walter was nothing but muscle, but his voice was effeminate in the way of Michael Jackson, soft and amused. He played the drums in his spare time—a football player with a hobby!—not the wild John Bonham kind of drums but Buddy Rich style, a hepcat working the brushes. In his first years, he dressed like Rerun on *What's Happening!!*: bell-bottoms, snap-brim hat, platform shoes. He was a terrific dancer. Several times a year, WGN showed his appearance on *Soul Train*, in which he had danced up a storm. It was that funky seventies kind of dancing, too, with lots of hand claps and splits.

Embodied in this one player you had the yin and the yang, the sugar and the salt, the smash mouth and the ballet that make football such a great game. Here was a culmination of Bears history, a resolution of opposites. At once brutal and refined, Nagurski *and* Grange, Butkus *and* Sayers. On certain carries, he was as slick as the Galloping Ghost, running forever, engaged in a kind of parallel play. On others, when only a yard was needed, he was as punishing as Ditka, lowering his head, bulling through. Near the goal, he did something I'd never seen: whereas most backs crash into the line, Payton would take the ball from a pitch, run toward the scrum, then leap, sailing clear over the top, landing on the crown of his head, bouncing back to his feet, as if his neck were a tremendous spring.

He had a rough start: zero yards on eight carries in his first game. He was cold, homesick, and alone. Chicago glowed around him like a coil, electric, unknowable. "I felt it immediately," he said. "I felt the greatness of this city. I felt it when I started playing and I didn't have performances as good as they should have been. I felt the wrath of the city then."

Following a poor midseason performance—zero yards on ten carries in Detroit—Bears head coach Jack Pardee benched Walter. As he watched from the sidelines, his belly churned. Like many players, it was not hope that motivated Payton. It was fear. Fear of failure, humiliation.

Payton said that that day on the bench, five games into his first season, was a hinge. It put a scare in him, showed him, just for a moment, the life that awaited if he failed. Very few players make it to college, fewer still to the pros, and most of those, stars at every other level, flame out. You see them years later, pushing a broom or carrying boards at a construction site. Walter's older brother, Eddie, a high school and college star, was an NFL bust, appearing in a half a dozen games with three teams over three seasons. He was the guy asking the bouncer to double-check the list: Eddie. Eddie PAYTON. Walter's brother! Eddie's memoir, published in 2012, is called *Walter & Me: Standing in the Shadow of Sweetness.*

After that, Walter played every game with an almost graceful fury. Most impressive were his durability and hustle. As James Brown was the hardest-working man in show business, Walter Payton was the

Walter Payton running for daylight, November 11, 1984

hardest-working man in football. Even late in the day, when a game was as good as over, he never stepped out-of-bounds but always turned upfield to deliver a blow. It gained him an extra yard or two and sent a message: when you tackle Walter Payton, you pay the price. He credited his college coach for the wisdom that determined his style: "Never die easy. If you're going to die anyway, die hard."

Payton would eventually pass Jim Brown as the NFL's all-time rushing leader, a record once considered unbreakable. He'd surpass O. J. Simpson's single-game record, as well as his record for the most consecutive hundred-yard games. But in the end, Payton's most impressive quality was his toughness: thirteen seasons and he did not miss another game. "The fact that Walter survived thirteen years in the NFL, missing only one game, especially with the beating that a running back takes, is the most amazing thing," said Jim McMahon. "He was the strongest guy I've ever met. Pound for pound, he was muscle everywhere."

Every fan has his favorite Payton run, but aficionados agree: the best came in his third season, against Kansas City. It was one of those plays, you keep thinking it's over, they got him, and suddenly he emerges from a crowd, shrugging off, stiff arming, high kicking. "It was the first time I saw him," Jim Brown said. "He fought for every inch. He must have twisted and knocked three or four guys over. Spun around, accelerated. And I said, 'Oh, my goodness—what kind of animal is this?'" The following week, playing with the flu—he had a 103° fever; you could see him suffering on the sideline—Payton ran for 275 yards against the Vikings.

Here's how good he had become: Gale Sayers turned testy; in interviews, he spoke of the pureness of the Gale Sayers style. Payton was, indeed, a different kind of player. Sayers ran seemingly without effort; there was ease in every pivot. Payton was like a car with its engine showing. You could see the pistons firing, the shafts cranking. He was a man at work, ham and eggs, meat and potatoes, a great runner but a great blocker, too. He did everything. He was the team's backup punter. Now and then, he would throw. In 1984, when McMahon went down, Payton played an entire half at quarterback. He set up in something like the single wing, playground style. *Go out, I'll look for ya.* When the linebackers dropped back into coverage, Walter dashed through the gaps. In the course of his career, he completed ten touchdown passes. A favorite moment from 1985 was a trick play: McMahon pitched to Payton, who raced around the backfield, attracting the attention of every defender, planted and threw a high-arching rainbow that Mac caught as he crossed into the end zone. It was a backyard play, drawn with a finger in the dirt: I toss to you, you toss to me. For years, I had a picture of it taped to my wall: McMahon's eyes bugged out, looking at the ball all the way in.

"There are a lot of great Hall of Fame backs, the Jim Browns of the world, the Gale Sayerses of the world, the Tony Dorsetts of the world, but none of those guys blocked," Johnny Roland told me. In addition to being a good runner in his own day, Roland was the Bears' running back coach. "But Walter was a great blocker. He was backup punter, backup field goal kicker. He threw the ball. He was our disaster quarterback. If you wanted him to, he could go up into the stands and sell popcorn."

But it was Payton's spirit that was valued most. At the end of every play, after he had been taken to the ground, he would extend his arms, placing the ball a few feet upfield. This was Sweetness in a drop of rain, always angling for a little more. "After every run, he'd push the ball forward a few inches," Ditka said. "The ref would move it back, but maybe over the course of his career Walter gained fifty yards that way."

Payton was the ideal player for a mediocre team. He gave the fans something to care about on the worst days. He transcended the game and seemed to represent the city itself. He was Chicago as Chicago wanted to be: a fighter, a hitter, a hustler who's been knocked down but always gets back up. "When I played, I never ever sat on the bench," Plank told me. "You know why? I wanted to watch Walter. I would stand on that sideline and just look: the way he hustled, even in games when we were hopelessly behind, you could learn from that. If you put on a tape and watch a player and cannot tell from the way he plays whether his team is ahead or behind—that's who you want. And that was Walter. Watching him was my pep talk. I'd tell myself, 'That's how you need to play. When you go back out there, bring it.'"

Payton's workouts were marathons of self-punishment. "I tagged along on one of those," Plank told me. "He jumped off cliffs, climbed up ropes, did suicidal stuff. When we finished, I said, 'Walter, I admire you, but I'm working out alone next time. I want to get strong, but I don't want to die.'"

Each morning, Walter "ran the hill." This started at college, in

Jackson, Mississippi, where he raced up a hill beside Highway 220. As there are few actual hills in Chicagoland, he resorted to a landfill behind his house in Arlington Heights, a trash heap with a steeply pitched grade. According to the *Chicago Tribune*, it covered fifty feet at a forty-five-degree incline. Payton would ascend in sprints, ten or fifteen trips up and down in a row. Trying to explain what this felt like, he said, "Have you ever jogged up 25 flights of stairs and run down? It burns. Your legs, your buttocks, your back, your chest, your stomach—everything wants to leave you."

"He'd run that hill in Mississippi, and he had a hill here in the suburbs, and he'd leave guys who were trying to stay with him half-dead, puking their guts out at the bottom," said Ditka. "If he had any fat on him, you couldn't have grabbed it with a pair of pliers."

Early one morning, I drove to Walter's Hill. I'd woken up sick but went anyway, first to a doctor's office in Northbrook, then to a Walgreens, where I got antibiotics, before finally heading west on Dundee Road. The hill is in Arlington Heights, past Buffalo Grove High School with its stadium and state championship banners. I turned onto Kennecott and went by subdivisions. I drove into the park that's been landscaped atop the landfill. I got out of my car and followed a trail out onto a promenade. Suddenly I was standing where Sweetness stood each morning at the end of his run, at the apex of Walter's Hill. It was cold and clear. A man in a Bears sweatshirt went by with his dog, a Scottie in a Bears sweater. Number 34. I saw joggers. A woman pushed a stroller. The trees were yellow. Looking east, I could see more yellow trees scattered amid the housing grids, the slate roofs as well ordered as circuits in a transistor radio. Payton lived in one of those houses. Behind his house, this hill. Atop this hill, a bench and a plaque that shows Walter's face and lists his accomplishments. Otherwise, there seemed no evidence of the man who ran the hill. That's the thing about work. It vanishes like a memory of pain. Only the results are remembered.

Walter Payton is a model for all those engaged in arts that don't properly value effort. How many times have you heard a person say, "He was a great player but just did not work hard enough," as if work were different from talent, more prosaic, something anyone could do if he wanted. But as I've gotten older, I've come to believe the ability to persist is as much a gift as speed or soft hands. Not everyone has it. Those who don't, fail. Those who do, leave no proof of it in statistics. Walter's Hill is the only monument I know to that invisible quality without which everything else would be impossible. Payton was a great athlete, but hard work was his outstanding talent. It was the bedrock upon which the Bears would finally build a great team.

9

READY, FIRE, AIM

Iron Mike mixing it up with 49ers fans at Candlestick Park
in San Francisco. December 15, 1987

Mike Ditka played his last game for the Bears in 1966. His final years in Chicago were miserable. He felt unappreciated, unloved. He'd given his knees and hips and youth to the team, but Halas refused to pay him what he was worth. "I never understood why he never saw my value for the way I played for him," Ditka told Jeff Davis, author of *Papa Bear*. "I played hard for him. I'm not even saying I played good for him. I played hard. Every down, I played hard . . ." When Halas learned that Ditka had been involved in negotiations with the Houston Oilers of the rival American Football League, and had been paid, he cut Ditka's salary 10 percent. That's when Iron Mike spoke those piercing words: the old man throws around nickels like they're manhole covers. "I think it was at a banquet," Ditka said. "I'll tell you one thing: you couldn't say much in Chicago that Mr. Halas didn't know about. It would come back to him. He had a powerful network of people . . . It made Halas furious when he heard about it."

Ditka signed his last Bears contract the following summer: $25,000 for one season. He got that much only by threatening to hold out; he would skip training camp, even the season. Halas still refused. In the end, it was Mugs who inked the deal. "As you got to know [Halas], you found out he played a game with people and knew how to play it as good as anyone," Ditka said. "He was crafty. He had a way to maneuver and manipulate and change and end up getting it done the way he wanted it done. I guess all great people do."

The final blowup came in 1967. It resulted from a bit of loose talk.

"The thing that really made [Halas] mad was once I called him a cheap Bohemian," Ditka wrote later. "He came right to me. I was getting dressed and he called me in and asked me about it. But I said I just said it in jest. I told him I could have called him a cheap SOB but the Bohemian thing was something I was just being cute with. He said, Don't be cute with my nationality. I said, It's like you saying I'm a dumb Polack or something. Why would that bother me? He was right, though. It was a stupid thing to say. Those are things you do when you are young and trying to be cute."

Ditka had inadvertently violated one of Halas's principles. He believed in freedom, hard work, winning. He did not believe in ethnic determination. It's what made him a great coach, open to anyone who could play. If I'm cheap, he might say, it's because I lived through the wars and the Depression and was forced to learn the value of a dollar, not because my ancestors came from Czechoslovakia.

By the end of the week, Ditka had been traded to Philadelphia, a graveyard for players. Halas did not just want to get rid of Ditka; he wanted to bury him. Many Bears fans mark the start of the team's decline to this trade, which sent the club's heart and soul to the Eagles for quarterback Jack Concannon.

The Philadelphia years were the worst of Ditka's career. "I cried like hell," he said. His family stayed in Chicago, meaning Mike was out there, tired, wounded, alone. The Eagles were awful. The games were awful. Ditka spent much of his time cursing on the bench. "I'm sure if there is such a thing as purgatory on earth, I was in it there," he said. He haunted the local bars, staring at his face in the mirror. It was one of those trials that come in every life, a moment in which you know, just know, that if you weaken or lose focus, you'll be washed away by malaise, slide into dissolute wandering. Why not sit down on the riverbank with this bottle, just for a minute, an hour, a short nap beneath the trees? "The whole year was a real low point," he said. "I had an apartment in downtown Philadelphia. My family was still in Chicago. Basically, every night I would go out. I drank a lot. I was not playing and it was just ridiculous. I was about to kill myself with the drinking. I was in bad shape. Nothing else to do. I was a mess."

In the Ditka scheme of things, a man needs only himself—determination and will should be enough to get anyone through. And yet, when he touched bottom in Philly, it was not self-love or zipperoo

that saved Iron Mike: it was a voice on the phone, another human being reaching out across the dark. "I would have quit the game if Landry
hadn't called," Ditka told me. Tom Landry, the head coach of the Dallas
Cowboys, had a tremendous effect on anyone lucky enough to fall
in his orbit. (Note all the Texans named Landry.) He spoke with a
twang, his voice sharp but encouraging. He said, "Mike, this is Tom
Landry over in Dallas. Now you tell me the truth, Mike: Do you think
you've got anything left?"

You show a man at sea a raft, he will swim for it.

Ditka stopped drinking, stopped carousing. He spent months running and lifting weights, living like an ascetic. When he showed up at
Cowboys training camp in 1969, he was in great shape, ready to give
the orange one more squeeze. He would play four seasons in Dallas,
nearly as many as he'd played in Chicago. It was a gift that allowed him
a late-career florescence, the sort afforded only to those who are lucky.
He described them as "the best years I ever played." He did not make as
many catches as he had in Chicago, but he was thrown the ball in key
situations. On January 16, 1972, Ditka caught a touchdown in the Super Bowl, a Roger Staubach pass that found him in the end zone.

These seasons reframed Ditka's career, completed it. If he'd retired
in Philly, if his story had ended there, sadly, in a bar, he would have
been remembered as a buzz cut from the sixties, a product of a certain
time and place, a one-act athlete frozen in black and white. But in Dallas,
he made the transition to the full-blown, woolly 1970s, where he became
a beefy, mustachioed Cowboy surrounded by hippies. "Everything was
radical," he said. "Nobody wanted the Vietnam thing. Everybody had
their own philosophies. Everybody was against the government. It was
a different breed of person coming out. . . . Then all of a sudden we got
that smell around the locker room. We would say, 'What the hell's that
smell?' . . . I guess it was called hemp or rope."

The end came slowly, then all at once. "I had lost weight," said
Ditka, "my back was killing me." He'd lost speed, too, and some of the
fearlessness that had always been crucial to his performance. It's a matter of split seconds. At the beginning, you hit, then think; at the end,
you think, then hit. "You [believe] it's going to last forever," he said.
"You figure the Good Lord gave you this body and it's going to keep
working and it's not going to get hurt. You're going to wake up every
day with enough enthusiasm to say, 'Yeah, I'm going to play the game.'

All of a sudden, after you've been doing it for eight or nine years, even if you're healthy, then the mind starts playing tricks on you. It makes it tough. You start saying, 'I don't know if I'm going to catch that one coming inside . . .' "

Before a game against San Francisco, Ditka pushed back his chair and tried to get up from a poker table but couldn't stand. His back locked, the pain came in waves. A few days later, he went into Landry's office: *That's it, Coach. I'm done.* Then, a few days after that, as Ditka was wondering what he might do next, he got his second life-shaping call from Landry. *Do you want to work with the receivers, Mike?* Perhaps no one else would have considered Ditka for such a position. A coach is supposed to be even-tempered, rational, sane. Ditka was a hothead, a tantrum thrower. One night, after not liking his hand in a game of cards, he ripped a deck in half. You have to be incredibly strong to do that—and also a little nuts. But Landry recognized a quality in Ditka, the way he seemed to motivate everyone around him. He became the Cowboys' special teams coordinator. He could be seen screaming on the sideline, throwing a clipboard, kicking a cooler. The mustache was there, the polyester pants, the whistle, the turf shoes, the temper. Around the league, he was accused of schooling his players in dirty tricks. "We teach that when you come to block you close your fists and come up with your hands underneath the guy's solar plexus and hit him in the stomach," Ditka said. "It stops you from being called for holding and helps you deliver a blow. Nothing illegal about it."

"Mike was black-and-white," said Danny White, a Cowboys quarterback and special teams player. "There was no gray area. He yelled at me once after I shanked a punt. He was used to yelling at kickers. I yelled back at him. I said, 'Yeah, right, Mike, I did it on purpose. Fine me.'

"We played a lot of racquetball," White went on. "It was a great way to stay in shape. Rafael Septien, our kicker, and I would play [Coach] Dan Reeves and Mike, two of the most competitive human beings. Rafael was an A-plus player, coming from Mexico. I was pretty good. They couldn't beat us. Their only chance was to bang us around, intimidate us. Mike would finally reach the point where he wouldn't even aim at the wall. He would aim at Rafael. My plan was to stay away from Rafael because Mike might miss Rafael and hit me. And Mike would hammer the ball. He'd drill it at you. It really hurt. He didn't care. He wanted to drive you to the point where you quit. Not a finesse guy, a bull in a china closet. That's the way he played football, and it made him a great coach. There was no middle ground. You either get the job done, or you were gone."

Landry taught Ditka how to coach, how to lead, even how to live. He taught him to internalize his fury, play a long game: *You don't have to tell everyone what you think every time, Mike!* "If there is a compassionate side to Mike, it's because of Landry," White told me. "Ditka learned professionalism from Landry. He learned that, as a coach, you have to control your passions. I think those years in Dallas made Ditka a coach. It calmed him down."

When I laughed at this—it's hard to imagine anyone less calm than Ditka in the third quarter, down by ten points—White said, "Yeah, try to imagine Ditka without the influence of Landry. He would have been a raving lunatic. So I think, believe it or not, Landry had a huge effect. He helped Mike control his emotions. A normal person loses their composure and screams at someone, then feels bad. But Mike never felt bad. Until Landry. Then he began to realize, hey, these are human beings. He still yelled, but now he felt a little remorse. He might not apologize, but he felt it."

Ditka coached nine seasons in Dallas. While there, he was akin to the young Moses, a phony Egyptian prince living in the wondrous palace of Pharaoh. His life was good, his future assured, but he was not with his people, not fulfilling his destiny. When the Cowboys faced the Bears, he caught himself wishing that he was on the other sideline: Moses feeling a strange rush of sympathy when the overseer clubbed the Hebrew slave.

In 1981, the circuit filled with rumors: the Bears would soon fire their head coach, Neill Armstrong. That's when Ditka made his move: "I wrote Halas a letter," Ditka said. "It was a simple letter. I just said I wanted to renew our friendship. I told him I knew he had experienced some troubled times. I said, 'I just want you to know if you ever make a change in the coaching end of the organization, I just wish you would give me some consideration.' That's all. It was a very nice letter."

Why was George Halas still running the Bears?

After Halas retired from the bench, he stepped away from the front office as well, turning the operation over to George Jr. A dark-haired man, Mugs spent much of his life in his father's shadow, following him up and down the sideline, hanging helmets in the dank locker rooms of the old NFL. He joined the Bears front office as soon as he graduated from Loyola University on Chicago's North Side. Mugs had two children and two wives. When the first wife filed for divorce, she cited "mental cruelty." According to the *New York Times*, she claimed, "Football took precedence over our marriage and our children."

Mugs might've been brilliant, but you'd never have known, as his story was so completely overwhelmed by his father's. Part of this is likely because Senior outlived Junior, always a tragedy: Mugs died on the last day of the 1979 football season. According to an autopsy, he'd suffered a massive coronary; he was fifty-four. The news was kept off the radio until the old man could be found. Tim McCaskey, Virginia's son, was dispatched to tell his grandfather. The situation was biblical. It was about patriarchy. Halas had one male heir. Everything depended on him. Mugs would carry the name, the team, and the spirit into the next century. This was the old man's legacy. The future was an abstraction, but Mugs was real. Until he wasn't.

With Mugs's death, logic would seem to dictate the ascension of Ed McCaskey, the only other family member who worked in the executive suite. But logic would also dictate an end zone nowhere near a brick wall, retiring Butkus's jersey, and a postgame pep talk more eloquent than "You're all a bunch of cunts." "[Mugs's death] set the Old Man back dramatically," said Jerry Vainisi, who had served as team treasurer since 1972 and would take over as general manager after Jim Finks. "His whole preordained plan was to live forever. If the unconscionable happened that he died, certainly Mugs would run the club and live forever. It was *never* to go through the McCaskey family. Part of it was the Latin primogeniture, that everything goes to the oldest male, plus he was the one running the team."

At eighty-five, Halas announced his return to the helm, saying, "Only a Halas can run the Bears." It was a jolt. Here was this relic—was he really still alive?—of the ancient leather-head days returning to a game that had long since passed him by. Stan Jones, who played guard and defensive tackle for the Bears, compared it to "Orville Wright coming back to run United Airlines." Halas reasserted control, firing or isolating many of the people closest to Mugs. In January 1981, he called Ditka, who, years later, still remembered the old man's exact words: "Kid, this is George Halas. I want you to get on an airplane and fly to O'Hare. Don't tell anybody. Take a [car] and come to my place at 5555 N. Sheridan."

Halas was called the old man even when he was young. He was eighty-six when he reached out to Ditka, grouchy, grizzled, heartbroken. He told Mike to travel in absolute secrecy. The press, the big shots, the sportswriting bums—none of them were to know anything. "It was like foreign intrigue," Ditka said. "[Halas's assistant] Max Swiatek picked me up in a black Lincoln Town Car. He drove me to Mr. Halas's apartment, and we went upstairs and sat at the kitchen table. The first thing he said, and I always remember this, was, 'Tell me about your coaching philosophy.' I said, 'Coach, what do you want me to do? Bullshit ya? My coaching philosophy is the same as yours: I want to win.'"

"We did a deal right at his kitchen table," Ditka wrote. "My contract for 100K was by far the smallest in the league, but that's OK. That wasn't my worry. I wanted to prove to Mr. Halas that he made the right decision."

When the news hit the papers—Ditka to coach the Bears—the sportswriters went wild. That hothead? That hard-drinking, all-night-carousing pop-off artist? "The old man was on his deathbed," said Bears quarterback Bob Avellini, "and here's a guy writing a letter to that old man who's been . . . what? A special teams coach for the Cowboys? And he gets the job? The odds of that happening are monumental. You don't go from special teams to head coach. If there's a coach on a lower rung than special teams, I can't think of it."

"Nobody else in the National Football League would have hired me, no question," said Ditka. "Too many drawbacks. There's an NFL image you have to be and maintain and I probably wasn't it."

"There were people right in the Bears organization who didn't want me, who thought I was the stupidest hire of all time," Ditka explains in *In Life, First You Kick Ass*. "But Papa Bear had the say-so—*he started the Goddamned NFL!*—and he gave me the job."

"Some of the people who have known Ditka best . . . wonder if there is a punch line to this joke," the Chicago columnist John Schulian wrote in *The Sporting News*. ("Hiring Ditka would be madness.")

"I don't know what was in George Halas's mind when he hired Mike Ditka," Bill Tobin, a Bears general manager, told me, "but I do know that Halas wanted physically aggressive teams, and that's what Mike wanted, too. Halas knew Ditka and what Ditka stood for and what Ditka wanted from a team. The players that we'd been drafting from '75 until Ditka got there came from the same cloth: hard-nosed, physical, intelligent people. Ditka was supposed to bring it all together and give us that identity."

Before Ditka left Dallas, Landry offered a last bit of advice: "Whether you succeed or not, do it your way," he said. "Don't ever leave yourself open to doing it somebody else's way, and then blame them if you fail."

Ditka held his first team meeting as head coach in the summer of 1982 in Halas Hall. He was forty-three, a big man with a gaudy mustache and curled hair. He wore coach pants and a short-sleeve shirt stretched tight across the chest. He paced, chewing gum as he barked out words. He chewed so hard and fast you actually felt sorry for the gum. Every player in the locker room would remember this meeting as a pivotal moment, the end of one kind of life, the start of another. "I'll never forget the first day I saw him, this tightly wound spring with close-set eyes that darted from side to side," Mike Singletary wrote in *Calling the Shots*. "Intensity oozed from his skin. The first day, you knew change—for good, for bad, nobody was sure—was ahead."

"I remember the first time Mike introduced himself as head coach so clearly," Brian Baschnagel told me. "We were in Halas Hall in Lake Forest. Most of the guys were sitting in back—the first three or four rows were spotty with people, which was typical of team meetings. He comes in and doesn't say a word, just looks at every one of us. There were probably fifty guys. After he had viewed every one of us, he says, 'Hi guys, this is Mike Ditka, your new head coach. We're going to the Super Bowl.' And of course we all kind of nervously look at each other. Then he says, 'I don't know what year we're going to the Super Bowl, but we're going. It's up to each and every one of you to decide whether or not you'll be with us when we do.'"

"Size matters," Doug Plank told me. "Having a guy five five walking in front of your team saying, 'Hi, I'm the head coach, blah, blah,' that's one thing. But Ditka walking in at six three and looking like he's been through a hurricane? Immediate respect. It didn't take people long to figure out the terms he was coaching under."

"I let them know there was going to be change," Ditka told me. "We were going to win a Super Bowl but a lot of them weren't going to be with us when we did. I didn't say it to be cruel. It was just a fact."

"There's three kinds of coaches," said Plank. "First, there's the aspirin coach. He's the guy that comes in and feeds you a bunch of baloney and makes you feel better initially, but nothing changes. Then there's the penicillin coach. He comes in and fixes *almost* everything. The problems, the illnesses. But there's one thing he can't fix and that's cancer on a team. What's cancer? Guys don't like each other, the offense versus the defense, huge attitudes. You need the third kind of coach for that: the chemo coach. Bill Parcells, Mike Ditka. The chemo coach comes in, man, he's the new sheriff in town. He's so powerful by the way he looks, his presence, his actions. If you got a bad attitude, you don't buy into his system? He doesn't care who you are—you're gone."

That July, the Bears had minicamp at Sun Devils Stadium in Phoenix, where, in the summer, the grass heats up to 120°. Ditka selected it with care: he did not believe the Bears' failures had been caused by lack of talent alone but resulted from a losing attitude that can spread from player to player, a disease that must be sweated out. "If you accept defeat, you're going to be defeated," he said. "You can be gracious in defeat, but you better be doing flip flops inside. If you're not churning, you'll get your ass whipped, that's all there is to it."

When James Scott, a Bears star receiver, showed up late for practice, his equipment was put in a garbage bag and dumped in the hall. He was eventually cut. When Ricky Watts, a second-round pick in 1979, showed insufficient hustle, he was handed his own equipment-filled bag. (Ditka did give Watts another chance, but he was relegated to special teams and never started another game.) The fact that Scott and Watts were talented only emphasized the point: I don't care who the fuck you think you are—you're in, or out. Ditka wasn't just getting players in shape, he was changing expectations. "The culture changed immediately," said Kurt Becker. "The nonconformists were gone. And some of these were players, guys that had produced. It didn't matter. If you weren't with the program, goodbye."

The practices that followed were as tough as any in the history of the league. Ditka ran 'em, pushed 'em, challenged 'em. If a guy doubled over, the bile filling his mouth, Ditka would say, "Look at it this way. You could be working for a living. And really, what can you do? I don't think half of you are smart enough to get a job. We don't need you. If you want to leave, get a better deal, fine, go." Some players started calling Ditka "mad dog."

"For all the pounding, the most important things were done subtly," Baschnagel told me. "For example, he gave us two rules. Just two. First, we had to go unsupervised before practice and jog around the field twice; second, we had to do ten chin-ups on our own. If you can't do ten chin-ups, do ten sit-ups. Those were his rules. And of course we all looked at each other and said, 'Well, what's the purpose of that?' But those were the rules. And he'd watch: Which guys would try to get around doing those two laps and ten chin-ups? Maybe they'd do three or four chin-ups, or pull up after running a lap and a half. The guys that cheated on those two rules weren't around for very long. I guess his point was that you have to do all the little things to be successful. All he had were two rules; if you couldn't adhere to those, you weren't going to sacrifice what was necessary for the team."

Ditka was in a peculiar position. Though he was the Bears' head coach, he controlled only the offense. The defense was coached by Buddy Ryan, who'd been hired by Neill Armstrong. When a head coach is fired, his staff usually goes, too. But in this case, when rumors of Armstrong's ouster began to circulate, the team's defensive standouts, who loved Buddy, took preemptive action. The Bears had remarkable defensive leaders: Alan Page, a Hall of Fame defensive tackle who now sits on the Minnesota Supreme Court, and Gary Fencik, the Yalie whom Mike Singletary described as "hit man bitch, reader of Kosinski and Fowles, world traveler, blues freak, fluent in the language of love." As Ditka was writing to Halas, Page and Fencik, who believed the defense had made a breakthrough the previous season, were writing a letter of their own, which they carried around the locker room for every player on the defense to sign.

Dec. 9, 1981
Dear Mr. Halas,
We the undersigned members of the Bears defensive football team
are concerned about the future of our team. We recognize that with
the disappointing season the Bears have had this year that there
may be changes in our coaching staff and/or administration of the
team. Our main concern is over the fate of Buddy Ryan and the

other defensive coaches . . . Buddy has maintained the discipline,
morale, pride and effort that we need in order to play well
defensively, in spite of the fact that we haven't had much help from
the offensive team . . .

"We knew Halas was supposed to be tough and not sympathetic to players, but we felt we had built something worth protecting on the defensive side," Fencik told me, "and saw no other way to protect it. We had to reach out to the owner. We knew there'd be a coaching change, but we wanted Halas to keep the defensive coach. Everybody loved Buddy. We thought the defense was great."

A week after Fencik and Page sent the letter, Halas showed up at a team practice, something he hardly ever did. He was a frail old man with blue eyes and a lantern jaw, more skeletal with each passing year. In the summer, he sped across the fields in a golf cart, "but it was winter, a cold, snowy day," said Fencik, "and we were working out at the Great Lakes Naval Training Center, practicing indoors. It killed the older guys because we played on a cement floor. Halas told our coaches to take a hike. He wanted to talk to the defense alone. When they left, he said, 'I got your letter. Your coaches will be back next year.'" Halas also responded in writing:

> *. . . This is a magnificent letter! It is a beautifully written letter! It is*
> *the highest tribute a coach could receive!*
>
> *I can tell you without fear of contradiction that this is the first*
> *time in the 61-year history of the Chicago Bears that such a letter*
> *has been written about a Bear coach . . . I'm so fortunate to have*
> *you boys on my team . . .*

For Ditka, it must have been maddening. He was head coach but had little control over the defense—he could talk all he wanted but did not have the power to fire Buddy Ryan. The result was a rift between offense and defense, a rift and a rivalry. The squads traveled on separate buses, attended separate meetings, followed separate codes. Ditka and Ryan were often at war. It was not an act: these men truly hated each other. It was the energy behind everything; it was there at halftime, at the beginning and end of each practice and game. "Every now and again, when things weren't going well on the field, Mike would come by and make some suggestions," Ryan said. "I'd just tell him to go blank himself, and he'd turn around and walk off."

In an unintended, roundabout way, this dysfunction actually helped the Bears: as squad went after squad, every practice turned into a battle and the players drove each other to the heights of ferocity. Asked to name the best team he faced in 1985, Ditka said, "the Bears." "When you went out for a normal practice, you wouldn't wear as many pads," Plank told me, "but when Mike came to town and Buddy was the defensive coordinator, you went to every practice thinking, You know what? A game could break out here at any moment. I'm taking everything."

"Our sidelines were a joke during the games," Jim McMahon told the writer Steve Delsohn. "I bet if people really knew what was going on back then, they would be amazed that we could win. They were fighting each other all the time. Ditka would yell at him to run a certain defense, and Buddy would say, 'Fuck you, I run the defense, get outta here.'"

"I give Mike all the credit," Plank told me. "Not many CEOs could manage circumstances like that. Imagine being the boss of a company and half the employees don't have to answer to you. But he figured out how to make it work. He knew the right buttons to push. Sometimes it was defensive buttons to get us angry or drive Buddy up the wall. He manipulated us, figured out how to push us where we had to go. The goal was winning. To do that, we needed to be a unit. If that meant getting players to hate coaches, fine. In the end, he showed an unbelievable ability to change a situation that hadn't changed since 1963. The Bears had been wallowing in mediocrity for years. It took Ditka along with a defensive coach that became his nemesis to make it work. There weren't a handful of people on this planet that could have done it."

For a fan, a new coach is like a new boyfriend. At first, it's heady talk and promises of you and me, walks in the moonlight, singing telegrams on your birthday, but sooner or later you figure out what this guy is really all about. Ditka arrived in 1982. By the end of his first season, most of us had realized he was insane. Now, when he appears on television and occasionally turns up in movies, what you see is a parody: Ditka at seventy-four playing Ditka at forty-four—a cartoon that, even in the memory of most fans, has replaced the coach as he was in '82, flipping off reporters, kicking benches to smithereens.

Rick Telander, a *Sports Illustrated* and *Sun-Times* writer who lived in a house beside Halas Hall, tells a story in the book he wrote with Ditka (*In Life, First You Kick Ass*) about a construction worker who, while patching Telander's roof, got into it with the coach. Telander heard the construction guy say something, followed by a few shouted words. A moment later, he came downstairs, "terrified."

What's wrong? asked Telander.

"Ditka yelled at me."

"What did he yell?"

" 'Use your hammer, not your mouth, jackass!' "

Ditka was moody and tantrum-prone. After a loss in Baltimore, he punched a wall, breaking his hand. Before the next game, he waved his cast at his players, saying, "Win one for Lefty." Jerry Vainisi admonished Ditka, saying, "Your technique is coach by crisis. You always have to have some crisis to overcome. It diverts attention from the game. The players don't understand it. They think you're crazy."

"We call him Sybil after the girl in the movie who had all those personalities," said McMahon. "Mike will be calm one minute, then throw a clipboard the next. People don't understand that, but we do. The players figure he's just going from one stage to another. He's merely Sybilizing."

Jim Finks described Ditka's method as "Ready, Fire, Aim."

Over time, a team takes on the personality of its coach. If he's strong, the team will be strong. If he's weak, the team will be ineffectual. But what if he's insane? Ditka's temper galvanized many Bears, got them hustling and hitting. But it was different for the skill players. What fired up the bruisers could be the undoing of a passer, that gridiron aristocrat who must do more than pound his way through. Even Ditka's admirers acknowledge that he was a terrible handler of quarterbacks. He bullied, shouted, undercut, threatened, punished, and chewed them out in front of teammates—in other words, he treated them like he treated everyone else. But a quarterback is not like everyone else. He's a delicate instrument, a jockey riding his own sense of self-confidence, out there on an audible and a spiral. "Ditka called plays we didn't even have," Bob Avellini told me. "I'd signal time-out, walk over, and say, 'Mike, we don't have that play.' And he'd shout, 'Shut up, and run the fucking thing.'" The list of quarterbacks terrorized by Ditka is illustrious: Bob Avellini, Mike Tomczak, Rusty Lisch, Jim Harbaugh.

"One time, we were on our own one-yard line," said Avellini. "We had ninety-nine yards to go with three seconds left in the half. Ditka sent in a play. Willie Gault is the split end. Ditka said, 'Throw the bomb.' I said, 'The defense is laying off thirty yards. There's nothing good that can possibly happen from this. I can take a safety, get stripped . . . what's the best that can happen? A thirty-yard completion?' He said, 'Just run the fucking thing.' Another time, we were supposed to run a sweep right. I saw something so I called a sweep left. It went for thirty yards. I get back to the sideline and Ditka is pounding his fist, slamming his clipboard. He'd rather have a shitty play that he called than a play that actually succeeded."

Avellini continued, "Everything he did was based on fear. It works for a short period but you can't continue on fear. I remember the first practice. We're running a two-minute offense. I threw the ball right where I was supposed to, but one of the guys ran the wrong pattern: it got picked off. I was supposed to run the whole two-minute offense but Ditka said, 'Avellini, you're out.' I said, 'What about the guy that blew the pattern?' Ditka said, 'You want to pack your bags and get the hell outta here?' I said no, but at least I stood up to him. When we got back to the locker room, the guys all said, 'Bob, that was great.' I said, 'Yeah, guys, thanks for backing me up.' I was always walking a tightrope. He'd threaten me: I'm gonna cut your ass. I'm gonna cut your ass. I went in against Green Bay when McMahon got hurt. I didn't even have a chance to warm up. I threw an incompletion. When I get back to the sideline, Ditka says, 'I'm gonna cut your fuckin' ass.'"

In a game in Seattle in 1984, Ditka told Avellini that under no circumstances was he to audible—that is, change the play sent in by the coach. Even if he saw an opportunity, the wide receivers wouldn't hear the change. The Kingdome was probably the loudest stadium in football. The Bears got to the goal line. Avellini was under center—he saw something. "I hear Ed Hughes, our offensive coordinator, say, 'Oh, no,' said Ditka. I yell: 'What is it, Ed?' He says, 'That son of a bitch is audible-izing.'"

Avellini threw to a receiver who was supposed to be in the corner of the end zone but wasn't because he hadn't heard the call. The interception resulted in a Seattle touchdown.

Ditka: "Bob comes out of the game, and I say—I'm trembling—'Bob, why would you do that, son?'"

Avellini: "Well, I thought—"

Ditka: "Don't THINK!"

After several deep breaths, Ditka went on: "Bob, if you ever do that again you will never—ever—EVER—play another down for me! DO YOU UNDERSTAND ME?" On another occasion, under similar circumstances, Avellini did the same thing with the same result. When he got back to the sideline that day, he was greeted by Ditka in full Ditka: "Don't you like me, Bob? Don't you like your teammates? Do you think we're stupid and don't give you good plays?"

When Avellini tried to explain, Ditka shouted, "That's it, you're done!"

"Then he looked at me," Ditka remembered, "and said, 'You never liked me anyway.' I was going to kill him. Right there. Tear his flesh off like a jackal. I was so mad my neck veins had veins!"

Avellini finished his career with the New York Jets.

In a game against the Chargers, Ditka swore at quarterback Rusty Lisch—he had fumbled—until he was out of breath. A few minutes later, when the Bears got the ball back, Lisch refused to play, saying, "I don't think I can go in after the way you talked to me."

"Hey Rusty," said Ditka, "I was *kidding!*"

"I got mad at Lisch for carrying the ball like a loaf of bread," Ditka explained. According to several players, Mike Tomczak, the Bears' third-string quarterback in 1985, was ruined by Ditka. "He once told me he was getting treatment from a sports psychologist to help him deal with the harsh criticism he received from Ditka," Dan Jiggetts wrote in *"Then Ditka Said to Payton . . ."* "He said the sessions helped him maintain his personal confidence and perspective."

Of all the Bears quarterbacks of the 1980s and '90s, only McMahon figured out how to handle Ditka, which is probably why only Mac won a Super Bowl. "T-Czak, T-Czak, I always told you how to deal with Ditka," McMahon said, laughing. "You just look him in the eye and say, 'Go fuck yourself.' If you did that, he'd leave you alone." McMahon was a goof, a talented flake who simply did not take it to heart when the coach blew up. *He's just Sybilizing.* He let even the titanic rages flow around him, leaving his inner quarterback compass untouched. Ditka called a play, Mac changed it, the Bears scored, Ditka went nuts. "He was the perfect quarterback for that team," Danny White told me. "First of all, when they needed a big play, he'd come through. He could throw down the field and had a hell-bent-for-leather approach that matched the team. But it was his temperament that was crucial. McMahon was the only quarterback who could put up with Mike Ditka. He would not let it get to him. Because McMahon was just as crazy as his coach."

Ditka met Halas once a week, master and protégé lingering in the fading light of a December afternoon. Prospects, plays. Till the very end, the old man had ideas. The body fails, but the brain keeps churning out solutions. In Ditka's first game as head coach, the Bears were on the Detroit 1-yard line with seconds left. They had two chances to get into the end zone for a tie, handed off both times, and failed. When Ditka got to his office the next morning, there was an old playbook sent over by Halas. It was opened to the QB sneak. From then on, that's what Ditka called whenever he got near the goal line.

Though he was an old man by then, Halas still took time to mentor select members of the team. He was a teacher at heart, which is why he took so long to leave the sideline and what made it so hard when he did. "I stopped in after a game when the offices were downtown," Plank told me. "I had a visit with [general manager] Jim Finks. George Halas stuck his head in and said, 'Doug, I'd like to talk to you for a few minutes if you have time.' So after I got done with Finks, I sat with Mr. Halas. He started talking about general things, what was happening on the team, then went into our most recent game. I was amazed by the detailed nature of his knowledge about each play. He picked up key things, crucial things, I'd missed. He'd say, 'Doug, on that long pass, their second possession in the third, I noticed that you started about twenty feet off the hash mark. But if you cheat a little, move five or ten steps closer to center, I think you'll get a helpful jump. Also, Doug, I thought you could have been wider on that punt return; it would have given you a better angle at the block.'"

"After one practice, a bunch of us were just sitting around Mr. Halas," Fencik said. "He was showing us how to hold a football so you wouldn't fumble. He asked for a ball, put his index finger over the point, and said, 'Here's the way!' It was such a perfect detail. You weren't really expecting it out of the owner of the team."

Mike Singletary: "I remember one day, after a miserable game, Halas just roared at our offense: 'This is football. Hold on to the fucking thing!'"

"The game had passed him by," said Avellini. "Is it sacrilegious to say that? One time he called me on a Friday and I'm in bed and everything, and he says, 'This is Coach Halas.' I said, 'Yeah, right,' thinking it's one of my friends. 'No, this is Coach Halas.' 'Okay, Coach, what's up?' He said, 'I want you to run this play.' Well, his play was something out of the 1940s. I'm sure you've seen it on film—in black and white, never in color. You take the ball and toss it backward to a guy like Gale Sayers and he just outruns the defense. But we were playing the Cowboys that week and I said, 'Boy, Coach, I don't know. Too Tall Jones could catch that ball in the air his arms are so long.' 'No, no,' he said, 'just run the play.' The result was Walter Payton having the most unbelievable run for a two-yard loss I've ever seen.

"I went to his apartment in the city," Avellini went on. "If you're from Chicago, you'd know it. A pink building around the 5600 block North, off Lake Shore Drive. It was one of these old buildings. I go up, and there's Halas sitting with Sid Luckman. And Sid starts telling me how to throw the ball. He says, 'You gotta throw it from your shoulder.' I said, 'Mr. Luckman, if I do that, I'm going to hit these guys in the head. I got to release the ball higher.' And the old man says, 'What do you know? You're a rookie. This is Sid Luckman!'"

"He came to our meeting room one day in my sixth or seventh year," Plank told me. "This was in Lake Forest, and he said, 'I'd like to talk to the team, share a few memories.' He then gave one of the most detailed breakdowns of the game I've ever heard any coach give. He goes to the blackboard, draws the field, [then divides it into sections]. He points with the chalk, saying, 'This is the red zone, this is the blue zone, this is the white zone.' It was the first time I'd ever heard the term 'red zone.' Think about how often 'red zone' is used today! He tells us what you do in each area. These are the plays you call, this is the strategy that works, here's how many yards you need per attempt. He backed it all up with an incredible breakdown of statistics. Here was a man who founded the league, who excelled as a player, a coach, and an owner, and he was sharing this knowledge with us. Come on! You've got to be kidding me."

In the spring of 1982, Halas was diagnosed with pancreatic cancer. He hadn't felt right for a long time. Knowing the name and prognosis of the disease—six months, a year—pushed him downhill. Patrick McCaskey realized his grandfather was near the end when, after his eighty-eighth birthday, he suddenly stopped swearing. He never again said a bad word about anyone. No more cocksuckers, no more mother-fuckers, no more pop-off artists. A profane voice had retired from the scene. He stopped drinking, he stopped yelling. He was in and out of the hospital, where he sat, propped on pillows, meeting friends and coaches. "I went to the hospital all the time," Ditka said. "He was very lucid. He asked about the draft and about the players. I told him he would like [Jimbo] Covert because he was just like Joe Stydahar. He would smile and say, 'That's good.'" A few months before he died, Halas sent Ditka a bottle of Dom Perignon with a note: "Mike, don't open it till you win the Super Bowl."

Virginia and Ed McCaskey wanted the team to be run by their old-est child, Michael. "Halas, who thought his grandson lacked the tough-ness to run the club, rebuffed them," Jeff Davis wrote in *Papa Bear*. "As unfair as it may have been to Michael, in many ways the eldest grand-son paid the price for his grandfather's enmity toward the senior Mc-Caskey." The story turned monarchical, Tudors and Romanoffs, words whispered outside the room of the dying king. According to Davis, Halas spoke these words shortly before he died: "Anybody but Michael."

George Halas died on October 31, 1983, Halloween, the streets filled with goblins. At the time of his death, the franchise, which he had purchased for $100, was worth millions. It passed to his daughter, who's watched its value grow and grow. Virginia Halas McCaskey's net worth is currently estimated at $1.3 billion. The *Sun-Times* ran the old man's obituary under the sort of banner usually reserved for declara-tions of war. Here's the lead: "George Halas is dead, they say. But he can't be. The Old Man is too tough to die." The funeral was held at St. Ita's on the North Side. There were twelve hundred mourners; storied figures from every era of football filled the pews: Pete Rozelle, Wellington Mara, Art Rooney, George McAfee, Gale Sayers, Tex Schramm, Lamar

Hunt, Gene Upshaw. Sid Luckman was a pallbearer; he rested his hand on the lacquered wood. Halas had many sons, but, after Mugs, Sid was the most beloved, the Brooklyn boy who returned, like a dog with the kill, with title after title in his teeth. "I have vivid memories of the service," Fencik told me. "The whole team went down on the bus. Everybody came from the NFL. The last guy in was Al Davis, the owner of the Raiders. He was in a black leather trench coat. It was very gestapo. He and Halas had fought like mad over the years, yet here he was, paying his respects."

Virginia Halas McCaskey made the announcement eleven days after the funeral: Michael would be the new president of the Bears. Mike McCaskey, who, at thirty-three, was nearly as young as some of his players; Mike McCaskey, a preppy, the product of Notre Dame High School and Yale; Mike McCaskey, once a member of the Harvard faculty and the author of a book on management; Mike McCaskey, a consultant who'd studied the art of corporate warfare; Mike McCaskey, who seemed to have everything but the one thing that mattered: the old zipperoo. He was, in fact, a fascinating, even brilliant man. Once upon a time, he wanted to be a priest. He served in the Peace Corps after college, teaching science and English in Ethiopia. But he was erudite and refined in a way that set him apart in the hypercharged world of the NFL. Despite the team's success in McCaskey's first years at the helm, he would never be truly accepted by the players. In his relationship with his grandfather, McCaskey stands for my generation in our relationship to the tough old America: we inherited a country we did not build.

As Halas sickened, Ditka, along with Jim Finks, Bill Tobin, and Jerry Vainisi, assembled the pieces of what would become the 1985 Bears. It was done via trades and the draft, the players appearing one after another, each taking a turn on the screen, smiling or sneering as a narrator fills in the backstory: this one because he can shoot the whiskers off a mule; that one because he can throw the blade.

Dan Hampton, six five, 264 pounds, a monster who could kill you with a single halfhearted blow, was drafted in 1979: the anchor of the defensive line, the thumping bass that made everything rock. In twelve seasons, he would break every finger and destroy every joint. He had at least a dozen knee operations. I worked out at the same gym and once saw him with his leg on a massage table, stretching. Sweat beaded his hairline, there was agony in his unfocused eyes, but you knew he'd be back out there on Sunday.

Otis Wilson, a linebacker from Brownsville, Brooklyn, was drafted in 1980, as was Matt Suhey, a fullback from Penn State. Suhey's grandfather played for the Canton Bulldogs against Halas in the industrial days of the NFL. Keith Van Horne, a key on the offensive line, was drafted in 1981, as was Singletary. He showed up late to camp his rookie season, part of a negotiating strategy. Singletary was of mixed parentage: African American and part Cherokee Indian. His features have an almost Asian cast. Buddy Ryan was all over him that first summer, running him, breaking him, calling him "the fat Jap." "You're nothing, 50," he'd shout. Singletary was known around the league for his grunts and curses, the intensity of his eyes. (When I asked former Eagles quarterback Ron Jaworski about the '85 Bears, he said, "I still see Singletary's eyes.") Plank gave Singletary his nickname. It happened on the sideline, when Buddy asked the safety why he hadn't run the play he sent in with Singletary. *'Cause I couldn't understand a word he said. That guy sounds like a fuckin' samurai.*

Jim McMahon was Chicago's top selection in 1982. The Bears had not used a first-round pick to take a quarterback since 1951, but Mac was special. Ditka saw in him the leader of the Bears as Terry Bradshaw had been the leader of the Steelers. He was small for a QB, his arm was questionable, and he had a bad eye, but he knew how to win. Ditka was always less interested in where a prospect ranked than in what he had inside. In McMahon's junior year at Brigham Young, he led the Cougars to one of the great comebacks. It was at the Holiday Bowl in 1980. BYU was down 42–25 with four minutes left. Fans were streaming from the gates. McMahon got into a shouting match with his coach, who threw up his hands, turning the game over to the QB, who somehow, just like that, led the team to two quick touchdowns, then, with time running out, beat SMU with one of those high, arching Hail Marys that is everywhere a sign of desperation. It's still known as the Miracle Bowl.

Ditka and Finks supplemented their draft picks with trades and free agent pickups. Gary Fencik was invited to camp after being released by the Dolphins in 1976. Emery Moorehead came over from Denver in 1981. Steve McMichael was signed after the Patriots cut him. "[The general manager in New England] called me into his office and said, 'McMichael, do you know why we're cutting you?'" McMichael remembered. "''Cause we think you're the criminal element in this league.' Thank God an old criminal in Chicago was still alive. When I met Halas, he said, 'We want you to be the person you are.'"

And what sort of person was Steve McMichael?

Big and scary. Fat now but made of iron then, a screw-loose sort of guy you approach with extreme caution. They called him Mongo after the Alex Karras character in *Blazing Saddles*. They also called him Ming the Merciless after a Flash Gordon villain. He was a bruising, durable defensive tackle who often led the rush on the quarterback. He would make over a hundred consecutive starts for the Bears. It usually took two linemen to stop him. He never seemed to be having anything less than a fantastic time. When McMichael first came to the Bears, Hampton picked him up at O'Hare. He had a single piece of luggage, a burnt orange garment bag emblazoned with a University of Texas logo—that's where Mongo grew up, where he played college ball and studied to be a dentist.

The early days in Chicago were a struggle. He made little money. One afternoon, when he was on the practice field, his car was repossessed from the parking lot. He wore his helmet high, his fists were bloody. He did not win all the awards, but the players in the league feared him. Not long ago, McMichael told Chicago interviewer Mark Bazer that he'd been playing a role in those years, a character named Mongo. "I'd go stand at the fifty-yard line and stare at the other team before the game," he explained. "I wouldn't warm up with the guys. I would just stand and stare. Wade Wilson, a quarterback from that time, looked me up at a convention. The first thing he said was, 'Steve, do you remember me?' I said, 'I remember you, quarterback. I'm like a vicious predator on the Serengeti. I remember all the wounded gazelles.'"

Drafting is an art. Those with the genius are able to discern not only who is good but who will be good. It's soothsaying, intuition. An acceptable draft might yield a player or two who stick. A great one might bring in two or three long-term starters. But now and then, a team will hit the daily double. In 1983, the Bears drafted seven starters, including four future All-Pros: Jimbo Covert, a guard from western Pennsylvania; Willie Gault, an Olympic sprinter who became the Bears' deep threat; Mike Richardson, a cornerback from East Los Angeles; Dave Duerson, who played safety; Tom Thayer, an offensive lineman from Joliet. In the eighth round, they took Richard Dent, a skinny defensive end with bad teeth. As part of Dent's contract, the Bears agreed to pay for his orthodontia. He started gaining weight as soon as his teeth were fixed; it had always hurt him to eat. He put on fifty pounds in two months. He's now in the Hall of Fame. Mark Bortz, also taken in the eighth round, started for eleven seasons in Chicago.

When I asked Bill Tobin what explained this success, he said, "Well, we looked for character. Character is huge. It's a saying we had: When in doubt, bet on character. That's why we ended up with the Leslie Fraziers and Jeff Fishers and Ron Riveras and Mike Singletarys. When your best players are also your best people, you got a lot going for you. We had some ornery kids but we didn't have any bums."

"It was like putting together a jigsaw puzzle," Ditka told me. "You've got to get those missing pieces. We needed a quarterback, we drafted McMahon. We needed a left tackle, we got Covert. We needed a speed receiver, we got Gault. We already had Singletary, Otis, Fencik. We got Duerson and Richardson for the secondary. We had Hilgenberg and Van Horne. We got Thayer. We had Suhey and Payton. We didn't have any tight ends, so we brought in Emery Moorehead."

In 1984, the Bears used their first pick on linebacker Wilber Marshall, perhaps the best athlete on the team. In 1985, they took William Perry, a huge, gap-toothed tackle from Clemson. Perry was 220 pounds in seventh grade, 13.5 pounds at birth. "I was big even when I was small," he said. After collapsing during an early practice, Perry was placed in a dehydration tank. "He's just a big overweight kid," Buddy Ryan told the press. "He was a wasted draft choice and a waste of money."

"I thought he was one of the most dominant college players I watched," said Ditka. "He could dunk a basketball. He had a great vertical leap. He had great explosion. He was fast for twenty or thirty yards. He had no endurance to run a mile, but he could do those other things pretty damn well."

Perry was listed at 310 pounds, but when defensive tackle Dan Hampton saw him at camp he laughed and said, "That kid's a biscuit away from 350." This explains Perry's first nickname on the team: Biscuit. His second was also credited to Hampton, who, seeing Perry without a shirt, said "It looks like a mudslide." But the nickname that stuck had been given to him in college by a teammate who, feeling trapped when Perry squeezed into an elevator behind him, said, "My God, he's like a refrigerator."

10

THE FRIDGE

William "Refrigerator" Perry spiking the ball during Super Bowl XX

In 1983, I made out with Christine Conner on the grass be-
hind North School. In the summer of 1978, I canoed the rivers of
Michigan's Upper Peninsula. That August, I walked through Charle-
voix from the hardware store to the lake in bare feet, eating an ice cream
cone. In 1981, I set the high score on Defender at Big Al's in Glencoe. In
1990, I drove all night from New Orleans to a town in South Carolina,
where I ate bacon and eggs and slept on the beach. In 2005, my oldest
son was born. In 1977, my tickets to Bozo's Circus arrived in the mail.
On July 30, 1975, I saw a cool big-kid bike parked in front of my
house. When I asked who owned it, my mom said, "You!" It was
my birthday. In 1983, in Eagle River, Wisconsin, I threw a wild punch
that connected, felling a bully who'd been terrorizing the kids at my
camp. For several weeks, I was regarded as a hero. In 1988, I dated a
girl many of my friends considered out of my league. Each of these is
a wonderful memory, a treasured moment in time. But looking back,
it's clear that none of them stands up to the collection of memories that
accumulated from the fall of 1985 to the winter of 1986, when the
Chicago Bears came into their own.

The team had been getting better every year. They went 8 and 8 in
1983 but finished with five wins in six games. So bad a few seasons
before, they were rising quickly through the ranks. They went 10 and 6
in 1984, winning the division—their best showing since 1963, when
Ditka led them to an NFL Championship. The Bears had died after
Iron Mike left, and with Iron Mike they were being reborn.

The team made the playoffs that year, but no one expected much from them. In the first round, they faced the Redskins, who were favored. The Bears were minus McMahon, who had lacerated his kidney in the fifth week of the season. Without Mac, the offense resorted to its old playbook: Walter right, Walter left, Walter up the middle. He ran for 104 yards. The crucial score came on a trick play that Ditka probably thought up in the shower: quarterback Steve Fuller pitched to Payton, who cavorted down the line, turned, and threw a wobbly pass for a touchdown. Chicago, 23–19.

As the Bears turned their attention to the NFC Championship, everyone in the city seemed to have the same realization: they could actually go to the Super Bowl! At the end of the week, the team went to San Francisco to play Bill Walsh's 49ers, one of the great powers of the era. I watched on the kitchen TV, my hands balled into fists, waiting for the offensive release that never came. I was all knots inside. The defense kept the Bears in it long after the offense quit. Finally, in the third, worn out by all those minutes on the field, each brilliant stop made futile by another offensive failure, the defense broke. That's sports: you have a hero, knowing that, at some point, you'll see that hero fail. I sat by myself, tears streaming down my face as Fencik gave futile chase to a 49ers rusher who burst into the end zone as Candlestick Park exploded with noise. In the fourth quarter, the San Francisco fans seemed to be laughing at the Bears, mocking the team's inability to do anything with the ball.

In the last seconds, Joe Montana handed off to a 264-pound offensive guard named Guy McIntyre, who lined up at fullback. Bill Walsh called it the "Angus formation." To a fan, it might seem like another big man killing the clock. To Ditka it was a coded message sent sideline to sideline—the 49ers coach saying, "I don't even need a real running back to beat you." "I thought it was just Bill Walsh being a jagoff," Hampton said. "But Ditka didn't forget."

For the Bears, the game ended in the best possible way other than victory: in taunts and curses, the sort of trash talk that burns. As Hampton and McMichael headed for the tunnel, the 49ers were shouting, "Next time, bring your offense." The final score was 23–0. "I read the newspapers for a week after they beat us," said McMahon, who stayed in San Francisco after the game. "I wanted to vomit. The whole idea they were putting across was that we didn't belong on the same field with them."

Payton cried in the locker room. Talking in that effeminate voice that broke your heart, he said, in essence, It took me ten years to get here; I'll never get back. "Quit holding your head down," Otis Wilson told him. "Next year, we're not just gonna knock on the door, we're gonna kick the damn door down."

Winter went by. Spring came, then summer. A few days before training camp, Ditka got hold of Rick Telander, a legendary Chicago sportswriter—he is a hero of mine—who lived next to Halas Hall. A workman went up to Telander's roof with a bucket of paint. In huge numerals, he wrote 23–0. Ditka wanted his players to see the score of the San Francisco game every day. The '85 Super Bowl run was driven by the anger and shame of that loss. It was the response. "Next time, bring your offense." The Bears were determined to make the 49ers and everyone else eat those words. It's one reason it's so hard to repeat: If you're out to prove something, what drives you after you've done it?

The season began with a string of wins: the Bears concussed Tampa Bay, crushed New England, roughed up Minnesota, embarrassed Washington. A few games linger, live in the memory, defining contests. The first of these came in week six, when the Bears returned to San Francisco. In Chicago, it was hyped as a shot at revenge. McMahon was back, which would be the difference. That's how it was: the defense dominated, but the team's fortunes depended on the quarterback. When Mac played, the Bears almost always won. Ditka stood before the press that week, giving a typically pugnacious assessment of what had happened, what would happen, who had laughed, who would be laughing and from what side of his face: the other fucking side. *Last time we were the hit-ees; this time we intend to be the hit-ors.*

There's footage of McMahon examining the field a few hours before kickoff, in sweats and tennis shoes, or maybe flip-flops, or maybe his feet were bare, grass between his toes, walking the grounds as the Cheyenne Indian Chief Two Moons walked the riverbank in the sweltering dawn before the arrival of General Custer. (Asked how long it took to defeat the Seventh Cavalry, Two Moons said, "As long as it takes a hungry man to eat his dinner.") The Bears started with the kind of flashy drive they hadn't been able to muster once in the previous encounter, Mac leading his team downfield one wounded duck at a time. Now and then, he would uncork a beauty, a classic old-school spiral. He was like a punk who could sit down and sing like Sinatra.

Payton carried the ball into the end zone. In five minutes, the Bears had scored more points than they had scored in the entire '84 NFC Championship game.

The Bears beat up San Francisco for the rest of that brief, satisfying afternoon. It went by like a dream. By this point, I was watching games—unless I could wangle a ticket—with my father on the twenty-two-inch Zenith in the family room. Sometimes friends came over, but usually it was just me and my old man, my personal Halas: me in full regalia, him in boots, jeans, and the cowboy hat he insisted identified him as a High Plains Drifter. "Billy the Kid, he was from Brooklyn, too." Like Ditka, my father is a man of slogans. If Sweetness executed a particularly miraculous fake, he'd say, "The key to walking on water is knowing where the stones are." If an opposing coach seemed to have no answer to the Bears, he'd say, "Failing to plan is planning to fail." If the camera zoomed on Michael McCaskey in the owner's box, he'd say, "The meek shall inherit the earth, but not its mineral rights."

Despite his instincts, my father had come around to the Bears, slowly at first, then with enthusiasm. By late September, he was committed. When I asked how a person could change his opinion so radically, he reminded me that he wore two watches, one on each wrist, because "a man with one watch believes he knows the time, but a man with two watches can never be sure."

My father loved Ditka, McMahon, the defense—all of it. When Wilson, Marshall, and Dent crowded the line, then, at Singletary's direction, began to swarm, he'd say, "Here they come!" A lot of these games had the feel of a heavyweight fight. When I spoke to Wilson, he compared the '85 Bears to Mike Tyson—the young fighter in plain black shorts, a killer from Brownsville, Brooklyn, waiting, probing, locking in, then ending it with a blow. As a Bears fan, you knew it was only a matter of time: it might come in the first quarter, or it might happen late, but the blow that broke the other team would come. When it did, my father would light his cigar, the flame dancing before his eyes, then, through a cloud of smoke, say, "The Buccaneers are in big trouble," or "The Packers are in big trouble," or "The 49ers are in big trouble."

The Bears were winning 16–10 at the half, but it was never much of a contest. From the first quarter, Chicago had the game in hand. At one point, when Payton executed "the Utah draw," a beautiful shovel pass of a play, the announcer said, "What a contrast in coaching. The rough-and-tumble Mike Ditka, against a *perhaps* more sophisticated Bill Walsh." *Perhaps* was the qualifier that saved the announcer from calling Ditka a savage. The Bears sealed it with a characteristic drive: slow, plodding, clock consuming. If you want to defeat Joe Montana, keep him on the bench. Payton rushed for over a hundred yards, but, late in the game, when Ditka was running out the clock, it was not Sweetness who got the ball. It was William Perry, the massive defensive tackle known as the Fridge. Buddy Ryan hadn't been using him on defense—Buddy called Perry a wasted pick—so Ditka brought him over to the other side. "I've got to break him in somewhere," Ditka said.

It's startling to see such a big man lined up at fullback. He seems miscast, in the wrong costume, on the wrong stage. "Here comes William Perry waddling onto the field and into our huddle," McMahon wrote. "'Gimme da damn ball,' he said, all hyper. Most of our linemen thought it was a joke, until they realized they'd have to block for this 325-pound mountain. They were afraid he would run right up their backs and crush them to death." Perry carried twice, picking up close to zero yards, which was not the point. "They ran a big, fat offensive lineman against us last year," Hampton said. "We thought we'd run a big, fat defensive lineman against them this year."

Those first feeble runs made William Perry a star, first in Chicago, then in the country, then in the world. It's hard to believe it happened. The Fridge T-shirts and the Fridge hats, the Fridge memorabilia, the Fridge commercials, the Fridge dance, and the big-boned cheerleaders who called themselves Fridgettes. For some, mention of the '85 Bears brings just this image to mind: Fridge, ripples of fat, gap-toothed smile, big cheeks, and size-22 cleats, maniacally dancing in the end zone of a poor sacked city. "It was revenge for me," Ditka said. "Yeah, I'll admit it. A little bit. Maybe a lot. Even though my first thought about using Fridge back there was, This big fellow can really block. I'd watch him in sprints in practice, and for the first five yards or so there was all this dirt flying up from under his shoes. Looked like a rototiller. I didn't like it when they used McIntyre in the backfield against us, that's for sure. So here's a response."

The Ditka paradox: having experienced Bill Walsh's use of the Angus formation as an insult, he responded with the Fridge. Even Don Corleone would call that justice. But then, having taken revenge on Walsh, Ditka continued to use the Fridge in the backfield against teams that had done him no wrong. The Packers. The Patriots. He deployed the Fridge as a blocker for Payton, as a fullback, even as a receiver. In doing so, Ditka was taunting other coaches in the exact way he had been taunted. Of course, by that time, the Fridge had become a phenomenon. At the end of games, fans would chant his name until Ditka probably felt he had no choice but to send him in. As any reader of science fiction can tell you, sooner or later the mad doctor loses control of his creation. When challenged by reporters who considered the Fridge a circus act, Ditka said, "Think about it. How could *you* stop a man that size coming directly at you? . . . Call it a sideshow," he added. "I call it beating their ass."

But the big story was the Bears defense, which had emerged as the most devastating force in football. "You describe it—please," Walsh told a reporter. "Use any adjective you want. I'll say it was intense and ferocious. They gave us a good, sound beating."

Amid the postgame mayhem, Ditka went on Chicago TV and told the city that he planned to celebrate on the flight home. He had purchased a case of wine on a trip to Napa Valley. Iron Mike tasting zinfandels and pinot noirs in wine country, swirling and spitting, closing his eyes, searching for that hint of raspberry, is an image worth swirling in your own mind. Ditka had promised to share the wine with his players if they won, but the booze never made it to the main cabin—Ditka sat in first class with McCaskey, while most of the team sat in coach.

How much wine did Ditka drink?

How many bottles are in a case?

"We were at 40,000 feet," Ditka wrote. "I was drinking white wine. If a lot is two bottles, then I had more than a lot."

Back in Chicago, several players noticed their coach's stumbling walk as he made his way to the parking lot. A few offered to drive him home, but Ditka just mumbled—*Angus, Fridge, Fucking Genius*—before roaring off in his car. "He damn near ran over a couple of guys," McMahon wrote. "Ditka was all over the road."

The players Ditka passed coming out of the lot saw him again a few minutes later: handcuffed on the side of the highway, surrounded by cops, party lights flashing. Having seen the coach boast on TV, an industrious patrolman set up just outside the airport. "When we caught up to where he'd been nailed, we saw his car on the side with a police chaser," wrote McMahon. "Nobody pulled over. We just honked our horns and drove on."

"I celebrated too much," Ditka said. "I was arrested and later convicted of drunk driving. It was the most embarrassing thing that could ever happen to me. I was stopped on I-294 shortly after leaving O'Hare. I was driving home. The officer handcuffed me and I didn't think that was necessary."

Copies of the ticket, which Ditka had been required to sign that night, made their way around Chicagoland. Someone showed me one at school. The violation was described, the time of arrest (12:14 a.m.), the name of the arresting officer. There was Ditka's drunken signature, all loops and bravado. Beneath it, in a section set aside for "comments," in letters that actually seemed to slur, he'd written, "Fuck you Jack." Ditka lost his license for six months and was required to take classes. As a fan, you wanted more than a legal resolution; you wanted a moral. What can it tell us? What does it mean? Perhaps it's the other side of all that exuberance, the price paid by the high-intensity boy; perhaps it's the comeuppance of a prideful man, the inevitable result of the fatal flaw that Ditka shared with Odysseus, whom we were studying in English: pride. Perhaps it was the reappearance of the devil that had ridden Iron Mike since his earliest days in the game, the beast that caused him to pop off about Halas. In the end, it seemed like just another part of the drama, another act in the circus: "Call it a sideshow. I call it beating their ass."

In week eleven, the team traveled to Dallas to play the Cowboys. This game was important on two levels. First, there was the hatred every Bears fan had for the Cowboys. We believed it was the culture of the team we hated: the Cowboys cheerleaders with their white go-go boots, their posters, and their appearance on *The Love Boat*; the Cowboys coach, stern and emotionless in his fedora; the holier-than-thou Cowboys' prayer circle; how Dallas had been anointed "America's Team." But it was really their excellence we could not stand, the machinelike perfection that returned them to the playoffs season after season. Then there was Ditka's relationship with Landry. As a coach, Ditka was the child of Landry. He learned from Landry, loved Landry. Ditka was thus returning to the house of his father, not with small talk and pastries but an army of brutes determined to trash the joint, wipe their bloody paws on the drapes. It gave the encounter a Freudian charge, the sting of patricide.

For a Bears fan, a thrashing of the Cowboys could justify an entire season. You can have the playoffs and you can have the Super Bowl and you can have the Fridge and the State Street parade—just leave me that Sunday afternoon in Dallas.

Before the game, Everson Walls, a Cowboys cornerback, shouted at Hampton, "You guys might be 10 and 0, but you haven't played any-one yet."

Describing the game is difficult in the way it's difficult to describe a hurricane: the devastation was everywhere, all at once. The signature play came early—in the first quarter—though "signature" might be too decorous a word to describe what happened. It was more like a knock-out punch, a blow that broke the will of a willful team. It was near the Cowboys' end zone, where much of that game was played. Dallas was like a man with his back to the sea. Nowhere to go, nothing to do but fight and die. Danny White, the Dallas quarterback, took the snap and dropped into his own end zone. Then, before he even had a chance to look downfield and find his receivers, he was surrounded, over-whelmed, on the floor of a collapsing house. McMichael, Singletary, and Fencik flying in from safety. White stumbled and threw, just to get rid of the thing, just to unload the dingus. Hampton reached up one of those meaty hands, blood, tape, and busted fingers, and batted the ball, which wobbled like a struck bird. It was up there for a long time. Richard Dent grabbed it and busted into the end zone. Touchdown. First score of the game, and the first touchdown of Dent's career.

Football is the ultimate team sport. If Hampton does not reach the ball, Dent does not make the play. And it was a career of such plays that put Dent in the Hall of Fame. Dent is there because he was great, but also because he played beside Hampton, who is himself in the Hall of Fame because he played beside Singletary, who is in the Hall of Fame because he played beside McMichael and Wilson and Marshall and Fencik, who will never be properly recognized because there are al-ready too many Bears in the Hall of Fame.

The camera zoomed in on Ditka. It was only later, after the Bears visited England, that he began wearing that Savile Row crap; this was still Ditka as Ditka, an angry man trying to prove himself to all the pop-off artists. He wore the same basic outfit every game: coach pants—possibly rayon, possibly polyester—coach shoes, white like a nurse's sneaker, a blue oxford shirt beneath a Bears sweater-vest. After big plays, Ditka showed minimal emotion. When things went wrong, that's when he exploded. He just nodded and spit when things went right. He probably spit in the dirt after big plays in Aliquippa, too. I know he did the same when he played at Wrigley. Spitting in the dirt after driving in the stake is a bit of code as old as the schoolyard.

From there, every step for Dallas was a step down. You could see the shoulders of their linemen sag, heads low in the huddle. The pupils of Danny White's eyes turned into asterisks. He was looking everywhere, focusing on nothing. He was sacked as soon as Dallas got the ball back. Otis Wilson coming from the blind side. White lay there for a long time, like a raised seal on the Texas turf. The Bears were relentless, blitzing again and again. In the course of the afternoon, the 46 defense revealed itself as something terrifying and new. "The images were shocking," Ron Jaworski wrote. "My study of the game feels more like an autopsy than a film breakdown: that's how violent Chicago's performance was. Seen 25 years later, it's still frightening."

"By the middle of the first quarter, my only thought was—it's the only time I ever thought like this—get the ball out of my hands as fast as I can," White told me. "Whether I threw it away or handed it off, I just wanted to get rid of it."

White was knocked out in the second quarter. Otis again—it was probably the best game of his career. He caught White in the act of throwing. When the camera moved close, you could see that White's eyes were closed, his face as relaxed as that of a sleeping child. As Buddy Ryan liked to say, "It's time to open a new can of quarterback."

Gary Hogeboom, a twenty-seven-year-old QB from central Michigan, came in for Dallas, but it didn't get any better. The Cowboys' offensive line had broken. The Bears came like water through a sieve. "Those poor Dallas quarterbacks didn't know whether to shit or go blind," Ditka said. "I can still see their backup Gary Hogeboom, when he was already on his way to the turf, and Singletary hit him so hard before he could reach the ground that I thought Mike had killed him."

Danny White came back for the second half. When I asked why he did this, he laughed and said, "Good question. I guess my ego got the best of me, pride or something. I wasn't going to let them knock me out and just sit over there watching this massacre. It was like watching your kids getting beaten up by somebody and just sitting there. These were my teammates and I was the guy they were counting on."

The second knockout came in the third quarter. Otis again, number 55, driving his helmet into White's spine. He went down in sections, folding like a card table. "He pinned my head into my chest," White said. "I thought I broke my neck. I remember the relief when I moved my head and realized it was still attached."

"For years, people in Texas would say Danny White is a terrible driver," Wilson told me, "'cause he flinches every time he sees the number 55."

"The Bears beat people up," said Jim Brown. "Most defenses in the NFL have maybe five hitters . . . The '85 Bears had eleven hitters on defense. The pressure they exerted was severe. Forget about the quarterbacks having time to pass—the runners couldn't even get started."

Coaches had begun to accuse the Bears of putting bounties on quarterbacks: take out Danny White, get ten thousand; take out Joe Montana, get thirty. Buddy Ryan just seemed too certain when he said, "We're gonna get to know their second-string quarterback." When I asked Bears linebacker Jim Morrissey, he said, "Nah, we did it for free. Who doesn't want to go after the quarterback? It's why we loved interceptions. It's the one time you can take a free, legitimate, big-time shot at the quarterback. Buddy talked about it religiously. When we intercept, the first thing you do is go find that quarterback." By the fourth, the game had become an embarrassment. Ditka took out his starters. He didn't want to run up the score on Landry. But Buddy kept his in— what's more, he was still blitzing, going for the kill. Ditka asked Buddy to "call off the dogs."

"Fuck off," Buddy told him. "It's my defense, Ditka."

"Dad never could stand Dallas," Buddy's son Rex said recently. (Rex Ryan is the head coach of the Jets.) "He wanted a beat-down. He wanted to kick their ass."

Ditka: "What was it, 44–0 or something? And we're still blitzing at the end of the game? That makes a lot of sense. I had to tell [Buddy], 'Quit blitzing, what the hell you gonna accomplish? You knocked out two quarterbacks.' I mean, it's crazy. And that game was embarrassing to me because there's no man in football I had more respect for than

Coach Landry. It was just our time. We were a better team than them, period. Let it go at that."

As Dallas fans streamed out of Texas Stadium, Wilson and Marshall started barking on the sidelines. John Madden, calling the game for CBS, said, "My God, they're barking like dogs down there."

The final score was, in fact, 44–0. It was the first time the Cowboys had been shut out in fifteen years. On the way off the field, Ditka shook Landry's hand and said he was sorry. "Don't be," Landry told him. "You have a heck of a football team."

"I felt good, but I also felt bad," said Ditka. "Here we were, doing what we could only dream of doing. And yet it was the worst thing. We had our picture taken before the game, Coach Landry and me, with our arms around each other. This was the guy I'd learned everything from."

Hampton found Everson Walls after the game, the cornerback who'd said, "You guys haven't played anyone yet." "And you know what," said Hampton, "we still haven't."

On CBS, as the camera sweeps the stands in a final goodbye, a fan holds a sign that says CHICAGO BEARS: YOU LOOK MAHVELOUS!

11

A RACE TO THE QUARTERBACK

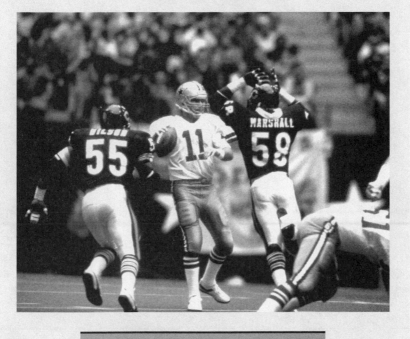

Linebackers Otis Wilson (55) and Wilber Marshall (58) closing in on
Dallas quarterback Danny White. November 11, 1985

Of all the '85 Bears, I was probably most excited to interview
Gary Fencik. If anyone could explain the team, I figured it would be
him. Here was a man of two worlds: the world of the suburbs, a public
school world of penny loafers and paisley, and the hyperviolent world
of the NFL. Fencik seemed like a kind of undercover agent, a medium-
size man in a big man's game. He attended Barrington High School;
his father was an assistant principal. He graduated from Yale and got
an MBA at Northwestern. He's spent his post-football life in private
equity, in the exact kind of job occupied by every kid I knew growing
up. He lives in Lincoln Park, in the exact kind of apartment where
I might live if I lived in Chicago. He looks like the guys I grew up with,
too. Ditka is a bear with ruined hips. Otis is a killer in a tracksuit.
Plank has titanium shoulders. Dent is broken-down and walks like
John Wayne in *The Searchers*. But Fencik is a regular guy, handsome,
with dark hair and a bent nose. He's you raised to the highest power, a
kid who wished the same wish, only his came true.

Size has a lot to do with it. The dimensions of professional football
players set them apart, mark them as a distinct species. Hampton was six
five, 264 pounds when he played. McMichael was six two, 270. Dent was
six five, 265. Today's players are still bigger. In some cases, much bigger.
You cannot imagine yourself playing in their game. You'd have to be
nuts. But when I met Fencik for brunch, I was gratified to see that, de-
pending on my shoes, he and I were roughly the same class. The Bears
listed him at six feet, 194 pounds, but I'd put him closer to five eleven.

Nor was he terribly fast when he played. Fencik was, in fact, an average-size American who had a talent for making big hits—he sped up when a normal person would slow down. "Deluding yourself, that's the trick," he told me. "You have to work yourself up into such a state that you forget just how much bigger than you some of these guys are."

"And that worked?" I asked.

"Well, yeah, but not all the time," he said, laughing.

He thought for a moment, remembering. "One night, after a game, I met up with Dan [Hampton] and Steve [McMichael]," he said. "They were hours ahead in terms of relaxing. After I had a couple beers trying to catch up, maybe a couple too many, I told Dan, 'I bet, if I were as big as you, I could whip your ass.' It made him crazy. He picked me up like a two-by-four and lifted me over his head and started shouting, 'But you're not as big as me! You're not, you're not!' He threw me down onto the floor. It really hurt. Then McMichael picked me up and cradled me and said, 'Hey, Hamp, be careful, you're going to hurt the little fella.' That's when you realize, these guys—well, they're great, but they're also very strong. I had some big friends."

Fencik was the hiker who had fallen in among grizzlies, the fan who'd gone through the looking glass but would always remain a fan. He rooted for the Bears as a boy, reading up on Butkus and Sayers, filled with Super Bowl dreams. He was a good player in high school, "not great," he said, "but I got better at every level. We had a good junior team at Barrington. The quarterback went to Arizona State, the wide receiver ended up at Minnesota. I got recruited simply because I was in film with those guys—it's the only reason college coaches happened to see me."

Fencik visited Yale in the spring of 1972. The white stone, the ivy—he fell hard. "There was just something about Yale that went beyond football," he told me. "I wandered around and looked at everything and thought, Oh boy, I really want this experience!" He played both ways freshman year, a receiver on offense, a safety on defense. Junior year, Coach Carm Cozza limited him to offense. "I had the longest reception in Yale history," he told me. "We ran a halfback option against Princeton from the one and I went ninety-nine yards for a touchdown." He was drafted by Miami in the tenth round in 1976, "the only team that had gone back and seen film of me playing defense. They said, 'Look, you have no chance of playing receiver in the NFL, but you could possibly make it as a defensive back.'"

In those days, a draftee would sign that first contract as soon as it arrived in the mail and not think about it again until a year or so later, when he realized he'd been screwed. But Fencik happened to be taking a class taught by Howard Cosell. I mention this partly to give a sense of the distance between Fencik's college experience and that of, say, Payton, who attended Jackson State. "It was a seminar with twelve students," Fencik said. "Every week Howard would come in with someone from sports. We had Pete Rozelle address us. We had Bob Wood, the president of CBS. We had Bob Woolf, who's considered one of the first great sports agents. He represented Larry Bird. On draft day, Howard invited me to New York. The Giants had just signed Larry Csonka and I remember walking in Manhattan with Cosell, Csonka, and Csonka's agent. I had dinner with Howard and his wife, then Howard had a car take me back to New Haven. When I got the Dolphins contract, I asked Howard what to do. He said, 'I'll have Bob Woolf take a look.' Bob made a few fixes, gave it back, and said, 'Now it's fair.'

"I was excited to be going to the Dolphins," Fencik continued. "They were just a few years off their undefeated season. Bob Griese was the quarterback, Mercury Morris was the halfback. They had the great 'No-Name Defense.' I worked like a dog in training camp. I ruptured my lung the first month—broke a rib, which popped the thing. They didn't tell me about that rib in Miami. I only found out when I was with the Bears. I got hurt during a drill and went to the locker room for X-rays. The doctor asks, 'When did you break your rib?' I go, 'Never.' He said, 'Yeah, you busted a rib in the last couple of months.'"

Miami cut Fencik in the last weeks of preseason. You think the final roster has been chosen, that last bullet dodged, then get a tap on the shoulder: *Coach Shula wants to see you, and bring your playbook.* (In football, the playbook is like the briefcase with the nuclear codes; it must never fall into the wrong hands.) Miami had traded for a veteran safety, making Fencik redundant. Shula later described the release as among the worst decisions of his career.

Jerry Vainisi contacted Fencik and asked if he wanted to come by Halas Hall and try out. The Bears were always looking for hometown prospects, players fans could identify with. "I was on my way to become a baby banker in the Citibank management training program in New York when they called," Fencik said. "I was going home to see my parents anyway, so I figured, what the hell, and went for a one-day tryout.

The next thing I know, I'm sitting with Jim Finks and he's welcoming me to the team. My God, after all those afternoons in Wrigley Field, I was a Bear! When Finks flipped through my Miami contract, which the Bears had to honor, he was perplexed. He said, 'No rookie gets all [these guarantees]. Who the hell did this for you?'"

Fencik appeared in thirteen games his first year, mostly on special teams. By his second, he was a starter. He played safety beside Plank, who trained the Yalie in the school of big hits. They came to seem a perfect pairing, a duo in the way of Captain & Tennille. (Plank told me that fans still call him "Gary Plank.") Fencik stood up receivers, Plank finished them off. Late hits, low hits, high hits: they were dirty and mean, carrying on a Bear tradition of operating on the legal line. They were known as the Hit Men. Plank was knocked out of the NFL in 1982. Fencik continued alone. Well, not alone—Plank's spot was taken first by Todd Bell, then by Dave Duerson, but it always seemed like Fencik was alone without Plank. When Fencik, appearing in "The Super Bowl Shuffle," called himself "the Hit Man," it made me sad. Hearing it, you could not help but think of the other hit man who got injured a few seasons too soon.

Fencik played twelve years in Chicago, beginning in the dark days when the team was an embarrassment. Thus, he was in the perfect position to understand how the team became what it became, how, on defense, it went from mediocrity to maybe the best ever. When I asked about this—"I mean, how the hell did it happen?"—Fencik smiled. "Well, now you're talking about the 46," he said, "and if you want to understand the 46, you've got to start with Buddy Ryan. Remember, I'm the guy that wrote the letter that saved Buddy's job. I'd always remind him about that."

Buddy Ryan grew up outside Frederick, Oklahoma, on a farm in desiccated country ringed by low hills. The family lived in a four-room house without plumbing. He was up each morning before first light, dragging himself to the barn to milk the cows—an antiquated, old-time American childhood. Scarcity was his god, as having nothing makes a boy tough. Years later, at training camp, he'd stand in the bathroom and watch the prospects shave. He looked for those who shut the faucet between swipes of the blade. The kids who let the

To defensive coordinator Buddy Ryan, you were either an adjective or a number. Here he is with number 55, Otis Wilson, celebrating a victory over the Giants in the second round of the 1986 playoffs.

water run were fancy boys and could not be trusted; those who conserved grew up with well water, far from town, and were the sort who would play in pain. The rougher the childhood, the more promising the recruit.

Buddy played high school football, a tough number who punched above his weight. At sixteen, he joined the National Guard. He needed the money—$40 a month. "Then the sumbitches went and mobilized us," he told *Sports Illustrated*. This was during the Korean War, when the fighting was hot. He arrived in the vicinity of the 38th Parallel in 1951. At night, he walked the perimeter of camp, a pistol on his hip, his mind filled with formations. Everything about the army, from the barracks to the men marching in rank, reminded him of the game. He was promoted to master sergeant, where he learned to haze the privates, shout in their faces, break 'em down and build 'em up—it was the way of the army, and, long ago, before the sports agent and the union, it was the way of the NFL.

Buddy led a platoon in Korea, saw action, then went home. The G.I. Bill put him through Oklahoma A&M, where he played guard on the football team. A big mouth, he loved nothing more than giving the boys a hard education, turning them from a rabble into a unit. Less than a year after graduation, he was hired to coach a high school football team in Granville, Texas. For Buddy, it never much mattered if he was leading seventeen-year-olds or pros—coaching was the thing, building the unit, taking the hill. Ed McCaskey might ask God to convert the Communists, but Buddy was going to force conversion at the point of a gun, a free runner, a blitz. Everywhere he went, his defenses hurt people, and his teams won games. By 1960, he was climbing the ranks, eventually becoming the defensive coordinator at the University of Buffalo. According to the former Cleveland Browns coach Sam Rutigliano, "Even then, Buddy Ryan was the kind of guy who'd pull the trigger before the target was up."

In 1968, Buddy was hired as defensive line coach of the New York Jets. He'd stay with the team for several years, but the epiphany came in his second season, as the Jets were preparing for Super Bowl III. Buddy spent the week in meeting rooms, listening as the game plan was laid out by head coach Weeb Ewbank. In describing his strategy, Ewbank kept stressing the same point: We've got to protect our quarterback Joe Namath. He's the key. We lose him, it's over. "If we gotta block eight, we block eight, but Namath doesn't get hit." After about the ninth repetition of this speech, a synapse fired somewhere in Buddy's brain. *The quarterback!* If Weeb will give up so much to protect this one player, he must be the key. If he protects with five guys, I'll rush six. If he protects with six, I'll rush seven. No matter what, I must kill the quarterback! "This clearly made an impression on Buddy," Jaworski wrote. "He figured that if Weeb thought it was so important to keep Namath from getting hit, then, as a defensive coach, Buddy needed to come up with whatever he could to hit the quarterbacks of other teams."

The story of Buddy Ryan is the story of this one big idea; the rest is commentary, the steady unfolding of packages, formations, and schemes as the coach fiddled until he found the best way to concuss the quarterback.

In 1974, he took a job with the Vikings, where he helped build the defensive unit that came to be known as the Purple People Eaters. In 1976, he was hired as the defensive coordinator of the Bears. Buddy was forty-five, a barrel-chested, theory-stuffed genius. He wore wire-frame glasses and was constantly sticking his finger in the faces of his players, yelling, smirking, or brushing the sandy hair from his fierce eyes. It was in Chicago that he finally got a chance to flesh out his ideas, mold his troops, run the show.

In many ways, Buddy never stopped being a master sergeant, a hard-ass of the break-'em-down-and-build-'em-up variety. He knew all the tricks of the cult leader, how to sweeten the hours of pain with a scrap of praise, a hand on the neck, a tap on the helmet at the end of practice. In Chicago, he put himself at the center of worship. He was charismatic, intense. You'd follow him to the edge of your strength and sanity because you wanted to be acknowledged. It did not matter where you were drafted or how much you got paid: Buddy made you earn your spot. Everyone started at the bottom, where you were mocked and humiliated, name-called and worked over, until he could see you had broken and were ready to submit. Then he remade you into a killer, a kamikaze who would fly into the aircraft carrier. "Buddy operated by numbers," Plank told me. "There were no names. You were either an adjective, and not a very complimentary one, or you were the number on your jersey. I was 46. Being a number was an honor. It meant you weren't an adjective. Here comes this master sergeant from the Korean War and he started to develop and encourage pride in being part of a special unit, a defensive squad."

"Buddy had a grading system when we watched film," the linebacker Jeff Fisher, currently the head coach of the St. Louis Rams, told the writer Steve Delsohn. "He either said nothing about you, which meant you did your job. Or he said you were horse shit, a dumbass, or an asshole. If you were horse shit, you missed a tackle. If you were a dumbass, you made a mental error and let up a big play. If you were an asshole, you were probably going to be on the streets pretty soon."

Singletary: "The NFL didn't have limitations as to what a coach could do back then, so Buddy would break a man down of everything he had, then allow him to build himself back up. There is something psychologically brainwashing about this process."

Singletary added a kicker that tells you he was among the brainwashed: "Underneath it all, you knew that Buddy loved you."

"He would beat you down, beat you down, beat you down, then build you back the way he wanted," Jim Morrissey told me. "I'd have done anything for Buddy Ryan."

Asked when the defense coalesced, every Bear identified the same moment. "It was in '78, Buddy's first or second year with the team," Plank said. "We hadn't played well the day before. In fact, the defense had been pushed around. Buddy came in smoking a pipe, looking serene. We went into the defensive meeting room. Now, there's a line used in the military: they don't care how much you know, until they know how much you care. Buddy was breaking down the game. Then he stopped and looked at us and said, 'You know what? I'm just disappointed. I thought we were better than that. I thought we would give more effort.' He said, 'If there's one thing that I have a hard time with as a coach, it's turning on a film and seeing players playing below their ability.' And as he was talking, a tear rolled down his face. I'm getting emotional just remembering it. We became a family at that moment. After that, whatever he asked us to do, no question, we'd do it."

In his first years in Chicago, Buddy was coaching mostly mediocre players. On many afternoons, the Bears were outclassed. It was a moment of asymmetrical despair that led to the 46. Playing on Monday Night Football in 1981, Detroit defeated the Bears 48–17. It was a time for radical solutions. To compete, he had to improvise. "He was experimenting with defenses," Plank told me. "He was going wild, looking for some way to generate a pass rush. You'd go into a meeting and see a bunch of crazy formations on the board. He'd go through each and say, 'Okay, here's what we're going to try.' And someone would say, 'What do you call it?' Buddy didn't use X's and O's. When he put things on the board, it was numbers. He named formations after the number in the center of the formation. So one morning we go in and sure enough there's a new defense with my number in the middle: the 46."

"Ryan . . . moved balls-out safety Doug Plank to middle linebacker," Tim Layden writes in *Blood, Sweat, and Chalk*. "He called it the 46 because that was Plank's jersey number, and it would challenge evolving NFL offenses like no defense had before."

In the standard defensive alignment, called the 4–3, the center was not covered. This usually allowed him to double-team a rusher. But Buddy moved a linebacker to the line of scrimmage, then shifted Plank into the gap left by the repurposed man. This meant none of Buddy's rushers could be double-teamed. On a blitz, another linebacker or safety would creep up to the line and hide behind a big defensive end. As a result, there were more rushers than blockers, which is why, in 1985, it often looked as if the Bears had too many players on the field. Buddy called the hidden blitzers "free runners." "Confuse the offense until they have no idea where you're coming from—that's what creates a free runner," Plank told me. "A free runner is an unblocked defensive player, and he gets to the quarterback so much faster. He doesn't have to shed a blocker and he's running full speed. When a free runner hits the quarterback, the quarterback flies through the air."

Here's Ron Jaworski's jargon-filled description of the 46 defense: "Buddy moved Plank from his safety position into the box, as if he were a linebacker. The other two safeties, Fencik and Fisher, were also sent in at key moments to apply additional pressure. Something was different about the Bears down lineman. The weak side defensive end lined up outside the offensive tackle in a wider pass position, while the other defensive end and defensive tackles set up directly over the guards and the center. This became known as a 'reduced front' and it forced the interior offensive linemen into awkward and difficult one-on-one matchups. It became the defining feature of the 46."

Here's how the same defense was experienced by a fan: in fulfilling an age-old playground fantasy, Buddy had decided, fuck it, and seemingly sent all his guys after the quarterback with a simple mission: *Nail him.*

There was an inherent weakness in Buddy's system. Or as the competing coaches put it, "The 46 is unsound." In overloading the line, the Bears sacrificed coverage elsewhere. Look at film from 1984 or 1985, you see receivers wide open downfield. Buddy's gamble was that the quarterbacks would be first too hurried, then too terrified, and finally too beat up to find the open men. As with Danny White, they would have just one thought on their mind: get rid of the ball. "The 46 became a fucking nightmare to coach against," Bruce Coslet, a defensive coordinator for the Cincinnati Bengals in the 1980s told Tim Layden. "It was something nobody had seen and nobody knew how to prepare for it. Buddy changed football with that defense."

"Scary"—that's how Jaworski described it. "Abnormal. Different. It was blitzing. It was chaos. It was impossible to prepare for. Just impossible."

The 46 was the logic behind the modern T-formation come full circle: Halas had raised the quarterback to such a place of preeminence,

The 46 defense: The quarterback-rattling alignment as drawn for me by Doug Plank, who explained the mechanics in an accompanying note: "This was the original alignment for the 46," wrote Plank. "The entire defensive line was shifted down with a defensive tackle playing over the center. The 2 linebackers aligned over the tight end. One of these linebackers always rushed the qb. My position was later replaced by Singletary, and Duerson replaced [Jeff] Fisher. Jeff and I could drop back and play deep 1/2 on some coverages. Jeff and I blitzed, covered outside receivers, and had run support duties. Every assignment was based on what the offense did. If they stayed to block, we would have coverage duties. If the running back ran routes, we would blitz."

turned him into such a finely calibrated piece of offensive machinery, that he became almost too valuable for the team's own good. Rather than cover everyone, Buddy would short-circuit the offense by taking out the QB. As the boxers used to say: Kill the brain and the body will follow.

"Football is chess," said Plank. "You can capture all my pawns, but if I tip over that king, I win."

Plank told me the defense was called the 46 merely because it happened to be his number on the board that morning, but it was more than that. The fact is, Doug Plank, the twelfth-rounder out of Ohio State, the kid recruited by Woody Hayes merely to stick it to Joe Paterno, was Buddy's ideal player: the vicious, all-out, big-time hitter who made the wheels go round. If you wanted to play on the 46—at first, the formation was not used every down—you had to play with the intensity of Plank. "Buddy loved the way he did his business," Steve McMichael wrote. "That's why it was called the 46 defense. It was built around a safety like Doug making plays."

Over time, the 46 became something more than a mere alignment of players. It was an attitude, a way of competing. "Attack, attack, attack—that was the mentality," Plank told me. "You weren't going to be a friendly dog eating puppy chow. All of a sudden, you were going to be a hungry man looking for meat. Buddy used that defense to change the mind-set of that whole defensive team. He would ridicule and embarrass you until you played the way he wanted you to play. He turned us into an elite group, like the Green Berets. I'm not going to tell you how guys politicked for certain positions on the 46. Because certain positions were given the opportunity to hit the quarterback. And the recognition that you would get from that was like winning the presidential election. If you're in a room and you have a group of grown men screaming and clapping and patting you on the back, talking about something you did on Sunday, well, who doesn't want that?"

The 46 made its debut six days after that terrible loss to Detroit. Ryan felt a special urgency: the Bears were facing the best offense in the NFL. I recommend this game, played Sunday, October 25, 1981, for study by future generations. Here you had the soaring pass-drunk offense that Don Coryell devised for the San Diego Chargers, with quarterback Dan Fouts sending a magnificent array of receivers downfield, meeting the 46 in its first sketchy incarnation. Elegant precision faces the howling mob, eleven brutes with maces and helmets, barbarians wandering in the black forest of Soldier Field. It's the dialectic of history: when a system becomes arrogant, a competing system will arise to defeat it. "As organized and experienced as that group of players were from the Chargers, they'd seen nothing like it," Plank said. "Mad dogs. Wild men. Coming from every side. A jailbreak. By the end, Dan Fouts did not know where to look: Should he try to find the open man downfield, or should he simply brace for impact?"

"It's hard to overstate how much confusion this caused offensive lines of that era," wrote Jaworski. "They didn't know who they were supposed to block, because none of the defenders was where he was supposed to be."

It was this confusion, planted in the mind of the quarterback, that made the 46 hum. It was not merely pressure that devastated the offense; it was the perception of pressure. ("The anticipation of what might be coming was just as important as what actually did," explained Plank.) Even on plays in which the linebackers dropped back, the quarterback, sensing the rush that was not there, hurried himself into mistakes. In this way, the 46 got in the head of the quarterback. In this way, the 46 made even the best QB defeat himself by turning his own anxiety into a weapon.

The Bears beat the Chargers 20–17 in overtime. For Fouts, it was among the worst games in a Hall of Fame career. He completed thirteen of forty-three passes and was intercepted twice. A casual fan might believe he'd just seen an upset, a fluke, but it was actually the start of a new era. "We were going wild in the locker room," Plank said. "We were screaming and shouting and all thinking the same thing: My God, this can work."

Every week, there was a new feature or trick as players learned the intricacies of the 46: how to cheat, where to fake, when to go full tilt at the quarterback. At first used in spot situations, it became the Bears' standard defense. It peaked in 1984 and 1985. By then, thanks to draft picks and acquisitions, the Bears had great players.

It took a particular sort of athlete to excel in the 46. According to Jaworski, the scheme required defensive ends who could beat offensive guards one-on-one; linebackers who, if needed, could cover downfield; and a middle linebacker smart enough to direct the troops, a defensive version of Sid Luckman, "another goddamn coach on the field." You had to be versatile enough to swap positions in the middle of a play. By 1984, this meant McMichael and Hampton on the line; Dent, who, for about five seasons, was unstoppable; Wilson, who could cover downfield; and Singletary, who was one of the few men other than Plank with the smarts and intensity to command the 46. "Who are you going to double-team?" McMahon asked me. "You got Dent outside of McMichael, you got Hamp. On the other side—who was that other tackle?—Hartenstein? He could hit. You cover every lineman, Buddy just puts the linebackers up on the line of scrimmage. Now you've got to pick your poison. Who are you going to let run free? Somebody's going to come free and the rest are one-on-one. If the ball ain't gone fast, the quarterback's gonna get nailed. It was a combination of the system and the players. We had some of the best guys that ever played."

In 1985, the Bears deployed the final pieces: Wilber Marshall, a rookie linebacker who was ideally suited for the 46, and Dave Duerson, a third-year safety who played beside Fencik. (The safety is the deep man, the last line of defense.) Space in the lineup had been made by Al Harris and Todd Bell, staples of the '84 team who held out in 1985. They probably figured the Bears would suffer and Michael McCaskey would buckle. *Wait till Duerson gets burned on a few long plays.* But the new starters proved perfect replacements, and the Bears just kept winning. Marshall was actually an upgrade at linebacker, but Buddy never accepted Dave Duerson. No matter how well he played, Buddy would tell him that he'd be on the bench the moment Todd Bell returned. "Buddy just absolutely hated my guts," Duerson said. "I called my dad when I first got drafted and I told him, 'Dad, I didn't graduate college to go through this.' My dad believes every male child should do two years in the armed services . . . So he says to me, 'Well, it sounds to me like you're in the army.'"

Bell and Harris are a footnote to the Super Bowl—an asterisk, a cautionary tale. As they waited for McCaskey to meet their demands, their team went on a historic run. There was a party, everyone did something, even the offensive linemen got famous, but these sorry bastards missed it. When they returned in 1986, they carried the stink of tragedy. You could not look at Al Harris without thinking, Oh, the poor schmuck. Harris, who began his career with an afro and mutton-chops in 1979, ended it with a shaved head in Philadelphia in 1990. Todd Bell, who, once upon a time, seemed certain to enter the Bears pantheon, ended his career on a Monday in Philadelphia in a game against Chicago, in which, as McCaskey and Ditka looked on, he busted his leg and was carried away in agony. He drifted after that, eventually returning to the Ohio town where he had made them ooh and ahh a million Friday nights before.

Here's the mismatch that will always exist when a player sits to negotiate with an owner: the teams have the money and the stadiums and the television deals, while the players have only their talent and their youth, which, like everything that matters, is vanishing. If, in the modern NFL, the players make millions—in 2013, the Bears' average salary was just over $2 million—it's only because the owners are making billions.

Todd Bell died on March 16, 2006. He had a heart attack while driving through Reynoldsburg, Ohio. He was forty-seven. "Todd never let 1985 go," Al Harris said. "He felt betrayed. I had that feeling, too, but after a while, that's life."

The Bell and Harris situation had an adverse boomerang effect on the Bears and its president, Mike McCaskey, who, though he was treated as a hero by other owners for having stood up to the players and won anyway, seemed to learn the wrong lesson. "The precedent McCaskey established can mean only trouble," McMahon wrote in 1986. "If he believes the Bears—or any other team, for that matter—can afford to let good players not play, for the sake of 'fiscal responsibility,' then that creates problems."

By 1985, Mike Singletary and the other defensive leaders had mastered one of Buddy Ryan's greatest innovations. He had called it "Automatic Front Coverage," which Plank shortened to AFC. Buddy drew up a handful of formations—AFCs—each tailored to a particular offensive alignment. As middle linebacker, it was often Singletary's job to read the offense, identify the play, then, by shouting a code, shift his men to counter. Quarterbacks had been reading defenses for years, changing plays on the fly to create mismatches. Now the defense was reading the offense as it was itself being read. "This meant the Bears could, before the snap, change the angles from which their rushers came and flip what kind of coverage their defensive backs and linebackers were employing," wrote Jaworski. "This was virtually unheard of back in the eighties."

One afternoon, in New England, the Patriots quarterback got to the line, looked at the Bears defense, and changed his play. Then, as soon as the receivers and ends had shifted, Singletary, shouting like a samurai, told the defense what play the offense was going to run and moved his teammates again. The QB, seeing this new alignment, called another audible, which Singletary read and countered. The QB stood horrified, staring into the wild eyes of Singletary, who shouted, "Well, are you gonna change your play or not?" It had a huge psychological impact. It was like the moment in the sci-fi movie when the captain realizes the alien is not merely looking at him, but that he's actually being scanned. *My God, it knows what I'm thinking!*

"Every time the offense moved, we moved," Plank said. "It freaked the offenses out because if they started a motion from one side of the field to the other, we could go through three different coverages matching them."

"You could sense the fear," defensive tackle Tyrone Keys told me. "Especially when the quarterback shifted and Singletary shifted us right into the strip to where they were going. And you could hear them talking, saying, 'They know the play, they know the play!' Singletary was key—he was a coach on the field, and so was Fencik. Did you know that he went to Yale?"

When I wanted to know what it was like to play against the 46, I would just call a great player of that era and ask, "What's the best defense you ever faced?"

Cris Collinsworth, receiver, Cincinnati Bengals: "The 46 in Chicago. Physically they were unbelievable. They could put up points on defense, they could embarrass you. I still think Wilber Marshall belongs in the Hall of Fame."

Joe Theismann, quarterback, Washington Redskins: "My God, the 46. Inside you had Refrigerator Perry, outside you had Dent and Mc-Michael. What gets lost is that those front seven guys were really quick—they could beat anybody one-on-one. Singletary in the middle, Otis on the outside, Wilber on the other side. They beat the tar out of us. That defense was really an offensive unit. Their job was not just to tackle or create interceptions but to force fumbles, make plays, and put points on the board."

"People were afraid because a lot of guys got knocked out," Tyrone Keys told me. "I saw Singletary knock out Sammy Winder. Sammy was sound asleep. Like a baby. I saw Joe Ferguson sleeping like a log right in the middle of a football field. I saw Archie Manning after his career ended, and he said the reason he quit football was because of what the Bears did to him in '84. He got sacked eleven times, and if he got sacked eleven times, imagine how many times he got hit! We were vicious, man. Every play was just a race to the quarterback."

There were great defenses before 1985 and there have been others since, but none matched the '85 Bears. In the course of sixteen games, they gave up 198 points, fewer than 13 a game. In the playoffs, they outscored opponents 45 to nothing. There were games in which the other team barely breached Bears territory. "You can come up with comparative stats," wrote Singletary, "but the best way to tell is to take out the film of any team you want to compare us with: the Steel Curtain, the Purple People Eaters, the 2000 Ravens. Watch them. They're tremendous. Now put the '85 Bears film on and don't say a word. Our film will talk to you. What will it say? You'll know when you see it, because the film does not lie."

Ditka once knocked Buddy Ryan, saying, "On offense, you have to be smart. On defense, you just have to be brutal." It was a put-down, and it wasn't true. In Chicago, the innovations, the big strategic thinking, all came on the brutal side of the ball. The '85 Bears were thrilling on offense but they're remembered because of their defense. Nowadays, good defensive coaches say things like, "Bend but don't break." In 1985, in Chicago, this would have been identified as loser talk. When the 46 played, scoring was secondary—the main task was to break the enemy's will. If you do that, the rest will take care of itself.

12

SHANE COMES TO THE METRODOME

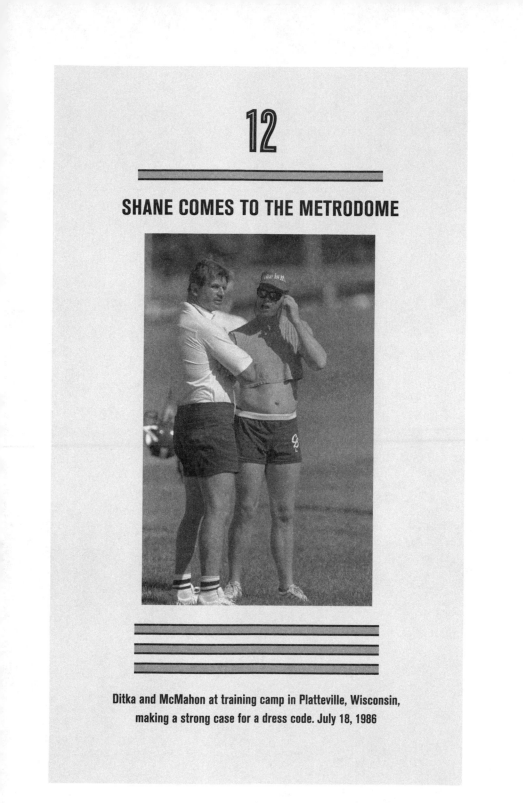

Ditka and McMahon at training camp in Platteville, Wisconsin,
making a strong case for a dress code. July 18, 1986

Every fan has a favorite game. Mine was played on Septem- ber 19, 1985, in the third week of the season, the Bears versus the Vikings in the Metrodome, which Mike Ditka, to the annoyance of Minnesotans, referred to as the Roller Dome. The Bears had defeated New England without incident the week before, but Mac had ended up in Lake Forest Hospital, where he spent two days in traction. Fans serious enough to read injury reports would have assumed number 9 wrenched himself while executing like a daredevil. No one played like Jim McMahon. Most quarterbacks avoid contact; McMahon actually sought it out. He loved hitting and getting hit. Ditka described him as a quarterback who thinks he's a linebacker. At the end of scoring plays, he'd racc downfield, twenty or thirty yards, in search of a lineman to head-butt. A football kiss. "No question that he shortened his career because of the way he played," Ditka said. "He ran, dove, hung on to the ball too long . . . He had no regard for his body. But I couldn't change him. It would have ruined him."

Only later did we learn the truth: McMahon had hurt his back not in the game but while sleeping on a water bed. Years ago, when I went to a neurologist complaining of numb fingers—I thought I had a brain tumor—he told me that I was suffering from a condition known as park bench palsy, a name derived from hobos who passed out on benches with one arm hooked over the top. It's also called honeymoon palsy, as it's common among new husbands, who, not wanting to be rude, let their brides sleep all night on their outstretched arms. Mac had suffered water bed palsy: a win over the Patriots, a drunken de-bauch, a stumble upstairs, a swoon into the watery waste, followed by hours of dreamless sleep in the most awkward position.

He showed up at practice in a neck brace. It was the sort of mon-strous thing you wear when trying to turn a fender-bender into a life-changing lawsuit. Ditka took one look at him and said, "You're not playing." This was Tuesday, and the game was scheduled for prime time Thursday. McMahon did not accept Ditka's decision. Asked about the game, he smirked and said, "There's no possibility I'm not playing."

"The one problem [McMahon] had was with authority," Ditka wrote. "He had a problem with his father, he had a problem with his Brigham Young coach, and he had a problem with me. Authority fig-ures. He was defiant just because he didn't want to be known as a con-formist, or a guy who would listen. He sure as hell didn't care about being the All-American boy."

Mac showed up at his next practice in street clothes and sat in the bleachers with Joe Namath, who was interviewing the Bears quarter-back for ABC. McMahon would not miss a chance to hang out with Namath. This was Mac's spirit guide. "I never was a hero-worshiper, or jock-sniffer, or autograph-seeker," McMahon wrote. "I liked Mickey Mantle, I think Jack Nicholson is super [. . .] if there's one person I identify with in sports it's Namath."

At the end of practice, when the press asked if McMahon would play, Ditka was more emphatic than ever: *Did you see him up there? No fucking way.* He then cited a rule in the manner of a judge citing legal precedent: "If you don't practice, you don't play."

"That's a high school rule," said McMahon. "There's no possibility I won't play."

Most of us believed the Ditka/McMahon feud was phony, ginned up for the press in the way of a subplot in professional wrestling. But when I floated this theory to Steve Zucker, then McMahon's agent, he said, "I was the go-between. I put the fires out. Believe me. It was real. They wouldn't talk to each other for weeks. But it was like father and son. They wouldn't talk but they loved each other. Sort of. In a way. They respected each other. They were both very stubborn men."

McMahon was told not to dress for the game, but there he was, in uniform, throwing spirals before kickoff. The Bears were in their white jerseys. Mac wore an Adidas headband to keep the hair out of his eyes, his bottom lip fat with chewing tobacco. He was concentrating on each toss, focused in the way of a fighter pilot who swallowed a handful of greenies in the hangar. Ditka, commenting on how sharp Mac seemed just two days out of traction, said something like, *I don't know what they gave him, but he came flying out of that tunnel.*

Interviewing NFL veterans, I sometimes felt like the kid talking to Clint Eastwood's broken-down gunfighter in *Unforgiven*:

KID: Was you ever scared in them days?
MUNNY: I don't remember, Kid. I was drunk most of the time.
  Give me a pull on that bottle, will you?

The ABC cameras found McMahon on the sideline, and, having found him, seemed reluctant to pull away. Mac was a star—he had that on even his worst days. Frank Gifford of ABC said there was no chance McMahon would play. Ditka had characterized his role as "Catastrophe Quarterback." Namath wasn't so sure. *Boy, I don't know, Frank. Jim told me there's no chance he won't play.*

The game started, then dragged. It got boring. The defense did what the defense did, but Steve Fuller, who started at QB for the Bears, could not produce. It was three and out, three and out. Most drives ended in a punt. The Bears defense began to lose faith. You could see it in the way they jogged onto the field after yet another failed possession. In the third quarter, the Bears were losing 17–9. And there seemed no prospect of putting up more points.

Meanwhile, McMahon was following Ditka up and down the sideline, talking, yelling, demanding: Put me in! Put me in!! Ditka ignored him the way a big dog ignores a yapping little dog until the yapping becomes intolerable, at which point he'd respond with a few ominous big-dog barks: *No I won't put you in! Do you know why? Because if you don't practice, you don't play!* This feud was more exciting than anything happening on the field; it was a high school soap opera, the coach driven mad by the flaky quarterback.

In the second half, McMahon had his helmet on and was playing catch on the sideline. Frank Gifford said McMahon was warming up on his own: *Ditka won't let him play.* You felt just how badly Ditka wanted to win without McMahon. He hated how talent seemed to give the quarterback permission to do whatever he wanted. In the last minutes of the third quarter, Minnesota took on the air of a team mopping up. It was all over. "The offense was sputtering, doing nothing," Ditka said. "I could see that Walter was not himself. And all of the time, as we were falling behind, McMahon was bugging the shit out of me. He was pouting down on the bench, then he was standing behind me, then he was following me around like a puppy. I turned around and almost stepped on top of him. 'Put me in,' he was saying, 'I can play. I'm fine.'"

Ditka finally threw up his hands and said, "All right, just go."

McMahon fastened his chin strap and ran into the game. From that moment, he would always be conflated in my mind with Shane, the reluctant gunfighter forced back into the fight, the man who, by his presence alone, changes everything. As soon as he got onto the field, you could sense a change in the weather. "Jim rolled in like a gunfighter strutting into Dodge City," Singletary wrote. "You could see the whole offense pick up." The running backs, the linemen, the receivers—they lifted their shoulders, their chests filled with air. Believing you're in it, that you have a chance—it makes all the difference. "Every good starting quarterback has got that confident arrogance—'I'm better than everybody else,'" said McMichael. "When I talk about the difference between Jim McMahon and Steve Fuller, I'm not talking about athletic ability, I'm talking about presence—the kind of person who everybody knows is around. It's like when you're at the high school dance and the most popular girl walks in the gym, all eyes turn to her." McMahon took a knee in the huddle, grinned, and said, "All right, boys, we're going down that field and getting six."

For McMahon, these few moments at the center of the world, at the still point of the spinning globe, made the rest of it—early mornings, practices, Ditka's tantrums—tolerable. Not being sure about McMahon's physical condition, Ditka sent him in with a conservative play: a screen pass. But when the quarterback got to the line, he noticed something. Having noticed something, he called an audible. That is, he changed the play. Ditka, on the sideline, having been turned into a spectator, cursed, threw his clipboard. McMahon stumbled as he took the snap and came very close to falling down. Later speculation attributed this stumble variously to his back, to being rusty, to the drugs that lit him like a Christmas tree, even to the aftereffects of a long night of partying. "I don't know if I should tell this on him," McMichael wrote,

"And I don't want [to say] anything negative about the boys in this book, but he wasn't supposed to play, remember. So yeah, he'd been out all night. Smelled like alcohol, you know?"

McMahon righted himself, then set up in the pocket. A Vikings tackler got through and was heading for number 9 with all the steam of a free runner. He would have ended the play, maybe the game, but, at the last moment, Payton, freelancing his way into the action, took the rusher out. This incredible block—Sweetness launching himself into the knees of a man twice his size—shows what made Payton one of the best backs in football history.

Payton had given McMahon an extra moment and he used it to find Willie Gault deep downfield. A screamer, a high flyer. Gault snagged it on the run. Just like that, Shane had picked off the first of the bad men, the leather-clad phantom hiding in the shadows on the balcony. One play, seventy yards, touchdown.

When McMahon got to the sideline, Ditka grabbed him, got in his face, and said, "Tell me, what fucking play did I call?"

"Screen pass."

"Then why the fuck did you do that?"

" 'Cause Willie was open."

It was not just the offense that McMahon brought to life; it was the defense, too. "I've never been around another quarterback that had that kind of effect," Plank told me. "He made everybody better, not just the receivers and tight ends, but the linebackers and safeties. He'd be head-butting the guys as they went onto the field."

On the Vikings' next possession, Wilber Marshall picked off a pass. A minute later, Mac was back on the field. Ditka sent in a running play. Mac saw something. He called an audible. Ditka kicked over a cooler. Mac rolled left, then hit receiver Dennis McKinnon in the chest as he crossed into the end zone. Two plays, two touchdowns. Bears 23, Vikings 17.

The Vikings came apart after that, took penalties, made mistakes. Is there a moment in the movie when some of the actors realize they've been cast as the bad guys? McMahon threw a perfect strike to Gault his next time on the field, but Gault dropped it. That was the rap on Gault: soft, he gave up the ball at the hint of contact. McMahon ran for a first down. "Gutsy little man, isn't he?" said Gifford. "Pinched nerve and all." A few plays later, McMahon found McKinnon in the end zone. He later described the audible that led to that score as "another sandlot maneuver." If I had known then what I know now, I'd have quit watching sports that day. It was never going to get better.

I snapped a mental picture of McMahon in the fourth. He was watching from the sideline as the final seconds drained off the clock on one of the great performances: seven passes, three touchdowns, 166 yards—in seven minutes. He'd taken off his helmet and fortified himself with another plug of chew. His hair was pushed back and he looked tough, with a three-day growth of beard. You could tell that he was admired, loved and admired, the sort of guy who would dominate even those nights when he was not around; everyone would laugh when his name was invoked, smile and say, "McMahon, that crazy fucker . . ."

I knocked on the door. A television, which had been blaring news of an outrage on the other side of the world, switched off. There were voices, then the door opened. A dark-haired woman shook my hand, then stepped aside, revealing a bald, medium-size guy in his midfifties. He was haggard, beat up in the way of a dockworker in his tenth year of early retirement. He was wearing a tank top that revealed sloped shoulders and shapeless arms, the arms of a once powerful man who, at some point, decided to take a rest, and liked it. The shirt was engaged in a dialogue with itself. In big letters, it asked GOT MILK? In smaller letters, beneath, it answered: GOT POT.

He nodded at me, then smiled, revealing the plug of tobacco tucked in his lower lip. After shaking my hand, he spit in a cup. His eyes were buggy. "Come on," he said. This was my first physical contact with Jim McMahon. On some level, I probably wrote this book just to meet the quarterback. I followed him to an office in back of the house. Mesquite and cactus, Weber grills, sauna and steam, sunshine all winter—Mac had forsaken Chicago a decade before, sold his house, moved to Scottsdale to one of the adobe mansions that run beside the low brown hills.

When I asked Steve Zucker what McMahon wanted from him as an agent, he said, "Jim wanted just one thing: enough money so that, when he stopped playing, he'd never have to work again." Here's how Mac described that fantasy in his autobiography, published when he was twenty-six: "And when I retire, maybe I can fulfill another dream.

You know how *Golf Digest* lists the top hundred golf courses every year? I'd like to just get on a plane and play them, one after another. What a way to live."

McMahon played his last NFL season in 1996 for Green Bay, where he spent most of his time on the bench. He'd been brought in as a mentor for Brett Favre, a sort of Merlin to teach the boy king the dark magic. That's football: first you're young; then, if you're lucky, you're old; then you're gone. He made it back to the Super Bowl with the Packers in 1996 but refused to play. ("[Coach Mike Holmgren] asked if I wanted to go in, but I said no," Mac told me. "I said, 'I played in this game when it meant something. I'm not going in to mop up.'") For a time, Mac hosted a golf tournament in Lake Geneva, Wisconsin, the Barefoot Classic, its only requirement being that players compete without shoes. Now and then, he shows up on a sports channel. In a particularly strange episode of *Reel Fishing*, he was seen drinking all afternoon, then peeing off the boat. In 2003, he was pulled over by the police in Navarre, Florida. He'd been weaving. If you compare the way McMahon reacted to the way Ditka behaved after he'd been stopped, it tells you everything: Ditka cursed, threatened, then signed the ticket "Fuck you Jack." According to the AP, McMahon told his arresting officer, "I'm too drunk. You got me."

"He was pretty well wasted," Officer Henderson agreed.

We spent two or three hours in his office, drinking beer, chewing tobacco, and talking. He was wearing shorts and flip-flops. He sat in a swively desk chair. His computer glowed. His shelves of memorabilia—footballs, awards, pictures taken on red-letter days, the young McMahon covered in grime, the old McMahon posed with presidents—looked down. His dogs came in—two Doberman pinschers who ran around smelling everything and a poodle who seemed to be in charge of the operation. Mac's girlfriend refilled drinks. Her name is Laurie Navon. McMahon has her name tattooed in Chinese characters on his arm. He has a gold hoop in his ear. He had houseguests. You could hear their happy voices in the distance, by the pool. Now and then, Mac seemed impatient to join the party, but mostly he had nothing but time.

He was unrecognizable when I first saw him, or nearly so, but as we talked, the years fell away and I found myself in the company of the quarterback I'd followed so zealously. This McMahon and that McMahon are the same person after all—the same house after a hundred years in the rain, when the ivy has penetrated the tuck pointing and the broken window lets the wind wreak havoc.

We talked about Chicago and the suburbs. McMahon has four grown kids and told me how strange it was to sit in the bleachers at his kids' games where every eye followed him and all the fathers seemed to want something. "The parents were a pain in the ass," he told me. "Especially the hockey parents. I actually got into a couple of . . . well, they weren't altercations, no punches were thrown, but words were exchanged. I'd try to sit away from everybody. I didn't want it. They tend to mouth off. I remember when my son was ten or eleven, playing in one of those rinks where you can stand behind the goalies. There were four or five fathers beating on the glass and I thought I saw a guy flip off the kids. Sure enough, a minute later, I see my son whack the glass—the guy is flipping him off. After the game, my son comes out of the locker room, and I see him jawing with somebody. I look over. It's the same guy. He's about six three, in a business suit, glasses, buddy-buddy with his friends. I tap him on the shoulder and say, 'Hey, tough guy, what's your problem? Why are you flipping off little kids?' He says, 'I didn't flip off your son, Jim. I flipped off the other kid.' I said, 'Does that make it right, asshole? I should beat the shit out of you right here.' I almost hit him but thought, No, I can't. So I asked my son, 'Do you want to kick his ass?' He said, 'Yeah,' dropped his bag, walked up, and jacked the guy in the chest, knocked him into the glass. The guy took a step toward my son. I said, 'You take one swing, pal.' He just stood there. I said, 'Yeah, that's what I thought,' turned to my boy, and said, 'Let's go.'"

I didn't know how to respond to this, so I asked about audibles—why did he call so many audibles? Was he doing it just to drive Ditka nuts? "Nah," he said, "that was a side benefit. Truth is, there were times when our offense was just not producing. Unless you did something, it wasn't going to happen. That's why, any chance I got, I'd throw it."

"Was it fun?"

"Was what fun?"

"Playing."

"Fuck yeah, it was fun as hell," he said, smiling. "But if you're not playing, if you're injured or backing up or whatever, that sucks. My last couple years, I didn't play much at all."

"Do you miss it?"

"Sundays were great," he said. "That's the only part of the game I miss. The week of work, dealing with the media and all that shit—don't miss none of it. Hanging out with the boys, being in the locker room— that's what you really miss. 'Cause they were some funny sumbitches. But I don't want to be young again. Have to do all that shit again. Feel that pain again."

McMahon gripped his right shoulder as he said this, thinking. While trying to untangle a knot with a fork when he was nine, he stabbed himself in the eye, permanently damaging his cornea. In Chicago, we used to joke that only the Bears would draft a half blind quarterback. When asked why he always wore sunglasses, even indoors, he would blame this childhood injury, saying it left him acutely sensitive to light. I always figured that Mac came up with the story to explain why he wore sunglasses indoors. After all, he didn't wear them during games, even on sunny days. But now, sitting close, his eyes did seem funky. He doesn't really look at you when he talks—he looks at a vanishing point over your shoulder.

"I still feel the pain of the game every day so I don't need to miss it," he went on. "I like doing what I do now, which is pretty much whatever I want. Didn't make a lot of money in the game, but I put four kids through college, so I did all right."

At his peak, Mac earned close to $1 million a year, his income significantly supplemented by endorsements. Every time you turned on a TV, there he was, hawking another product. He was lucky enough to be represented by Steve Zucker, who protected and increased the quarterback's money. According to Celebrity Net Worth, McMahon is currently worth $15 million, which makes him an exception among retired football players. Most of them struggle to earn for the rest of their lives.

"What's your typical day?" I asked.

"I get out of bed around ten. When it's nice out, which it usually is, I'll go lay by the pool for an hour or two. Check my mail. Watch some TV. For the last six weeks I had [a postsurgical] boot on, so I couldn't play golf. But now that I can play, I'll get out and play a little bit more."

"How are you holding up physically?"

Every player I asked this question responded with a catalog of woe.

"Not good," said McMahon. "My shoulders, my elbows, my knees— they're all pretty much gone. I'm probably going to need a new knee. They said if I screw this one up one more time, I'll have to get another.

My shoulders and elbows are what really bother me. I got memory issues. I got a deterioration in my neck, my upper neck, a compressed disk. And my lower back, lower spine, it's all degenerating."

The memory issues—that's what I wanted to know about. McMahon had joined hundreds of other former NFL players in a class-action lawsuit to force the league to take responsibility for the long-term effects of all those concussions and head blows. In recent years, doctors at the Brain Bank at Boston University have made a convincing case that many if not all football players will suffer from chronic traumatic encephalopathy, CTE, a disease that destroys parts of the brain. Symptoms include memory loss, depression, dementia. In recent years, several former players with the disease have committed suicide.

At some point, every conversation I had with a retired player turned to "the disease." Dave Duerson, an All-Pro safety on the '85 Bears, who suffered from CTE, killed himself in 2011. Duerson's former teammates spoke of the disease with a wounded sense of betrayal—they'd been betrayed by their team, their league, even their own love of the game. Here were men who played a rough sport they knew would extract a price in hip replacements and artificial knees, but to find out, twenty years after retirement, that it might also take their personality, their mood, their memory, their mind? In the end, you forget your own name. And there's no test, no way to know if you've got it until they do the autopsy.

When I asked McMahon about the lawsuit, he said, "Which one? I'm a plaintiff in this concussion case and I'm also doing a workmen's comp case and a disability or line-of-duty case. And then I've got my limo driver case. We were in a limousine coming back from Tahoe, and our driver fell asleep, went off the road, fuckin' . . . we should be dead."

"How's your memory?"

"Sometimes, I come into a room and have no idea why I'm there."

"That's not good."

"They gave me this memory test, a list of fifteen things, and they'd say, 'What do you remember of those fifteen?' I'd get two or three. And I'm like, 'Damn, you just told me that shit!'"

Whatever the state of Mac's brain, he's a pleasure to be around. When asked about a specific moment or play, he lights up. We spent the afternoon talking about his past.

Jim McMahon was born in Jersey City. When he was in grade school, his family moved to California. When he was ten, a coach arranged all the kids who'd signed up for Pop Warner football in a line on a suburban field. Each kid was handed a football and told to huck it, heave it as far as you can. There were wobblers, wounded ducks, scorchers. The coach walked until he reached the most distant ball, picked it up, walked it back, then handed it to McMahon, saying, "You're the quarterback."

Like Ditka, he was a high-intensity boy. When he was twelve, he was kicked off his Little League baseball team for smoking. In high school, he was suspended for vandalism. When he was sixteen, his family moved to Roy, Utah. McMahon was the kid from nowhere, the smartass who, at the end of the summer, turns up on the high school field and blows them all away. He could hit a man at thirty yards. He was tough, too, small but fearless, ready to shove the ball down the throat of a player twice his size. A kid like that attracts scouts. They sit in the stands with notepads, behaving like men at an auction.

In the spring of 1976, McMahon made the puzzling decision to attend Brigham Young, the Mormon university up the road in Provo. Why would a high-intensity boy who'd already been in trouble put himself under the jurisdiction of the Mormon honor code, which forbids tobacco, alcohol, premarital sex, and everything else Mac loved? He blamed his dad, or, more simply, his father's desire to watch him play. It was the last time, he later said, that he'd let anyone else influence his decisions.

McMahon threw his first touchdown freshman year and started as a sophomore. He would set fifty-five records at BYU and pass for more yards than any other quarterback in NCAA history. He was small and his arm was just good enough, but he had an uncanny sense of the game. Looking at a defense, he could quickly cycle through every possibility. "You could see in college he was one of those savants," McMichael wrote, "who takes a snap and as he's backpedaling has deciphered where to throw the ball already."

McMahon was trouble at BYU. It was not just that he violated the Mormon code, but that he seemed to take cavalier joy doing it. Reports were constantly making their way back to the dean: McMahon has been chewing tobacco on campus, as if Joseph Smith had never been martyred; McMahon was drinking at a party, as if the secret book had never been found in upstate New York; McMahon has been sleeping at his girlfriend's apartment, as if Brigham Young never led the faithful through the mountains. There were threats, second chances, probationary periods, then, finally, after the 1981 season, McMahon was expelled. He was told he might return someday, later, not now, to earn the credits to take a degree. It confirmed what McMahon always believed about authority: Ditka swears his religious devotion, then calls Mac a motherfucker every Sunday; BYU suspends Mac for violating the honor code, but only after they've gotten every possible bit of service out of his heathen body.

When I asked McMahon the hardest he'd ever been hit—he was a rag doll, known for taking a pounding—he did not have to think. "In college," he said. "We were playing New Mexico. Linebacker by the name of Jimmy Carter. I won't forget it, 'cause Carter was the president at the time. He knocked the fuck out of me. I was looking left. I was supposed to have protection on the other side. The blocker was a sophomore. He blew the assignment. Just as I'm getting ready to throw, Carter's helmet hit my wrist, and my own fist hit my chin. Then he picked me up and dumped me on the back of my head. I was out for ten minutes. But I got up. Or they said I did. They said I got up and walked to the sidelines and fell down. Then I was out again. That's the last thing I remember till Monday. But they said I went back in and played. I missed like two series. I couldn't remember the plays. I couldn't call them. That's what they said. I'd just call a formation and say, 'Get open quick.' They said I picked the defense apart. They said it was easy."

The Bears took McMahon with their first pick in 1982. He was not the biggest or the fastest, and his arm, well, I've told you about his arm, and his eye, and his attitude, but Ditka tended to go for the guy who struck him as a player.

"We thought we were getting close and we needed a quarterback, and he was the best," Bill Tobin told me. "We liked his toughness. We liked his aggressiveness. And he was a winner. He had that bowl game he won—that was pretty special. And he fit our mold. See, one thing that we never let bother us in our draft room was size and speed. We liked them big and fast, but we would break the mold and draft players as opposed to specimens. McMahon was not tall and he wasn't a great passer. He didn't have a superquick release. But he was a winner."

Halas seemed to like McMahon at first. "I'm well pleased," he said after the draft, "as this quarterback seems to have 'the touch.'" His optimism turned to scorn when McMahon dragged out contract negotiations. Mac finally went in to meet Halas. "He was kind of crotchety," McMahon told me. "I'd been sitting outside the office for an hour. I finally asked the secretary, 'What am I waiting for?' And she said, 'Mr. Halas is taking a nap.' I said, 'Well, wake him up, I got things to do.' When I got in there, he said I was asking for too much money, though even if they met my terms, I'd still be one of the lowest-paid quarterbacks in the draft. 'If we give you two hundred bucks a game, you're overpaid,' he said. 'You've got a bad arm, a bad eye, bad knees, and you're too small. Maybe you should go to Canada.' So I asked, 'Then why the hell did you draft me, old man?'"

By the early 1980s, Halas, having prospered with the television deals that have made the NFL fabulously profitable—the league generates $9 billion a year—was a wealthy man. In addition to the Bears, he owned several side businesses. And yet, perhaps conditioned by early years of struggle, he fought for every dollar. McMahon finally agreed to a four-year deal starting at $60,000, ending at $100,000. Paltry for the time, it's shocking when compared to today's salaries. In 2011, quarterback Michael Vick signed a six-year deal with the Philadelphia Eagles for $100 million, then had a terrible season. (In the course of ten games, he threw twelve touchdown passes and ten interceptions; his team finished 4–10 and his coach was fired.) But if players from the '80s and '90s feel they missed out, they're aware that the players from still earlier eras looked upon their $100,000 contracts with stupefied envy. When it comes to big money, everyone believes he arrived a generation too soon.

McMahon made his entrance in the summer of 1982. "[He] walks into Halas Hall and he's got a beer in his hand and a six-pack under his arm," Ditka said. "I think it was Miller, but it might have been something else. He has a wad of tobacco under his lip, too. First thing he says is, 'I was getting dry on the way in.'"

There had never been anyone like him in Chicago, a city where heroes were often of the role model variety. For those of us attracted to rebels and mavericks, he offered a way into the game. By my sophomore year in high school, the walls of my room were covered with pictures of Mac: in a headband, a wad of chew in his lip; cursing Ditka;

jogging into the end zone with unhurried ease; set up in the pocket like he has all the time in the world, an inspiration for all those who want to stay calm amid the storm of life.

He was terribly out of shape—this resulted partly from his own nonchalance, partly from his holdout. He'd been drinking on the beach long after the other guys had taken up the spartan ways of the season. The team introduced him with "the Bears Mile," an annual event at which, as the press snapped pictures, the squad ran around the track. McMahon was a mess, huffing and puffing. By the end, he stopped running altogether—it was the last time the team would ever invite reporters to watch the players run. "I remember his first year," Ditka said, "he ran a mile and a half in almost 13 minutes, walking the last part, looking like he was going to puke and die, finishing behind everybody but our very heavy offensive lineman Noah Jackson—but he was on board. I read that in 1984, even with his lacerated kidney, he'd gone out for Halloween with his teammates, dressed as a priest, drunk. He had a Bible with him, and I guess when you opened it, there were photos of naked women inside. Well, this was football, not religion."

"I was his roommate in the first minicamp," Tim Wrightman told me. "We were rookies. It was before the season. We weren't even signed. It was three days. Sunday was the last. He goes out Saturday, then comes rolling in at three o'clock in the morning, blind drunk. He throws up till about six thirty, then we go to practice. Jim somehow fights through it, then, at the end, Ditka says, 'Okay, we're going to run ten cowboys.' A cowboy was a sprint down the field, a walk back—a hundred and ten yards. Any other quarterback would have said, 'It's minicamp in May, it has nothing to do with the season; my hamstring's a little tight, I can't run those.' But Jim did every one of those cowboys, then threw up. That's why guys loved him as a captain and a leader. He didn't take shortcuts. If he partied, he didn't expect to get special treatment. It made you realize how tough he was—that's why guys respected him and loved playing with him."

Whenever I asked McMahon's teammates to describe him as an athlete, they laughed. "As an athlete?" said Kurt Becker. "Horrible. He couldn't scramble. He had a good arm but not a great arm. He wasn't a pinpoint passer. But he did have knowledge of the game. That was his biggest attribute. He knew who was going to be open before the ball was snapped. He wasn't a great specimen by any means, but he could read a defense."

"He didn't have the strongest arm, but he could get it there," said Brian Baschnagel. "He had a great touch on the ball. He always put it where it needed to be in relationship to the defenders. Sometimes the ball would wobble, but his throws were easy to catch."

Emery Moorehead: "He wasn't going to hit a guy sixty yards down field but he would scramble and see somebody and have the strength to get it there. He knew the game inside out. That's why he was able to stay in the league so long."

Tim Wrightman: "Physically he doesn't look like an athlete. He's soft, pasty. He looks like the Pillsbury Doughboy. He couldn't throw a spiral. Believe me, I caught lots of his passes. They never looked right. But he could read the defenses and he always found a way. He would switch the ball into his left hand on the goal line as he was getting tackled and throw it left-handed for a touchdown. He was just win at all costs. And he was smart. The guy could read defenses, and, most importantly, he was the only quarterback that could get along with Ditka."

Ditka tried to revamp the Bears offense when he took over. "He came in with a scheme that was finally something other than Payton left, Payton right, Payton on the screen pass," Moorehead told me. "That had been going on since Walter arrived. There was no diversity, no motions, everybody knew what was going to happen. It was pretty pathetic." Ditka added deep routes and trick plays, but the offense remained woefully conservative. "It was boring," McMahon said. "We ran the ball, not what I was used to. There wasn't a whole lot to be successful with at quarterback for the Bears. There was nothing to do. You get to throw on third and long. If you're lucky enough to get a first down, you keep playing. It was frustrating."

Mac changed that: he would run Ditka's plays only until he recognized a mismatch or a flaw in the defense, at which point he called an audible. This gave Ditka fits, but it finally made the Bears dangerous. But McMahon's greatest contribution was leadership. Even on bad days, the team played better when he was on the field. With number 9 in the game, they always believed they could win. "It was his personality, the fact that he'd fight," Plank told me. "If we needed a yard, he'd go headfirst. If it meant jumping off the ledge, he was going to jump off a ledge. I think the defenders looked at him and said, 'Wow, we wish he was on our side.' He was just one of those guys."

"He played with total abandon and he's not big," said Fencik. "He took a beating."

"Everybody rallied around him because he was willing to do whatever it took," said Moorehead. "Even though he only weighed 190 pounds, he was just as physical as our linemen. He would deny the plays Ditka sent in, be like, 'Nah, that ain't gonna work.' Then call a play of his own. And of course everybody really wanted to make that play work. Nine times out of ten, McMahon made the right call."

"Jim knew what he was doing," Ditka told me. "A lot of guys with audibles didn't. If you knew the game and studied the game, it didn't bother me if you wanted to change something. Nobody said the play I called was the best in the world. But I called it based on what I'd seen on film and everything."

McMahon became the starting quarterback November 6, 1983, a week after Halas died. It took him time to find a rhythm, but by the middle of the following season, he'd become as effective as any other quarterback in the league. His impact is overlooked: Mac was playing in the era of masters like Marino, Elway, and Montana. He never put up big numbers—probably no QB could have with the Walter Payton Bears—but he had a talent for scoring when the game was on the line. He didn't have the most passing yards, but he led in the only statistic that matters: wins. In one stretch, from 1984 to 1988, the Bears went 35 and 3 in games that McMahon started. There used to be a saying about Rocket Richard, the great hockey player: he's not the fastest, but there's no one quicker from the blue line to the goal. That was Mac. He could feel the end zone the way a surfer can sense the proximity of the sea: if it was on the wind, it made him wild. Though Halas was partly correct about McMahon—bad eye, weak arm—the quarterback did have the quality that Papa Bear prized above all others: the old zipperoo.

As we talked, McMahon kept making the same point about the '85 Bears: amid all the hysteria for the defense, the offense is not given its proper due. "We scored the most points in the NFC that year, and the second most in the league," he said. "We held the ball almost forty minutes a game. Tough to beat when you score that much and don't give the ball back. And it gives the defense a good long break. You can't win with just one side of the ball. Marino proved that in Miami. They had a great offense but couldn't stop anybody. If you don't perform on both sides, and have a good kicking game, you're not going to win championships."

"How do you think the '85 Bears would do if they were playing today?"

"We'd still be kicking ass. Maybe we wouldn't win a Super Bowl, but you have to remember, some of us are pushing sixty!"

It's an old joke, and we both laughed. Then I asked McMahon if he still works out. Plank is in the gym several times a week, titanium shoulders and all. Fencik is all over the North Side on his bike. But Mac laughed. "I haven't worked out in ten, twelve years," he told me. "There's not much I can do. I know I've got to do something. I'm fuckin' feeling bad. But when I start to work out, I'm like, There's nobody hitting me anymore, so why am I doing this? I did it for so long, it was my life for thirty-some years. It felt good to take the last few years off."

I asked if he could still throw. I had brought a football. It was in my car. I had just reread Roger Kahn's *The Boys of Summer,* published almost twenty years after the '55 Dodgers won the World Series—a stretch similar to the one that separated Super Bowl XX from my discussions with the '85 Bears. Kahn ended many interviews by asking some ancient Dodger to play catch. He would stand in the gloaming and toss a ball with a faded star. As he did, the years would fall away and the old men would again be as they had been on those dusky Ebbets Field afternoons, and Kahn, in the middle of life, would be as he'd been as a boy in the bleachers, when his heroes strode across the field like figures painted on a Greek vase.

I figured I'd do the same: me and Mac throwing the pill as the light went down. But football is not baseball, and the men I interviewed had been damaged by injury, consumed by surgery, recovery, implant, arthritis, depression. A few were all right, but many more were as dilapidated as old shotgun houses. In *Death of a Salesman*, Willy Loman objects to the indignity of capitalist America: "You can't eat the orange and throw the peel away," he says, "a man is not a piece of fruit!" But that's exactly what did happen to Willy Loman, and to a lot of old football players. Their youth is gone, and now only the peel remains, a husk filled with memories.

When I asked Mac if he wanted to play catch, he grimaced. "I haven't thrown in years," he told me. "My shoulder hurts so bad I can't even throw my car keys."

He sat a moment, then, hearing his friends in the pool, sighed, and said, "I'd better get back."

He stood slowly, painfully, unfolding one joint at a time, then walked me out. "When you see the boys," he said, "tell 'em Mac says hello." Then, in the way of Colombo saving the best question for that moment when he stands with his trench coat in the doorway, I asked McMahon if it had been worth it. "Knowing what we know, about the injuries and the brain and CTE?"

He smiled and said, "I'd do it all again in a heartbeat."

13

STAR-CROSSED IN MIAMI

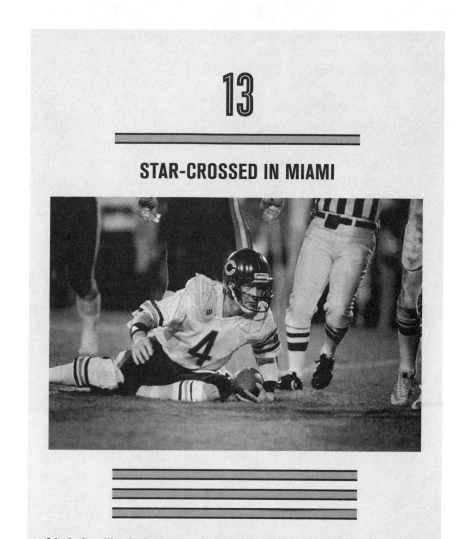

A typical position for backup quarterback Steve Fuller—on his ass, getting nothing
done—during the Bears' worst game of the season: December 2, 1985,
when Don Shula and the Dolphins lay in ambush

By Thanksgiving 1985, it looked as if the Bears might never lose another game. The defense was only getting stronger. In addition to Buddy's 46, opposing players had to master their own fear. "Before teams played the Bears, they weren't even *thinking* about winning," said Rex Ryan. "They were just hoping to survive—they didn't want to get the crap kicked out of 'em. The '85 Bears had teams beat before they even played."

All of which drew special attention to the Dolphins game, played December 2, 1985, at the Orange Bowl. The 1972 Dolphins remain the only NFL team to go unbeaten in the regular season and playoffs, then win the Super Bowl. The veterans of that team, which won Super Bowl VII, let it be known that they did not want the Bears to match their record. They converged on Miami; they'd cheer from the ramparts as Don Shula and Dan Marino fought off the hordes. Before the game—it drew the largest audience in the history of Monday Night Football—you could see the old warriors dressed in sports coats and slacks, broad-chested men flashing Super Bowl rings, shoving those jeweled monstrosities right down the throat of the cameras.

In ways that would become clear, the game had been arranged as a kind of ambush. In a Western, the Kiowa scout would take one look at the shadows emerging from the tall grass and scream, "Run!" The players and coaches, the mood of each team, the tenor of practices—it gave you a queasy feeling. For starters, there were all those '72 Dolphins, Bob Griese, Larry Csonka, Mercury Morris, who, in themselves, meant nothing—Csonka wasn't going to play—but suggested how badly the Dolphins wanted the game. Then there were the Bears—Hampton, McMichael, Wilson—who seemed almost haughty, certain they could not be beaten. Then there was Miami itself: the sun and the umbrellaed cocktails, the girls on the beach where many of the Bears spent Monday afternoon, drinking and laughing and studying the line where the water went from turquoise to aqua. Then Ditka, who wanted to prove something, wanted to show that his offense was more than Walter left, Walter right, Walter up the middle. He'd beaten Landry and now wanted to beat that other deity, Don Shula, and do it in a way the maestro would understand.

And don't forget Buddy, who rode into Miami like Custer, painfully unaware that he faced karmic payback. Shula had been the coach of the Baltimore team that Ryan, then with the Jets, helped defeat in Super Bowl III. For that game, Shula, young and stupidly ignorant of life's vicissitudes, had not prepared a plan, believing that whatever had been good enough to beat superior teams in the NFL would be more than enough for the Jets. He went in arrogant, picturing ticker tape and flowers. This time, it was Buddy who came in without a plan: in the previous weeks, the Bears had dominated, defeating Dallas and Atlanta by a combined score of 80–0. Buddy figured that whatever had undone the Cowboys would work on Miami. He'd come full circle: he was back in a big game, only now he was on the other sideline, among those who believe themselves invulnerable. As Buddy boasted about his defense, Shula was in his lab with eyepiece and slide rule, solving the riddle of the 46.

In every story of hubris, there's an ominous hint, which the hero, had he not been so intoxicated, might have heeded. For Buddy, it came from Jimbo Covert, a guard who protected McMahon on the line, a task he'd once performed for Marino at Pitt. Spotting Covert after practice, Ryan said, "We're going to blitz your buddy and knock him on his ass."

"If you do that," Covert said, "he'll kill you."

"That night, the Orange Bowl was the loudest stadium I've ever been in," Brian Baschnagel told me. "I was hurt, so they had me in the coach's box. I got such a headache from all that noise. It was deafening. The crowd was as rambunctious as they possibly could be. Everyone knew what was on line: Miami's undefeated season. We weren't intimidated, but it was intense, and kooky things happened. It was a star-crossed night."

McMahon was out of the lineup, hurt. With what? Who remembers? It seemed like he was wounded half the time. It was the shoulder, the back, the knees, the hand, the brain rattling in the skull fluid, the kidney, the water bed palsy.

Steve Fuller started at quarterback. He'd yet to throw a touchdown pass that season. The Bears defense would have to keep the score low. The Dolphins came onto the field, the stadium rocking. I remember Mercury Morris, a dazzling runner from the '72 team, screaming at Marino, urging him on. In 1983, when Morris should have been playing, he'd been in prison, sent away on a cocaine conspiracy charge, though the conviction was later overturned. I met him shortly after he'd been freed. He was big, shiny, and dark. His hands were as rough as leather. He told me the penitentiary had been so near the Orange Bowl that, lying in his cell on Sunday afternoons, he could hear the crowd. I asked to see his Super Bowl ring. He dropped it in my palm. It was an anchor, crusted with gunk.

Miami scored on its first drive. This hardly ever happened to the Bears that season. Marino did it by rolling away from the pass rush, then finding receiver Nat Moore downfield, where he was being covered by linebacker Wilber Marshall. Linebackers are big, and even the best have trouble keeping up with a speedy receiver—it was a mismatch that Miami would exploit. To a Bears fan, that first TD seemed like a fluke—until Marino did it again.

Miami had the worst rush defense in football, but Ditka kept calling pass plays. Some players believed he was trying to prove something to Shula. Coaches speak to each other in code. But Fuller could never keep up with Marino, who picked apart the Bears' defense with freakish ease.

How did it happen?

As I said, Shula had a plan, a solution to the 46. Rather than try to outmuscle the Bears, he used their own strength against them. Football jujitsu. *No one can beat the 46?* Fine. *Let's let the 46 beat itself.* He accomplished this with a series of plays in which the Dolphins' linemen were told, in essence, to let the Bears rushers through, step aside as they converged on the pocket. But when they got there, Marino, having rolled away from Richard Dent, was gone. It gave the QB a few extra seconds, just enough time to exploit the unsoundness of the 46.

Marino found receivers uncovered, or covered by the wrong kind of players. "I'll give Shula credit," Singletary wrote. "He played us for suckers. The game began and sure enough he sucked us in, showing a huge opening up the middle, through which we so magnanimously entered, only to be swallowed up by converging linemen."

It was a strategy perfectly suited to Marino, who had the quickest release in football—the ball left his hand superfast. "He was able to get outside the pocket and buy time," Plank told me. "I don't care what defense you're running, everything breaks down after six seconds. If the offense can get a receiver in the flat, it becomes individual match-ups. And they had great receivers, and Marino made great throws. It was the pass rush that failed the Bears that night."

"The Dolphins beat us because the 46 was predicated on getting to the quarterback before he could do anything," said Wrightman. "Marino was known to have the quickest release in the game. That's what beat us. He could get rid of the ball faster than our guys could get to him. He's the one guy that could have done it."

Even a Bears fan had to respect what Shula had done: he was a coach with a weaker team but a better plan. "There's a reason Shula's in the Hall of Fame," Tyrone Keys told me. "He did things we'd never seen before."

When Ditka realized what was happening—the defense had been tricked, forced into mismatches—he told Buddy to switch from the 46 to the "nickel," in which five defensive backs drop into pass coverage. "Mind your own damn business," Buddy shouted. "It's my defense."

"The Bears did not go with any nickel defense against our three-wide-receiver set until very late in the third quarter," Shula said later. "They played what they'd always played, because it had killed everybody else. Of course, everybody else didn't have Marino at quarterback. And Moore was great catching the ball against one-on-one coverage. Whenever I'm at a speaking engagement, I tell the audience that the best half of football I ever saw was what we did against the Bears that night."

The Bears stormed into the locker room at halftime, cleats clattering on cement. Thirty-one to ten: more points than the 46 had given up in its six previous games combined. Ditka was on Buddy's heels.

Goddamn it, Buddy, you stubborn fuck! Your defense ain't working. Wilber can't cover Nat Moore. Put in the fucking nickel.

Stick it up your ass, Ditka!

Fuck you, Buddy! Get somebody out there that can cover Moore!

As the players reached the lockers, Buddy turned on Ditka. He was red faced; the men went nose to nose. From there, the reports fork into competing narratives. In some, the players pull their coaches apart; in others, punches are thrown. Ditka denied it, proof being: If we had fought, I'd have whipped his ass. You saw Buddy. Did it look like his ass had been whipped? "It was a big [fight], no question," Ditka said. "I told him very simply, 'You want to go outside right now, we go. We can do it any way you want to do it. We can go right out back and get it on, or you can shape your ass up.'"

This moment, Ditka and Ryan face-to-face, is the core of the '85 season: each coach represented an opposing tradition. Ditka was a pragmatist. He'd excelled as a player and had nothing to prove physically. He wanted only to win and would employ any system that worked. Ryan was a visionary. Having never made it on the field, he was determined to leave his mark on the game's history. As an intellectual, he had staked his legacy on one big idea: the 46 defense. He would win with it or go down in a blaze of glory. Merely good on their own, these men were world-class together—they complemented each other—which would have been great had they not also despised each other. It was this hatred that gave the team its edge.

"Ditka was right," said Hampton. "He was basically saying, 'Buddy, quit being an asshole and put the nickel back in there on Nat Moore. Wilber can't do it. Buddy thought Wilber could jump over buildings, but he was getting his ass wore out."

"I think Buddy's pride got in the way, and we paid for it," said offensive tackle Keith Van Horne.

In the third quarter, the Bears finally started to play like the Bears. After scoring 31 points in the first half, the Dolphins would get just one more touchdown. But how that touchdown came about told you everything. "It was in the second half," said Fencik. "Mike Richardson, our left corner, got a real good break on the ball. Maybe he could have intercepted it, but the ball hit Hampton's helmet, changed direction, sailed over Hampton, sailed over Richardson, sailed over me, and landed in the hands of a Miami receiver, who was like, Where did this come from? [and] turned and ran into the end zone. I remember walking off the field with Dan [Hampton], laughing and saying, 'You know what? It's just not happening tonight.'"

Steve Fuller was knocked out in the fourth. Mac snapped on his chin strap and went in, sparking dreams of gunfight glory. Whenever I watch this stretch on DVD, part of me thinks that this time will be different. As McMahon moves downfield, I almost believe that history will change, and the Bears will come back, and be undefeated.

Ditka kept sending in pass plays, but, near the end, when the game was clearly lost, McMahon changed them to runs: Payton left, Payton right, Payton up the middle. Ditka screamed at his quarterback on the sidelines: *What the fuck are you doing?*

"We're not gonna win," said McMahon, "so let's get Wally his hundred yards." Payton was on track to break O. J. Simpson's consecutive hundred-yard-games record.

"Is he close?" asked Ditka, calming down.

"Very."

"Okay, you're right, let's do it."

(Payton would rush for 121 yards that night.)

The Bears changed in silence after the game, hurried to the airport, flew home to Chicago. They arrived to the stillness of 3:00 a.m. freeways, water towers and factories, glass buildings in the distance. In the coming weeks, various theories were posited to explain the loss. According to Buddy Ryan, it was a fluke: "We get a punt blocked before the half, and they end up scoring. Another time we had 'em third-and-long, Hampton's rushing the passer, and the ball hits Dan in the helmet. It goes up in the air about forty feet, and one of their guys catches it for a touchdown." According to Otis Wilson, Ditka, who insisted on passing when Walter could have gotten the needed points on the ground, was to blame. "Walter had a hundred-plus yards rushing, but Ditka had to match Marino. But you don't match Marino." According to McMichael, it was the result of too much partying. McMahon had been on the beach all day and some players said he reeked of beer in the huddle. "There was no doubt in my mind, if we'd have played the Dolphins at twelve o'clock on a Sunday, we'd have beat the shit out of them." Ditka's explanation was most succinct. It was honesty in defeat that made him a better headman than Buddy: "What happened? I'll tell you what happened. We were out-coached."

In retrospect, the loss was probably a good thing. A thumping was exactly what the team needed to pop the bubble of overconfidence. It got the attention of the players and made them realize they were not invincible.

The NFL is obsessed with winning: in no other sport do you hear such frequent mention of that word. Lombardi said, "Winning isn't everything, it's the only thing." Ditka said, "My coaching philosophy is the same as yours. I want to win." Halas said, "Never go to bed a loser." The best baseball team loses sixty or so games a year. In hockey and basketball, the championship is decided in a seven-game series, meaning you can lose three times in the last week and still hoist the trophy. Football's too rough for that—it takes days to recover from an hour on the field. A single loss at the wrong moment ends everything. In such a world, if you have to lose, it's better to do it early. The '85 Bears will not go undefeated? Good. Let them focus on the games that matter. "Losing to Miami was the best thing that could have happened," Tim Wrightman told me. "Now that the undefeated thing was off our back, we were all like, To hell with it, let's just go out and get our fucking Super Bowl rings."

It was the morning following the loss in Miami—just a few hours after the team plane had touched down—that the Bears shot the video for their ridiculously boastful "Super Bowl Shuffle." The players had recorded the song a month before. It was Willie Gault's project, his way out of the life, as the gangsters say. He'd been a world-class sprinter in college, a member of the 1980 Olympic team that had missed the games because of America's boycott. He was the Bears' deep threat, the speedster who stretched the defense. His game expressed his character: elegant but soft, a zipperoo-deficient blur of speed. He shied away from contact and sometimes dropped the ball in big situations. Then, just as you were about to give up, he would take a punt or a short pass and go the distance.

Willie planned to go west after football, make his name in Hollywood. He'd had a cameo in Rob Lowe's movie *About Last Night . . . ,* which he never stopped talking about. Everyone's known a guy like that, a beautiful dreamer, forever on the make. He wears a high hat, and each gesture tells you that he's bound for gaudier scenes. Five or fifteen or twenty years down the road he'll realize that this was his moment, back here, with a lot of people he didn't realize he loved. He'd been so busy planning the future that he never noticed the dream country from every window of the bus.

Dick Meyer brought the idea to Willie: a single cut by the increasingly popular Bears, with profits going to charity. Meyer owned a music company called Red Label. He got Willie on board, then Willie got the other guys. Twenty-four Bears agreed to participate.

Ditka frowned on it. McMichael laughed at it. Hampton called it pretentious. It was a lot of things, but not pretentious. It could have used a little more pretension. It was just a bunch of stiff jocks in blue jerseys and tight football pants dancing like robots as they rapped phrases about their identity and intentions. The music had been repurposed from "The Kingfish Shuffle," a rap based on the Amos 'n Andy character. The lyrical method, a peacock's self-portrait, is as American as Jack London. It can be heard in everything from Mark Twain's *Life on the Mississippi* ("I scratch my head with the lightning and purr myself to sleep with the thunder! When I'm cold, I bile the Gulf of Mexico and bathe in it; when I'm hot I fan myself with an equinoctial storm; when I'm thirsty I reach up and suck a cloud dry like a sponge; when I range the earth hungry, famine follows in my tracks!") to Bo Diddley's "Who Do You Love" ("Tombstone hand and a graveyard mind, just 22 and I don't mind dyin'") to the pre-fight patter of Muhammad Ali ("I done rassled with an alligator, I done tussled with a whale, I done handcuffed lightning, thrown thunder in jail!").

The Bears' take on the tradition was crude but wonderful in the way it seemed to blow out the mental detritus of a lifetime of losing. It opened with Payton dispelling any criticism of motives. Why were the Bears dancing like fools, he asked. Simple: to help the needy. Richard Dent called himself the Sackman and prophesied his imminent return, Gault characterized himself as a chocolate swirl, and Steve Fuller compared himself to thunder and lightning.

The video was shot at the Park West, a music venue on the North Side. Payton and McMahon refused to participate. "When the idea was brought to us, it was to feed the homeless on Thanksgiving and Christmas," McMahon told me. "It seemed like a nice thing. But I didn't know anything about a video—Willie only told us about the record. Then two or three weeks later, he said, 'Okay, now we have to make the video.' We're like, Shit, you didn't say anything about a video. And they had us taping it the day after we lost in Miami. Everybody got home at three or four in the morning—you had to be at the studio at eight o'clock. Walter and I told them, 'We'll do it after the season.' But they said, 'No, we have to release it with the record.' So we just didn't show up. They did everybody's part. Walter and I finally did ours a week later, after practice, in the racquetball court at Halas Hall. We weren't too happy about it."

The song was a smash in Chicago. More than half a million copies sold. James Joyce never won a Nobel Prize. *Taxi Driver* lost the Oscar to *Rocky*. Jim Thorpe had all his gold medals stripped. But "The Super Bowl Shuffle" was nominated for a Grammy. Whatever else you might say, it's catchy. A few verses have stuck in my mind: several times a year, they return like a case of tropical sprue. McMahon describing himself as the Punky QB, for example, or Wilson calling himself Mama's Boy Otis, or Fencik identifying himself as the Hit Man. "Fencik shouldn't have done it," McMichael said, "because he showed everybody how horseshit of a dancer he was."

Fencik's dancing *is* terrible, but Fuller's is worse; he was Eddie Murphy's parody of a white guy, the backup quarterback flailing his arms as he raps.

Like many vivid childhood memories, "The Super Bowl Shuffle" fills me with a special kind of shame today. My face turns red when I hear it; my neck tingles. As you grow up you become too tasteful to enjoy things that once filled you with pleasure. Past thirty, most of us become too smart for our own good.

At the time of its release, the greatness of the "Shuffle" was beyond question. I had the single and the video. I scattered it on mix tapes, so, now and then, between Springsteen and Dylan, it came as a surprise that made me smile. In the summer of 1986, some friends and I, members of a softball team called the North Shore Screen Doors, recorded our own version. I remember just one verse, written for my friend Mark, who, having contracted the "kissing disease," missed most of the season:

I swing like golf to psych a pitcher out
that's why they call me Mr. Rout.
Doc, give me a shot, so I can play,

cause the Doors are hot every single day.
He said sorry, son, I know how you feel
But you've got to stay in bed till your mono is healed.
And I said, look, I don't want to go out just to get a tan
I want to go do the Screen Door Slam!

The possibility of summoning the jinx—that's the only thing that concerned most of us. Boasting of a triumph that has yet to be accomplished is the worst kind of bad luck. You might as well break a thousand mirrors or walk under every ladder from Glencoe to East Wacker Drive. There was a terrible history of this in Chicago. In 1969, shortly before the Cubs collapsed, a few musicians recorded the song "Hey, Hey" with the chorus, "Hey, Hey, holy mackerel, no doubt about it, the Cubs are on their way!" In 1972, Steve Goodman, a folk singer from Park Ridge, released "Go Cubs Go!," the refrain of which ("Hey, Chicago, what do you say, the Cubs are gonna win today!") turned haunting when the Cubs crumbled. In 1984, a month before the Cubs imploded in the National League playoffs, a handful of players released a country single that seemed an ominous precursor to "The Shuffle." Leon Durham sang on it, as did Jody Davis and the ace pitcher Rick Sutcliffe: "As sure as there's ivy on the center-field wall, the men in blue are gonna win it all."

I remember an emotional phone call with my brother who was in law school. "The Super Bowl Shuffle" struck him as an act of madness. "The idiots!" he said, sobbing, "have they no memory? Don't they understand the importance of precedent?" (My brother was halfway through a first-year course on Constitutional law.) I defended the Bears—this team was different, I said, better and nastier, strong enough to whip the jinx. "The outcome is not a matter of curses," I said. "It's a matter of deciding who will be the hit-ees and who will be the hit-ors."

"You're too young," shouted my brother. "You don't remember. I sang 'Go Cubs Go' all summer in 1972 and look what happened!" Then he said something my parents said whenever a topic like the Cuban missile crisis came up: "To you, it's history, but it's my life!"

In the end, the Bears were saved by the very success of "The Super Bowl Shuffle," which resulted in copycats. The Dallas Cowboys released "Living the American Dream." The Cleveland Browns released "Masters of the Gridiron." The L.A. Raiders released "Silver and Black

Attack." The L.A. Rams released "Let's Ram It." When everyone courts the jinx, there is no jinx.

The story ended in a classically Chicago way. There was controversy regarding the money and how much of it would actually go to charity, participants felt betrayed, and the Illinois attorney general, Neil Hartigan, had to get involved. All these years later, it's still a sore subject. "There were a lot of hard feelings about it because even though money went to charity, many people thought more should have gone," Gary Fencik told ESPN.com in 2005. "Even the backup band wasn't happy with their cut. But it is what it is."

14

THE FERGUSON HIT

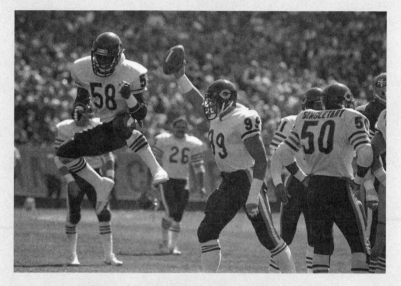

Wilber Marshall (58) and Dan Hampton (with the ball) celebrating during their
December 22, 1985, thrashing of Joe Montana and the San Francisco 49ers,
as Mike Singletary (50) gets back to business

Every now and then, a single play captures the spirit of a team. It can stand for an entire season. If you want to learn about the '85 Bears, you can talk to old players and old coaches about tactics, or you can simply say, "Tell me about the Ferguson Hit."

The Bears underperformed in the weeks following the Miami game, stumbling through the remainder of their schedule with workmanlike wins over the Colts and the Jets. There was something bleak about this part of the season. It was like the chapter in the book in which the golden boy is set upon by gloom and wonders about the purpose of life. After all, these games had little meaning, the Bears having long since clinched their division as well as home-field advantage in the playoffs. Ditka worried that his players would bring this bad mood into the postseason. The landfill of history is packed with teams that peaked too soon. The Bears needed a shot of adrenaline to wake the barking dogs.

They ended the season at the Silverdome in Detroit. The Detroit Lions were at best mediocre, but their general manager had traded for one of my favorite quarterbacks, Joe Ferguson, who, at thirty-six, was still a creative playmaker and a terrific scrambler. I wanted the Bears to win but expected to see Ferguson complete a few passes. It's a weakness of mine: I root for the old guys, their old guys as well as my own. What actually happened gave me a sense of what it must have been like for fans whose teams fell into the gears of the 46.

It was on the second or third play of the game. Ferguson took a snap, dropped back, looked downfield, but only for a moment, as the Bears were coming. He scrambled outside, doing his Ferguson thing, stumbled—watching it again, I think, *Go down!*—righted himself, then looked up just in time to see Wilber Marshall coming full steam, lowering his head, launching. The crown of Marshall's helmet hit the aging quarterback square on the chin. He went skyward, then dropped. You could see that he was out cold. He landed in the heavy way of an inanimate object. As this was happening to his body, his soul, his spirit, his consciousness, everything that made Joe Ferguson Joe Ferguson, was somewhere else. "I can still see the lick Marshall put on Ferguson," said Ditka. "My God, I thought he'd killed him."

The Lions' coach came out onto the field, followed by a trainer. Someone picked up Ferguson's arm and let it go. It dropped, lifeless. For the moment, he'd been turned into a cadaver. The backup quarterback, Eric Hipple, walked onto the field to talk to the coach. He stood there as the staff worked on Ferguson. It was a naturally occurring split screen: dead Ferguson and concerned coach; concerned coach and fresh quarterback emerging from his can.

A few minutes later, Ferguson, having been revived, sat on the sideline, helmet off, hair tousled, dazed. I've seen the same look on the faces of old hobos on the Bowery, methadone addicts on withdrawal, winos with delirium tremens. If El Greco came back, he might want to paint Joe Ferguson five minutes after that hit, his eyes as wide as saucers, a fog all around him, the roof of the Silverdome rising above.

Marshall's blow did not knock Ferguson out of the NFL. In fact, he stuck around for another four seasons, playing his last game for Indianapolis in 1990. But whenever I spotted him, I would think, But I saw him die in Detroit!

While working on this book, I decided to track down Joe Ferguson. It took about twenty seconds to find his number. He sells real estate in Arkansas. I got his machine. I was surprised by his voice. I had watched him play but had never listened to him talk: he had the thickest Southern accent I've ever heard; he sounded like a moonshiner from the Ozarks. Who'd buy a house from this guy? I left a message, telling him I wanted to discuss his career with Buffalo and Detroit, his playing style, his college glory, and maybe we could touch on the game against the Bears in 1985. He left a message for me a few days later, saying he'd be happy to talk, but he never returned any of my follow-up calls.

Around this time, I met Gary Fencik in Chicago. I told him about my back-and-forth with Ferguson. He laughed. "What's so funny?" I asked.

"Well, it's just that Ferguson's never going to talk to you about that play. I know, because I tried, too. We happened to be at the same golf tournament. And I said to myself, 'Hey, Joe Ferguson!' So I went over, really dying to talk about it, but before I got within ten feet, he puts up his hand and says, 'I know what you want to talk about and it will not be discussed. And besides,' he said, 'I'm the worst guy to talk to about it. I don't remember anything that happened the day before or for two days after. It's completely blank. I recovered, and that's all.'"

For the Bears, the Ferguson Hit was an elixir. It set the tone for the playoffs. It closed the season with a flourish, put an exclamation point on a body of work: four seconds of action that captured the essence of the 46. Especially telling is the fact that Marshall's play would now get you suspended. (He was fined.) Hitting with the helmet, hitting in the head, hitting a defenseless player, hitting to injure—it's everything officials are trying to drum out of the league. As Plank said when I spoke to him, "My entire career would be considered a penalty today."

It's a matter of special interest to veterans and coaches of the '85 Bears: When your entire style of play is banned, what does it do to your legacy? And what does it mean to fans who loved that team and writers who gloried in it? If you get pleasure from watching the Ferguson Hit, what does it say about you?

"What the league has done with the rules is right," Ditka told me. "You've got to protect the player from injury at all costs. Football's a collision sport. People collide at high speed. And what's happening, in my opinion, is that the helmet, once meant for protection, has become a weapon. They're trying to get people to quit leading with their head. There's a lot of other ways to tackle. Originally, when you were taught to tackle, it wasn't with your head. The new rules are just trying to get us back to that."

Other football men were less sympathetic. After discoursing on the glory of big hits, Bill Tobin, who worked for the Bears from 1975 to 1993, eventually becoming the team's general manager, told me, "And now they're saying, well, late in life, these injuries are showing up. Hey, if you're a coal miner, things show up. If you're a farmer, things show up. The liabilities are there and if you want to take them, go for it. If you don't, get up in the stands and be a cheerleader or join the band."

"They're sissies," said running back coach Johnny Roland, who was himself a stand-out ball carrier for the Cardinals and the Giants. "They can't even play football now. They don't even know how to tackle. They want to protect the quarterback 'cause they're making so much money and the fans want to see the quarterback. But if you get a good running shot at a guy, hell, that's why they call it football. They don't call it tiddleywinks, they call it football."

Hipple finished the game at quarterback for Detroit. He was sacked again and again but kept getting back on his feet. It was never really close, which made his performance inspiring. In the way of Hemingway's matadors, he seemed to stand for mankind in its fight against absurdity. Near the end, he was hit in the same way as Ferguson: square on the chin by an airborne Wilber Marshall. The ball was knocked from his hands and recovered by the Fridge, who went forty yards before being hauled down at the Lions' 20. It was a prized image in Chicago: the joy of the fat man in the open field. (Ditka: "Fridge is a big man with some fat on; not just a big fat man.") But what lingers is Hipple, a mile behind the play, struggling back to his feet.

The players were celebrating on the flight home from Detroit, getting loud. Finally, Ditka got on the PA system: *All right, ladies, listen up! There's nothing to celebrate yet. We have yet to win a single fucking thing that matters. I want you to spend some serious time over Christmas thinking about that and trying to find yourselves.* A moment later, as the players stared glumly at each other, McMahon came on the PA: *And after you find yourselves, ladies, come find me. I'll be in a gutter somewhere.*

15

THE YEAR WITHOUT A WINTER

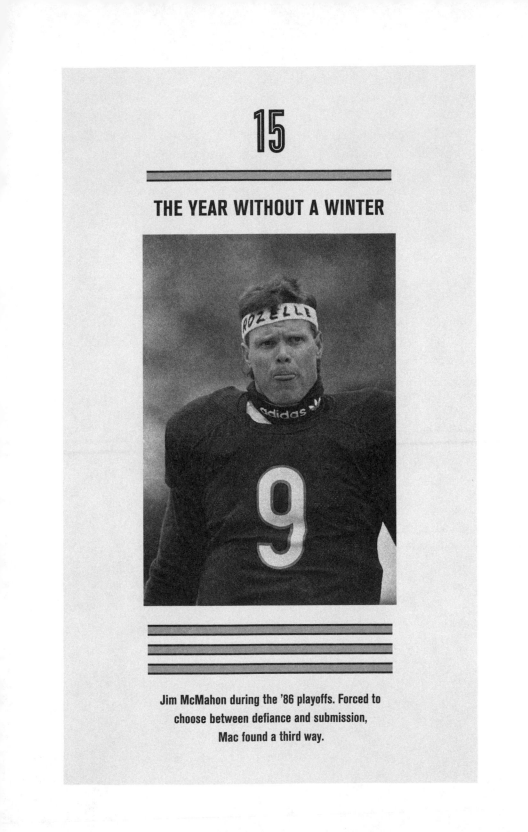

Jim McMahon during the '86 playoffs. Forced to
choose between defiance and submission,
Mac found a third way.

For me, Chicago will always be as it was in the mid-1980s.
That was the city as I loved it, the world at noon. It was Greek Town
and Wrigley Field and beers at the Checkerboard Lounge. It was days
at the beach and nights on the toboggan and house parties in Winnetka. It was being chased by the cops and sneaking out and the city in
the distance. It was Howlin' Wolf and red hots at Big Al's and frosty
malts and denim jackets and girls in penny loafers and stone-washed
jeans. Every other place is measured against the city when the world
was whole. That's when I was young and my parents were young and
my brother and sister were home and we huddled together when the
big snows came. When I look at my own children, I am filled with envy.
Everyone lives in Eden and everyone gets banished. Everyone falls from
grace just for being alive.

Chicago was the center of the world. It's where John Hughes set all
those movies, where the Belushis lived like shambling comedic saints
in Wheaton, where Big Twist & the Mellow Fellows played at Biddy
Mulligan's every Thursday night. The city had shaken off the torpor of
the 1970s: Jane Byrne was gone, Harold Washington was going. (He
died in office in 1987.) We would soon hand our fate to another Daley.
For what are the bad times but a nap between Daleys? It was the start
of a renaissance that continues, the rebirth of the greatest city. New
York has one foot in Europe. Los Angeles is a collection of suburbs.
Miami is café con leche. New Orleans is drunk. Seattle wears flannel.
San Francisco is beautiful vistas and empty streets. Boston is ancient.

But Chicago is America. The '85 Bears seemed to symbolize the city in its resurgence, the reawakening of the beast after a funka-delic slumber. It was not the fifteen wins—it was how they were achieved, the smash-mouth style that seemed to capture the spirit of the town.

In previous years, after the Bears played their last game, a melan-choly settled over everything like a cloud. It marked the beginning of the true winter, a dark stretch that did not end until March or April, a season of ice, in which the sun was off in another country. But in 1986, the Bears kept on winning. The *Tribune* ran an editorial: "What have the Bears done for Chicago? They have given us something to hope and cheer for in January, the time when ordinarily that bleak postholiday depression sets in and all we have to look forward to are subzero tem-peratures, blizzards and watching our cars rust. This January, cabin fever has been replaced by Bears fever."

In Chicago, 1986 was the year without a winter.

The Bears, having the best record in the NFL, earned a bye in week one of the playoffs, jumping directly to the second round. On January 5, 1986, they played the New York Giants. For Ditka, the big challenge was Lawrence Taylor, LT, the Giants' All-Pro outside linebacker. Many consider him the best ever to play the position. He was a disruptive force, fast and hard-hitting. He set up a few feet off the line, outside the tackle. When the quarterback dropped back, LT was coming from the blind side. If he got by the left tackle, he could shut down Payton and concuss McMahon. He could tip over the king. Before the Bears did anything else, they had to solve LT.

The Bears have a tradition of playing dirty, playing right on the line, that goes back to Halas. Barely legal is legal, which is how they dealt with Taylor. On the second or third series, as McMahon dropped back, Dennis McKinnon, a Bears wide receiver who was just the opposite of Willie Gault—tough instead of fast, he never flinched—sprinted downfield, seemingly following a deep pattern. Taylor forgot McKinnon as soon as he vanished from his peripheral vision, focusing instead on McMahon's eyes: Where's he looking? Where's he gonna throw? Once forgotten, McKinnon raced at Taylor from *his* blind side, lowered his helmet, and launched at the big man. It's a play feared by linebackers, a play many have tried to get banned: the crackback block. Delivered just right, it can end a career. Even a giant of a man is perched on very human knees.

McKinnon's crackback block—Taylor believed it had been ordered by Ditka—did not end LT's career, or even knock him from the game, but it did infuriate him. He lost his focus as he lost his temper. He began to look over his shoulder, wondering if some receiver was closing in for another crackback. When LT should have been hitting, he was thinking about getting hit. He'd gone from hit-or to hit-ee. At one point, he stood before the Bears' bench screaming at Ditka. He told Giants' linemen to hold Payton, *Stand him up so I can finish him.* The Bears did not have to worry about LT because LT took care of himself. Asked what the team had done to contain the great Lawrence Taylor, Ditka said, "Knocked the shit out of him."

It was 14° at kickoff, but the wind made it feel colder. It came from the lake in twenty-five-mile-per-hour gusts. It was nasty. The network broadcast a helicopter shot of Soldier Field. It was white as ice. The lake was blue. Ditka paced the sidelines in an old-time Bears jacket, the sort worn by college lettermen, a winter cap, sunglasses. Giants quarterback Phil Simms spent much of the afternoon on his back. New York's star runner, Joe Morris, went fourteen yards on his first run but never did much after that. In the end, he gained thirty-two yards on twelve carries. When he left in the second quarter, he was gripping his head. "We were hitting him so hard he said he got a migraine so he did not have to play," Dave Duerson told a reporter. "He didn't want to carry that rock." The camera zoomed in on Hampton's hands. They were wrapped in tape, and blood showed through like a steak through butcher's paper. Each finger was mangled, proof of his commitment. For stretches, the game seemed to return to football's origins: it was mob ball, where anything is permissible as long as the fool holds the dingus. When the Giants missed a field goal, Ditka did a triple fist pump. He chewed his gum like a fiend.

The sequence that broke the Giants came in the opening quarter. First Joe Morris was tackled in the backfield. Then Phil Simms was knocked down just as he got rid of the ball. Then Simms was dropped for a twelve-yard loss by Dent. After starting on the 35-yard line, the Giants ended the series at their own 20. The New York punter set up on the 12. His name was Sean Landeta. He was a twenty-three-year-old

Dan Hampton (99) leaping over the enemy to get to the quarterback. October 28, 1985

rookie. He blew on his hands. He was cold. If you looked closely, you could see confusion in his eyes. You could see his breath, too, a cloud of panic that drifted above Soldier Field. He caught the long snap with brittle hands, took two steps and lofted the ball, setting up for the kick. At the crucial moment, he made the mistake of looking up. The Bears were coming at him jailbreak fashion, howling and waving their arms. If the tightrope walker looks down between buildings, he sees a vortex. The earth drops away and he's falling. Landeta kicked the ball, but the ball was not there. *How strange. He missed it completely.* By then, the Bears were over the wall. Shaun Gayle, a cornerback playing special teams, scooped it up at the 5-yard line, took two strides, and was in the end zone. It was the shortest punt return for a touchdown in playoff history.

Landeta later claimed the wind had taken the ball, a mystery gust from a mystery system. I met him six or seven years later, interviewed him in training camp before another season with the Giants. He would play forever, or football's version of forever, taking his final snap in 2005, when he was forty-three. As soon as I identified myself as a Bears fan, he put up his hands in the way of Ferguson and said, "I know, I know, but it really was the wind."

He was such a nice man, and such a good punter, and so adamant that I believed him. At least until I spoke to the Bears who were on the field that day, all of whom laughed at the mystery wind. "He can say what he wants, but I was there!" Otis Wilson told me. "The wind blew no damn ball. Go back and watch. It's clear as day. That boy looked up at the wrong time and what did he see? The abyss. And when you look into the abyss, the abyss is looking right back into you."

The Bears won 21 to nothing. The Giants quarterbacks—plural, because, at some point, another can was opened—were sacked for sixty yards. They gave up more territory than they gained. McMahon threw two touchdown passes and Payton ran for ninety-three yards. John Madden, who announced the game on CBS, called it "the most dominant performance by a team I have ever seen on a football field."

A few days before the game, McMahon received a warning. He'd been seen wearing an Adidas headband on the field, which violated the NFL's agreement with advertisers. In flashing the name of his sponsor, Mac was selling something he did not own: network television time. He was ordered to cease and desist. When he protested, pointing out that he'd been wearing the headband most of the season without complaint, he was told, *Yeah, well, things change.* McMahon is a true individual, the sort of person who positions himself in opposition to authority by instinct. He does not like being told what to do, especially if it strikes him as arbitrary. If Ditka offered a legitimate criticism, he'd listen. If Ditka Sybilized, Mac flipped him off. If he'd been alive during the Revolutionary War, he would have been in a hemlock tree, picking off redcoats. As coaches in Chicago and at BYU had learned, the surest way to get him to do something was to issue a warning not to. He wore the Adidas headband during the Giants game, proudly, staring right into the camera. Pete Rozelle, the NFL commissioner, levied a $5,000 fine, which would increase if McMahon wore the headband on the field again. It became the story of the week: Would McMahon defy the commissioner, or would he submit?

This controversy was probably good for the Bears; it took the pressure off. As we all focused on Mac's headband, the team was preparing for the second round against the L.A. Rams. To some, they looked like trouble. They were weak at quarterback but had a player many considered the best running back in the game, Eric Dickerson, big and fast, a challenge to tackle. For several days, reporters wrote about the greatness of the Dick. He had gained 248 yards against Dallas the previous week. But when asked to comment, Buddy Ryan predicted a bad day for the running back: under 50 yards and multiple fumbles. "He'll lay it on the ground for us," Ryan said. "We expect him to lay it on the ground at least three times." This only fueled the fire, filling the air with nervous talk about headbands and defiance and Miami and comeuppance, and remember what goeth before a fall, and so on and so forth, with each round of reports stoking the old Chicago fear of collapse, and the '69 Cubs, and how good they looked in '84, and the '83 White Sox, and what about "The Super Bowl Shuffle" and the jinx, and *My God, Dickerson can fly!* until finally, in the way of a strong, calming father, Mike Ditka went on TV and explained the reality of the situation to the hysterical fans. "There are teams that are fairhaired, and teams that aren't," he told us. "There are teams named Smith and teams named Grabowski. The Rams are Smith. The Bears are Grabowski." He went on to explain how the Smiths would be coming to the Grabowskis' house on Sunday, where it's mean, where it's violent, and where, in the third quarter, it's going to snow.

It was in fact freakishly temperate on game day. Upper twenties, low thirties. When McMahon came out for warms-up, a plug of tobacco in his lip, throwing elegantly, each gesture exaggerated, he was wearing the headband. It portended an act of keen defiance, as Pete Rozelle would be attending the game in person.

The tenor of the day would be established in the first possession: either Dickerson was going to be able to run, or it was over. He was tall and lean, an exclamation point broken free from the page. He wore clear sports glasses, the strappy kind that hold fast and resemble skindiving gear. He was handed the ball on the Rams' first play. He went here and there, then ran bang into Fencik, who'd snuck up to the line. Any beginning that includes the safety tackling the star runner in his own backfield can be considered inauspicious. "Here's Fencik," said John Madden, "clean, nice guy, good-looking guy, Yale and all that, but when he gets that look in his eyes, it's Jekyll and Hyde."

McMahon soon took over, leading the Bears downfield. He got to the Rams' 16-yard line. The TV camera moved across the stands: a wash of faces, a thousand superfans, a million beautiful mustaches, ten million brawts, a billion links of sausage. He crouched behind center, read the defense, began to shout. He dropped back, looked and looked, spotted something, and took off, feet flying, head high. When McMahon ran, you knew you were seeing something. It was the way he moved, how he carried himself, wild, intoxicated. He went through the defense like a drunk going through a bar—filled with bad intent. He slowed as he crossed the goal line, raised his arms, then handed the ball to Kurt Becker, who spiked it with the joy of a lineman who, on most occasions, remains anonymous.

A moment later, Mac was on one knee on the sideline, grizzled, packed with chew, watching the defense. He was beside a warmer, a blowing machine. He turned and looked at the camera. No Adidas. He was instead wearing a blank headband on which he'd written ROZELLE. A small act of comic rebellion, it hit the city like a starburst. *McMahon!* Rozelle loved it: selling Adidas was one thing, selling the commissioner was something else. In the world of professional sports, which tends to be humorless, a joke can feel like a revolution. Given a choice between defiance and submission, McMahon found a third way.

The Rams had their best chance in the second quarter. They were moving. They gave the ball to Dickerson. He plowed ahead, vanished, then popped above the pile. He looked pained as he was stood up, driven back, and dropped. It was a violent collision, delivered by Singletary, one of those helmet-shattering hits that make everyone in the stadium groan. Writing about it later, Singletary sounded weirdly sexual: "Oh, what a shot! It was beautiful, orgasmic, a lightning bolt that resulted in a one yard loss. I screamed.

"I imagine kids fantasizing that when Otis or Wilber makes a sack it's them out there on Soldier Field playing before 60,000 fans," Singletary added. "Their whole week, their life, is made better, more meaningful, and we have something to do with it. It's therapy when we win."

In the course of sixteen possessions, the Rams went three-and-out eight times. They averaged less than two yards a play. Their longest drive went twenty-seven yards. Buddy was wrong. Dickerson did not fumble three times, but he did fumble twice, which will do in a pinch. In the second half, just as Ditka had prognosticated, it started to snow—not regular flakes either, but silver dollars that fell like happy tears. "God, it was beautiful," Ditka wrote. ". . . the big slow flakes coming down like in one of those Christmas snow globes, and it was perfect. Bears weather, Bears dominance, Bears success, Bears kicking ass."

Late in the third, McMahon changed Ditka's play at the line. You can tell by the way Ditka explodes as Mac drops back, rolls left, then finds Gault in the end zone. Touchdown. Mac races downfield, in search of linemen to head-butt. He walks over to Ditka, who glares, shouts, turns, stalks off. It's like the moment in the movie when the veteran chews out the flying ace: *Yes, it worked, but someday that kind of maverick stunt will get us all killed!*

Bill Murray is on the sideline, standing beside the blowers, wearing an iron-man-era leather helmet in the snow. He's laughing and smiling, as happy as any other fan who'd lived through years of collapse. "I wonder how Murray got on the sideline," says Madden. "The league office won't like that. They won't like McMahon's headband and they won't like that, either." At one point, the camera pulls back to reveal the city skyline. It's smaller than it is today, half the buildings, a third the size. It's a jarring image that reminds you that this story is set in the same place George Lucas set *Star Wars*: a long time ago in a galaxy far, far away.

All the while, you can feel energy building on the defensive side of the ball. It was one of the things that made Buddy's defense so hard to play: he never did what was expected. With a game in hand, most coaches would shift into a prevent formation, put in the backups, call off the dogs. But Buddy kept blitzing. The blitz has always been a rarity: an aggressive defense might blitz ten times all day. During a game in 1984, Buddy called up eight straight blitzes. He was like that crazy fuck at the roulette table who bets only double zero. A guy like that makes you nervous: either he knows something, or he's insane.

The Bears kept after Rams quarterback Dieter Brock. Something was going to happen. You could feel it. Then, with two minutes and fifty seconds left, something did. Richard Dent, coming from the blind side, unblocked, running free, crushed the Rams' QB. Brock's body, his poor weak human body, folded like a bad musical. The football came loose, bounded away. Marshall picked it up and took off. Just like that, he had men with him: the Fridge and Otis, a security detail racing toward the end zone as the stadium burst. And every beer was spilled. And every brawt was coughed up. And every card was dealt. And every cherry dropped in every slot machine. And every bride said "I do." "I was ten, fifteen yards behind the play, running like mad, trying to keep up," Fencik told me. "It was every dream I ever had coming true. It was every game of snowy backyard football going exactly as I'd pictured it. In that moment—my God, I will never experience anything like it again!—I was a player on the field, but, as I was chasing Wilber in the snow, I was a fan, too. I was a fan in a stadium filled with fans, and so happy because the Bears were finally going to the Super Bowl!"

The crowd counted off the last ten seconds: five, four, three . . .

In Chicago, you come into the street after a game like that and the city is one giant room and everyone is hugging and shouting and going crazy. I never had World War II; I never had V-J day; I was never a sailor and I never kissed a girl in Times Square—but I did have this.

In the locker room, Pete Rozelle presented Virginia and Ed McCaskey with the NFC Championship Trophy, which, in March 1984, had been renamed for George Halas. Payton hugged Virginia as Dick Butkus walked from locker to locker, shaking hands. Ditka got the team together. In an attempt at eloquence, he quoted Robert Frost but mangled it. In mangling it, he wrote his own poem, the song of the steelworker's son who's gone all the way. "You had to cry watching Ditka after the game as layer by layer Iron Mike began to melt," Singletary wrote. "He stood in front of us, smoking a cigar, head down, lifting it only to speak. You knew that he was thinking of Papa Bear—that he'd finally re-paid the old man's confidence. 'I just want to say, you guys have accomplished something special,' coach said. Down went the head, the feet shuffled. There were tears in his eyes when he spoke again. 'There's a poem,' he said: 'We've gone many miles, but there's more to go before we can sleep.'"

16

A BUNCH OF CRYBABIES

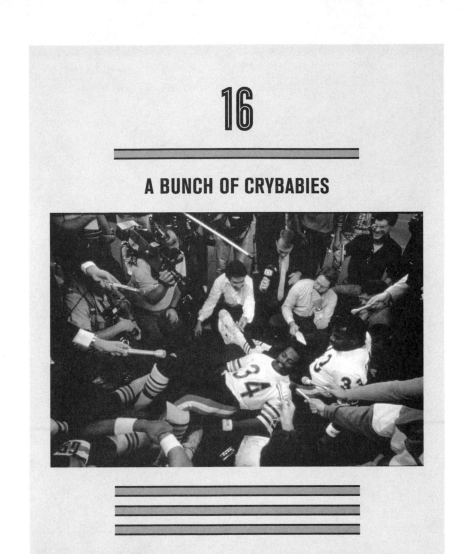

Walter Payton, voguing for the press during Super Bowl week, 1986

I arrived in New Orleans on Thursday afternoon. I checked into a motel in Metairie. I was staying with my friend Matt Lederer. Each day, we woke at 11:00 a.m., watched an hour of TV, then caught a taxi to the French Quarter. I was seventeen, in possession of money that I had not earned, decked out in Bears regalia, and filled with the old zipperoo. It seemed like the entire city of Chicago was down there, mingling and exchanging predictions. Everyone had a story: some of us had followed the team for years, remembered Ditka as a player and only wanted to live long enough to see one more championship; some of us were new to the team and believed this is how it would always be; some of us were born in the desert and had known nothing but this wandering life—but all of us fell upon New Orleans like parched rats, gulping down milk and honey.

As soon as the Bears arrived, they were awash in controversy. The first issue had to do with McMahon's ass, which he had bruised while sliding during the Rams game. "Yeah, I remember it," said Kurt Becker, who shared a room with Mac in New Orleans. "It's funny to remember a bruise on another man's ass twenty-five years later, but it was so disgusting. I couldn't forget it even if I wanted to. And I want to." Becker likened the bruise to a map on which different shades of purple denote varying elevations. McMahon believed the bruise could be properly treated only by a Japanese acupuncturist who'd helped him before: Hiroshi Shiriashi. But when Shiriashi turned up for the flight to New Orleans, Mike McCaskey wouldn't let him on the plane. McMahon used his first Super Bowl Week press conference to denounce McCaskey. It sounds silly, but for several days the main topic of conversation, even among old Chicago guys, was the condition of McMahon's butt and the effectiveness of non-Western medicine. The story reached its apogee midweek, when McMahon mooned a news chopper.

The second issue was more and less serious. Early one morning, a New Orleans DJ went on the radio and said that McMahon, while partying in the French Quarter, had been heard describing the men of New Orleans as stupid and the women as sluts. More serious because it resulted in death threats and turned Mac into a villain; less serious because the DJ later admitted he'd invented the story. The comments were out of character, anyway. McMahon never insulted civilians.

As fans, we worried that such sideshows suggested the Bears were taking the Patriots too lightly. Many players did indeed consider them pretenders. Chicago played New England the second week of the season, a game in which they sacked Patriots quarterback Tony Eason six times and knocked him down constantly. They beat him up and put a fear in him that, according to McMichael, never went away. Hampton said he knew the Super Bowl would be a romp that Wednesday, when he watched Eason at a press conference. He could tell just by looking at the quarterback's eyes. Worried, scared, he had not come to fight. He was hoping only to survive. Singletary had taken a room by himself in the hotel. He stripped a sheet off the second bed and hammered it to the wall, improvising a movie screen, where he watched hour after hour of film. As his teammates partied, the middle linebacker, awash in room service plates, searched the Patriots offense for weaknesses.

The Bears had a final meeting the day before the Super Bowl. Ditka said his piece, then the offense and defense split up for separate discussions. Buddy went through the game plan, then, at the moment when he'd normally offer some parting wisdom, just stood quietly, as if considering. There'd been rumors. Everyone heard them during the playoffs: that Buddy, after five years of battling Ditka, had finally been offered a head coaching job of his own and would soon leave for Philadelphia. If true, the Super Bowl would be his last game as a Bear, his last game at the helm of a defense he had shaped in his own image. Buddy was more than a coach. He was the leader of a sect, where hitting was a ritual and concussing was a triumph and getting concussed was a sacrifice. For many of these men, football was Buddy Ball. Playing for an ordinary nickel-loving coach was hard to imagine. And yet they were not naïve. They knew it was the same for coaches as for players: careers in the game being so vanishingly short, you take the opportunity. As the flanker tells the owner in the movie version of *North Dallas Forty*, "We're not the team. You're the team. We're only the equipment."

Buddy admitted none of this; talking about next year while the fate of the current season is yet to be decided violates league rules as well as a taboo. It's a mean, violent world: take your eyes off the prize, you're dead. It's exactly how heavily favored teams blow championships. But Buddy let his players understand the truth in his silence, his lumpy awkwardness. Then, when each man had stopped and considered and realized—the end of Buddy would be the end of the elite unit, the end of an ethos—he cleared his throat, pushed his glasses up his nose, and said, "No matter what happens after tomorrow, you guys are my heroes," then walked out.

There was a moment of silence. It distended. It went on. In it, you could hear sobs and great big men weeping, tears flowing down thick gleaming faces. "Guys were sniffling and crying. Real quiet," Ron Rivera, a backup linebacker on the '85 Bears and the current head coach of the Carolina Panthers, said later. "Then all of a sudden, out of nowhere, McMichael goes, 'What a bunch of crybabies. We're getting ready to play the most important game of our lives, and all you guys can do is whine about this?' And he grabs a chair and throws it across the room and it sticks in the chalkboard."

It's a story told and retold by Bears fans, painted like a scene from the Passion, done in stained glass. In it, McMichael performs the same service as the Polish cop on Michigan Avenue who said, "Get your heads up. Tomorrow is another fucking day." The chair stuck in the slate as it sticks in your mind, an image of the controlled rage of the 46.

Then Hampton jumped to his feet, screamed, and drove his hand into the film projector, which busted into gears and springs, and the men, whipped into a frenzy, charged out of the room, which is exactly how Buddy intended it.

Later, when asked if he was happy that Buddy was leaving, Ditka said, "Happy? No, I'm not happy. I'm elated."

———

I recently watched the television broadcast of the 1986 Super Bowl. I had not seen it because I'd been at the game—you actually see a great deal less in person than on TV, which is a predicament for experience collectors. Would you rather know how it feels, or what happened? What struck me, all these years later, was the tremendous silliness of the production: the regal pomp of introductions, old heroes paraded out, officials in golden jackets, smoke machines, plastic grass, and sparkly things. It's one of the reasons the Super Bowl is often a letdown— it's lost in its own ribbons and wrapping. In the end, it's still just a football game. When the announcer spoke to the crowd, he did it with a seriousness I recognized from synagogue: "The referee for today's game, Red Cashion, will now conduct the coin toss ceremony."

The camera sweeps across the crowd: more than seventy thousand people crammed to the rafters of the Superdome. I lean in as the shot lingers on some Bears fans: several wear McMahon jerseys; a few sport full-on movie-quality bear heads. A few years ago, a small plane, carrying two Packers fans home from Soldier Field, crashed. The pilot, who had removed his regalia, was killed instantly, but the passenger, still wearing his cheesehead, was uninjured. I remember where I was sitting that day, the section and the yard line, and am hoping to catch a glimpse of my seventeen-year-old self.

Payton was sent out to represent the Bears in the coin toss. Number 34. In his white jersey. With his headband and Jheri curl. Was he nervous? Sometimes, you get what you want but it comes too late; better if it happens when you are young, before you realized how important it would be. Payton won the toss, and elected to receive. In many ways, the kickoff is the best moment of any football game: the instant after the kicker has made contact and the ball hangs as if frozen and the players race toward collision and the fans hold their breath and it seems as if anything is possible.

The first play was a handoff to Sweetness: he ran seven yards. The second play went to Payton, too. He fumbled. New England recovered. A groan went up from those seats where the fans were dressed like Kodiaks. It was the old ache, the jinx, the disease. "Goddamn it all to hell," said a man behind me, "it's going to be the same story all over again." The Patriots kicked a field goal: 3–0. It was the last competitive moment of the day. As soon as the Bears defense got on, they began to terrorize Tony Eason. He'd been a star at the University of Illinois, six four, 212 pounds, a cannon for an arm. The Patriots had taken him first in the 1983 draft. He was at the start of a seemingly long career. But the Bears had him spooked. "His eyes were bugging out," said Dave Duerson. "He was terrified, really, every snap he was on the field. We were way inside his head."

For a quarterback, playing against the 46 was like surfing: if you didn't want to look like a fool, you had to get beyond the break, into the calm water. But Eason spent the entire afternoon close to shore, dashing here and there as the rollers broke over his head. The worse it got, the tighter he played; the tighter he played, the worse it got. He was chased, knocked down, sacked, intercepted. A nightmare, a humiliation watched by 127 million people. It was the culmination of Buddy in that room with the number 46 circled on the board. By the end of the first quarter, Eason had come to resemble the chicken on the hot plate: his feet were moving, but that didn't mean he was dancing. "I was adept at reading the offensive linemen," McMichael said later. "By their stance, you know if it's going to be run or pass. How do you know? If they're rocked back like they're taking a shit in the woods, it's going to be a pass. Once you've seen that, you look at the quarterback, look at his eyes to see if he's looking downfield, trying to read the coverage. But when I looked at Eason—and this was from the start, right after Payton fumbled and they scored that field goal—his eyes were wide open and empty."

Tony Eason is the only starting quarterback in Super Bowl history to finish the day without a single completion. He would finish zero for six, with three sacks and a fumble. ESPN rated his performance the worst in Super Bowl history. When the Patriots offense came on the field late in the second quarter, Eason stayed on the bench. He was replaced by the veteran Steve Grogan, who had not played in two months. Eason watched from the sideline, helmet off, confused. He was Sonny Liston refusing to come out for the seventh against Cassius Clay. He was Roberto Duran waving his gloves, saying, *No mas.* He was the old can of quarterback, tossed in the bin. He later claimed he'd had the flu, but I knew a kid at Tulane who played catch with him on the quad a day before the game. This kid talked about Eason's perfect spirals, the way the ball exploded from his hand. "Flu? Bullshit. He looked great."

If he did have the flu, it was in the way that Giants running back Joe Morris had a migraine in the middle of the first playoff game: a 46 migraine; a 46 flu. "Hell, what's the boy gonna do?" Otis Wilson said sympathetically. "The Patriots ain't blocking, and he's got these big monsters coming down on him like mad hammers. Shit, give the ball to Grogan and let the old man take the beating."

Eason continued in the NFL for several more seasons, but he was never really the same. He'd been broken by the Bears. I tried and failed to track him down. At last reporting, ten years ago, he was coaching basketball in Sacramento. He's otherwise dropped off the grid. A few years ago, at Super Bowl time, an ESPN reporter, having gotten ahold of Eason's home number, was brushed off by whoever answered. "Tony doesn't like to speak with anyone in the media," the reporter was told, "especially this time of year." When the reporter contacted the University of Illinois and asked if they knew the whereabouts of their former star, he was told, "Good question. We have no idea." Twenty-five years have gone by and Tony Eason is still running from Richard Dent. Like Joe Ferguson, he knows why you're calling and he doesn't want to talk about it.

Meanwhile, the Bears were scoring. McMahon ran for a touchdown, then ran for another; the Fridge scored, ditto Suhey. McMahon

The linebackers—Wilber Marshall (58), Mike Singletary (50), and Otis Wilson (55)—in the afterglow of their biggest win

completed twelve passes for 256 yards. He went off the rails with the headbands, though, coming out with a new one each series: this one to shine a light on juvenile diabetes, that one to remind people of the POWs still in Vietnam, this one a shout-out to his friend PLUTO. It was 23–3 at halftime. The only question was Payton: Would he score, or had he waited all these years to come away with nothing? The potential embarrassment—for Payton, who took these things too seriously—was sharpened by the fact that the Bears kept scoring. Even the scrubs were getting touchdowns. Fans would later point to a specific play as the lost opportunity, the moment Sweetness should've scored. The Bears had the ball on the New England 1-yard line: Payton lined up in the backfield beside Fridge, who everyone assumed would be the blocker and lead the way in. McMahon faked to Walter but gave the ball to Perry, who bulled his way across. "Walter Payton, I guess they figure they got a whole quarter to go," said the announcer, Dick Enberg. This play call was said to show Mike Ditka at his worst: by going with the novelty instead of the runner who'd carried the team for years, he was serving only his own legend.

Late in the fourth quarter, the Bears pulled their starters, including Payton. He sat alone on the bench, helmet off, sad face gleaming. The final score was 46–10. It was the most lopsided contest in Super Bowl history to that point. The Patriots gained just seven yards on the ground. "I'm not embarrassed," Patriots guard Ron Wooten said. "I'm humiliated." When the game ended, several players hoisted Ditka on their shoulders and several others hoisted Ryan. The coaches were carried off side by side, each borne away to his own destiny.

Payton headed straight for the tunnel. He went through the locker room like a shot, past the tubs filled with champagne, past the commemorative T-shirts, past the TV boys setting up for interviews, past Bob Costas loitering among the cables and gaffer's tape. Payton threw his helmet into the lockers—*bang!*—went into a utility closet, locked the door, fell to his knees, and wept. A handful of people gathered outside—Payton's agent, the team's PR chief. They begged him to come out. Walter moaned. When told his contract required him to give interviews, he shouted, "I ain't no damned monkey on a string."

"He was livid at Ditka for ignoring him and livid at Perry and

McMahon for hogging the spotlight and livid at himself for fumbling," Jeff Pearlman wrote in *Sweetness*.

At first, Ditka was confused—*I mean, hey, we just won the goddamn Super Bowl!*—but he eventually came to understand Payton's anger. "Here's a guy who set the all-time rushing record—one of the great players in the history of the game, or *the* greatest in my opinion—and to be on that big a stage in that short a time and not be able to do what he did best, I understood it. In the beginning, I didn't, because I had scored a touchdown in the Super Bowl and it meant nothing to me, it was just a touchdown . . . and then I could understand it because I was just a guy, but he was *the* guy."

"That was probably the most disturbing thing in my career," Ditka said in *Never Die Easy: The Autobiography of Walter Payton*. "If I had one thing to do over again, I would make sure that he took the ball into the end zone. I loved him; I had great respect for him. The only thing that really ever hurt me was when he didn't score in the Super Bowl, that killed me when I found out about it. I didn't think about it, I really didn't realize it. It just never crossed my mind, to be honest with you, that it was important. And then I realized how important it really was and I felt so bad about that over the years, but I couldn't undo it. In my mind, even when we were ahead 40-something to 10, or 30-something to 10, the only thing I kept looking at, and the only thing I kept thinking about, was winning the football game."

"He played for so long and had been the Chicago Bears for so many years and to see him not get into the end zone, it had to hurt," said McMahon. "But I don't think anyone recognized it during the game. I know I didn't. One of the touchdowns I scored was a play designed for Walter, but I spotted a hole and went in."

I'm with the Buddhists on this one: it does not matter who scored the points, only that the points were scored. The fact is, the Patriots' plan was built around stopping Payton. In such an instance, no matter what Ditka said later, the wise course was to use the star as a decoy, fake the pitch to Sweetness but give the rock to Fridge. Yes, Payton wanted to score. And Butkus and Sayers wanted to play for a championship. And Luckman wanted to quarterback in the era of big money. And Grange did not want to rip up his knee. And Halas wanted to live long enough to see the Bears win a Super Bowl. In fact, Halas did not want to die at all. "Here's where I will defend Ditka," said Bob Avellini.

"You win the Super Bowl and Walter walks off like he just lost his dog! It's a team game. If you win, that's all that matters."

"If you go to the Super Bowl, the idea is to win," Johnny Roland told me. "And we won 46 to 10. So my explanation to Walter was, 'When I came here in '83, despite all his individual accomplishments, he was still a loser 'cause the Bears never won. And you're only identified as a winner when you win. And the idea that the Gale Sayerses of the world, the Dick Butkuses, all the great players that have gone through this league—O. J. Simpson never got a sniff at a Super Bowl. Not only did Walter get a sniff, we won going away. And it's not like we didn't call plays for him. The first touchdown McMahon scored was an option. If you're a defensive coordinator, who are you going to take away, McMahon or Payton? So they take Payton, and McMahon scores. All those years he wanted to be in the Super Bowl, and obviously as a running back you want to score, but if it ain't to be, it ain't to be. And you feel bad but it ain't the end of the world. The end of the world is you go to the Super Bowl and you lose and nobody remembers you."

"Walter was always the focal point prior to Ditka and McMahon getting there," Kurt Becker told me. "Then, when Ditka took over, other people emerged: Otis Wilson and Hampton. And so now Walter had to share. I think that's what bothered him. The thing about it is . . . we wanted to win . . . and giving Walter the ball every play, you just couldn't win."

Payton finally got it together and left the closet, stood before the lights, did what was expected. "It would have been great to score one," he wrote later, "they would have had your name down as scoring a touchdown in the Super Bowl. In the days and weeks after the game, yes, I was bothered by it. But I was blessed to have parents who instilled in me that things happen for a reason. You may not understand it when it first happens, . . . but there will come a time when it will be shown to you."

That night, Ditka drank the bottle of champagne Halas had given him near the end of his life: "Mike, don't open it till you win the Super Bowl."

What happens when you have a dream and that dream comes true?

Ditka later spoke of the sense of anticlimax that washed over him almost before the game was over—it was like coming off a mountain.

You wake the next morning happy but sad and empty and without purpose. "Peggy Lee sang a great song, 'Is that all there is?' " Ditka said. "And it really felt that way. The game can never match what they build it up to be."

This feeling of melancholy, this loss of altitude or inspiration, it's felt not only by players and coaches. Fans experience it, too. I got up early the next day with a pit in my stomach. *What now? Where to?* I had gone out full and would return empty. I packed in silence. Lederer did the same. We caught a cab to the airport and got back on the Bears Charter, but the exuberance was gone. We flew home in silence. The superfans were sunk in their own girth. Even their mustaches seemed sad. It was the feeling you get on Sunday night after a long weekend times a billion. I looked out the window. What is this life? I asked my- self. What does it mean? Why does every minute pull me away from everything I love? I went back to Glencoe. I finished high school. I fin- ished college. When I was offered a job in New York, I went to my friends and told them I would take this job but only for a time as I did not want to live on the East Coast. I wanted to spend my life in the city I loved, Chicago, and, in case I got turned around, they had to call and remind me, otherwise I would be unhappy even if I thought I was happy. They said they understood and promised to call but of course they forgot. I got drunk in New York and made a fool of myself on sev- eral occasions and I met the love of my life and got married. I wrote a book, I had a kid, then another, then wrote another book, then had another kid, then moved to Connecticut, then, just like that, I was forty, then I was even older. In that whole time, the Bears never did win again. I missed Chicago but I did not go back. Nor did I get answers to the questions I had asked myself on the plane that day. I had come home after the Super Bowl and lived my life, hopeful that things might work out for me as they had worked out for the Bears. Fencik, McMahon, Hampton, Ditka, McMichael, Payton, Fridge, Marshall, and Gault— they had cured me of the defeatism of the Chicago fan. They had saved my life.

17

WHAT WENT WRONG

The Bears at Soldier Field on October 15, 1989, on their way
to another season without a Super Bowl

How good were the '85 Bears? Where do they stand historically?

The offense ranked second overall that season, and yet, despite the protestations of Jim McMahon, they were nothing special. A great running back a few years past prime, some good receivers, an exciting quarterback, but not in the same league as Joe Montana's 49ers or Troy Aikman's Cowboys or even Sid Luckman's Bears. Which is fine; they didn't have to be. The '85 Bears were about defense, and, if you go by statistics, you'd put them at the top, maybe the best. Over sixteen games, they gave up 198 points, which amounts to just over 12 a game. They intercepted thirty-four times, more than double the number of picks they threw. On seven occasions, the defense yielded fewer than ten points. They were even better in the postseason, when competition is supposed to stiffen. They did not allow a single point until the Super Bowl. They did give up a touchdown late in that game, but many of the starters were on the bench celebrating by then. Not long ago, ESPN's now defunct Page 2 put together a list of the best NFL teams ever: it had the '79 Steelers at seven, the '91 Redskins at four, the '62 Packers at three, Don Shula's undefeated '72 Dolphins at two, and the '85 Bears at number one.

It was more than the numbers. It was the quirkiness, the personalities—Danimal, Fridge, the Hit Man—a star quality that transcended the sport; it was the speed of the defense, the game-stopping hits, the collisions, the knockdowns; it was the dread that hovered over the enemy sideline, the way McMichael stood midfield, staring at the wounded gazelles; it was Marshall leaping over the line, Dent busting in from the blind side, Fencik sneaking up on the blitz, Singletary reading the quarterback and shouting signals in the way of a samurai.

Now and then, a sports commentator, speaking of a raucous stadium, will describe the crowd as the "twelfth man." For the Bears, the aura that surrounded the defense, the fear that preceded them, was not a twelfth man but a whole bunch of nasty fuckers who were going to beat you up as your mom watched. It's what Hampton meant when he said the Super Bowl was over on Wednesday, five days before kickoff. Because he looked into the eyes of the quarterback and saw a stunned deer. Other players, pro athletes who had excelled at every point of their lives, feared that Bears defense as they had feared nothing since their first days of Pop Warner football. As Howie Long told Lyle Alzado in the parking lot outside Soldier Field: *I haven't taken a beating like that since grade school.*

At times that season, it seemed as if the Bears had solved the problem of football, had cracked not just an opponent but the sport. They were on the same field as the other teams but were not playing the same game. It was tanks versus cavalry, dancers attempting pirouettes amid a pack of rabid dogs. That's a reason the Bears are not always mentioned when people speak of the best Super Bowl teams: teams are remembered for great games, barn burners, back-and-forthers with last-minute drives. There were no such situations for the Bears that year: every game was a mismatch, a thrashing. That's what made Marino's performance against the '85 Bears so remarkable, why Shula called it the best half of football he'd ever seen.

The Bears sent nine players to the Pro Bowl that season: Jim McMahon, Walter Payton, Dan Hampton, Otis Wilson, Richard Dent, Mike Singletary, Jimbo Covert, Jay Hilgenberg, and Dave Duerson. Thus far, four members of the squad have made it into the Hall of Fame: Payton, Hampton, Singletary, Dent. Five if you include Ditka. "It was a collection of oddballs and characters," Cris Collinsworth told me. "McMahon, the Fridge—they were never less than fun to watch. Unless you happened to be playing against them. In that case, they were scary. If only that team had repeated, they would be considered the greatest of all time."

It was something I heard again and again: if only that team had repeated.

In fact, the handful of teams usually considered the best did repeat, which is why they're called dynasties. Vince Lombardi's Green Bay Packers won NFL championships in 1961, 1962, 1965, and 1966, before winning the first two Super Bowls; Chuck Noll's Pittsburgh Steelers won three Super Bowls in the 1970s and another in 1980; Tom Landry's Dallas Cowboys appeared in five Super Bowls and won twice; under coaches Bill Walsh and George Seifert, the San Francisco 49ers won five Super Bowls in the 1980s and '90s. Bill Belichick's New England Patriots appeared in five and won three.

It did seem as if the Bears were poised to repeat: not only had they beaten everyone else, they did it with great athletes deployed in a defensive system that gave opposing coaches fits. They also happened to be the youngest team in the NFL. McMahon was twenty-seven. The Fridge was twenty-three. Dent was twenty-five. Hampton was twenty-nine, ditto Wilson and McMichael. Mike Richardson was twenty-five. Marshall was twenty-four. What's more, in the off-season, the Bears drafted a great running back from Florida, Neal Anderson, who could take pressure off Payton, who'd begun to slow. A running back at thirty-two is like a normal person at ninety: no one's taken more punishment.

If you had found me that spring and asked, "Hey, tough guy, how many Super Bowls do you think the Bears will win?" I'd have said seven. As of training camp 1986, it looked like nothing but blue skies and trophies ahead. "I thought somebody just invented this giant merry-go-round, and we were getting on, and we were going to ride it forever," said Ditka. "Then it all sort of ended."

The Bears remained an elite team for years, winning the NFC Central five times in six seasons. They lost only three games in 1986, but one of them was in the first round of the playoffs. After they posted the final score—Washington 27, Chicago 13—a gloom settled over my city; the sun was boxed up and carried away. The Bears won their division in 1987, 1988, 1990, and 1991, but no matter how well they did in the regular season, something always went wrong in the playoffs—it gave the era a doomed melancholy, a feeling of *what-if* and *should have* and *almost*. In Chicago, winning is a miracle; losing is forever. "It amazed me we didn't win four of them," McMahon said. "We lost eleven games in four years, but only got to that one Super Bowl."

It's one of the timeless questions in Chicago: What went wrong with the Bears?

There are many answers, many theories, many schools of thought. Here are some of the most compelling.

One: it was Buddy. He'd been the great motivator, the god each defensive player was working toward as well as the mad scientist turning the levers. When I asked Tyrone Keys why the Bears fell short in 1986, he said, "Buddy didn't come back. The defensive line coach didn't come back. None of the coaches from the defense were there. So the team went 14 and 2, but the chemistry was gone."

Ditka hired Vince Tobin to replace Ryan. Tobin had been coaching in the USFL and happened to be the brother of Bears general manager Bill Tobin. Vince continued to use the 46, but it became just another package. Then he refined it, trying to make a system that was unsound and irrational a little more ordinary. Vince Tobin was a rational coach, a man of percentages. He was never going to blitz eight straight plays, nor was he going to leave a receiver uncovered in a crazed attempt to open a new can of quarterback. Though the defense remained the best in the league statistically, they lost some of the mad-dog unpredictability that had terrified opponents. They were respected but not feared in the same way.

At times, Tobin seemed less interested in winning than in distinguishing himself from his predecessor. Whenever I mentioned the 46, he corrected me, saying, "I prefer to call it the Bears' defense," or, "Please, not the 46: the Bears' defense." Here was a manager brought in to return a guru-driven system to the straight and narrow: keep the good things, rein in the excesses, but the 46—excuse me, the Bears' defense—was all about excess. Once it lost that edge, quarterbacks started looking downfield. "Before I took the job, Mike said, 'I don't expect you to run Buddy's defense; run any defense you're comfortable with,'" Tobin told me. "So I brought my own playbook and philosophy, because I wasn't Buddy Ryan. Then, in almost every category in '86, we were actually better defensively than they'd been in '85."

Every category except the only category that matters: Super Bowl wins.

When I asked Otis if the defense was indeed better in '86 than it had been in '85, he said, "Hell no. No aggressiveness. Vince always said, 'We bend but don't break.' So, in other words, you're a boxer fighting Mike Tyson and this guy is telling you to let Tyson punch you in the face, then, when you get a shot, take it. But by that time, you might

Steve McMichael (seated left), Dan Hampton (seated right), and William Perry filming a McDonald's commercial in November 1985

be flat on your back. And when he blitzed, it was predictable. Inside the 20 everybody knew we were coming. So they're sitting waiting on you. It was a totally different defense after Vince came. We tried to make it work, but his shit wasn't going to work. If Buddy had just said, 'I'm going to humble myself and stay here for two or three more years,' we could have won three Super Bowls."

Two: it was the players. They lost their focus, went soft, bought into the hype. It was the Super Bowl itself that undid them, the narcotic of winning, the trophy and the parades and the party that erupted in every room they entered. In short, the Bears sold out. "We had the same players as the year before," wrote Payton, "but not the same desire, not the same hunger."

You've seen it in a hundred movies, every time some yokel wins the lottery or strikes oil: how quickly he forgets who he is and where he comes from—he leaves in denim and returns in velvet. During the off-season, when they should have been training like Spartans, several Bears, including McMichael and Perry, went on the road with the World Wrestling Federation, appearing in capes and tights, spangles and glitter boots, standing on the third rope, calling out Jake the Snake Roberts. By the end of 1985, ten Bears, including an offensive lineman, had their own radio shows. (If you pay attention, you'll notice that most NFL dynasties come in small markets, where there are fewer temptations.) By the first preseason game of 1986—played in London— Ditka had given up the sleeveless sweater-vest and coach pants that defined him as part of a style-starved breed. A Chicago clothier, spotting an opportunity, had begun to dress the coach. It was double-breasted and tweed from there: cuffs, pleats, snap-brim caps. Ditka opened a bar called City Lights, then a restaurant. It seemed every player owned an eatery. Mike Tomczak, a backup quarterback, opened T&T's in Joliet with guard Tom Thayer. Payton had two bars in Schaumburg and another out where the sun meets the corn. Fencik opened the Hunt Club on the North Side. McMahon opened Arena, a restaurant in Northbrook. Even Kevin Butler, the kicker, had a restaurant.

Ditka castigated his players for their spirit-sapping overexposure. *Stay off the goddamn TV!* Which explains one of the big complaints about the coach: hypocrisy. The fact is, Ditka did more commercials than the rest of them combined. He endorsed a plethora of products in the '80s: Peak Antifreeze, Dristan, Budget Rent A Truck, Talman Home Federal Savings and Loan, Hanes, Campbell's Soup, Chunky Brand. "He'd tell us to stay off television, then he'd turn around and do the commercials he made us turn down," Otis said. "When we did that 'Super Bowl Shuffle,' he told us he'd never, ever do a video. Then, all of a sudden, he comes out with the 'Grabowski Shuffle.'"

The nadir of the sellout was the Fridge on *The Bob Hope Christmas Special*:

HOPE: They said you can bench-press 465 pounds. Is that true?
PERRY: Yes. I get a lot of practice by lifting myself out of bed in the morning.

PERRY: People are making me out to be a lot bigger than I am. You know what that's like, don't you?
HOPE: Careful, Fridge.

Three: it was the 46 defense. Simply put, other teams cracked it. This was an endless topic of conversation in my interviews. Whenever I asked, "How do you beat the 46?" I'd get back a carefully considered answer. The introduction of the 46 was an evolutionary step in football. Beating it was therefore about more than the Bears: it was about the game, a sport that each of these men, even those who've been seriously damaged, love. They discussed the riddle of the 46 as an old general might discuss Patton's solution to Rommel. "Against that great defense, you wanted to play a very simple game," Jaworski told me. "The Bears weren't going to score a lot of points and you weren't going to score a lot of points, so don't take risks. Try to be close in the fourth quarter, then go for a big play."

"The best way was to block eight people, then send out two wide receivers," said McMahon. "That's what the Redskins did to us in '86 and it's how you beat the defense. If they're going to put pressure on you, block everybody and make your corners chase two guys around all day. As good as our guys were, they still couldn't cover all day long. If you don't get to the quarterback, the whole thing falls apart."

"That defense changed the way the game is played," Ditka told me. "'Cause if you bunch up your offense, the Bears' '85 defense would kill you. The solution was to spread everyone out. You do that, you can see where the guy is lined up without a blocker, hiding. Then pick him up.

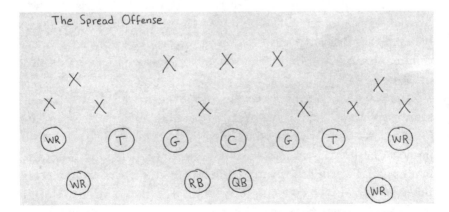

The Spread Offense. Variations of the spread are almost as old as football, but Mike Ditka told me it became a rage in the 1980s and '90s, in part as a response to the 46 defense. If you spread the offensive players out from sideline to sideline, the guards and tackles can see where the extra rushers are hiding and pick them up. Versions of this offense have come to dominate the game.

That's why, in today's game, guys line up from sideline to sideline. It's how they solved the Bears' defense."

"No matter how smart a coach or a scheme, the other guys eventually catch up," Jaworski explained. "You got all kinds of guys studying this stuff all the time. Coaches and scouts, everyone. Finding that weakness, that tip, that hint that could beat it. It's a game of adjustment. In the off-season, what these coaches do is remarkable. The time they put in, searching for the answer. So, by the end of the '86 season, the other coaches had figured out the 46."

Four: it was McMahon. I heard this again and again. McMichael: "We could have been the team of the decade if McMahon stayed healthy." Fencik: "'86 was an interesting year; we wanted to prove it wasn't just Buddy. But we didn't have McMahon." Baschnagel: "I think Jim alone, because of the injuries, was the reason the team didn't win multiple Super Bowls."

"Not having McMahon was key," Morrissey told me. "We talk about the defense, but there was no one better than McMahon—no one better at knowing where his teammates were, where the blocking schemes were, how to find the open receivers."

It was not just McMahon at quarterback the Bears missed. It was McMahon as a leader. When he was in the huddle, the players always believed they had a chance. As a result, everyone performed. It was a different team with him on the bench, which is where he spent most of 1986.

The play that ended his season still makes me mad. I was a freshman in college, watching at a friend's house on Prytania Street in New Orleans. The Bears were playing Green Bay. A Packers defensive tackle named Charles Martin had a white hand towel tucked in his waistband. In black pen, he'd written numbers on it, the jersey numbers of Bears he intended to take out. It was a hit list, the kind Nails Morton used to carry when he was working for Al Capone. McMahon's number was on the top. Early in the game, Mac made a bad throw, which was intercepted. But what matters is what happened after, long after—it seemed like five seconds, a football eternity. Martin grabbed McMahon from behind, lifted him like a doll, and drove him into the turf. It was the dirtiest play I'd ever seen, strangely disconnected from anything happening on the field. McMahon landed on his throwing shoulder, which had been reconstructed. He lay in writhing agony. Martin was ejected, but if I had the power of a mullah, he would have been executed. "It wasn't even a football play," Steve Zucker told me. "It was a criminal act."

McMahon was slow to return to the starting lineup. Ditka sought ways to pressure him, get him back on the field. Ditka was not the only one to consider McMahon a malingerer. At a meeting, Hampton accused Mac of putting his own interests above those of the team. *Look at my knees, look at McMichael's back! Don't you think we play hurt?* "We'll do it without you," Hampton said, "just stay out of our way." Ditka congratulated Hampton for saying what no one else had the guts to. That November, in what seemed like a ploy to motivate McMahon, the Bears acquired Doug Flutie from the Canadian Football League. Flutie had been a star at Boston College, the author of perhaps the most exciting football play in NCAA history—in 1984, Flutie defeated the University of Miami 47–45 with a last-second Hail Mary pass—but many considered him too small for the NFL. What's worse, he was cute: apple-cheeked and flip-haired, a kind of Michael J. Fox of the gridiron. He seemed an especially bad fit for this collection of night-crawling ne'er-do-wells and was hazed from the first. Flutie's Chicago sojourn was Hobbesian: nasty, brutish, short. "[The guys] felt like he was a usurper to McMahon's throne, so he wasn't going to be accepted," McMichael said. "Somebody even started calling him Bambi, not the manliest nickname in a football locker room. I don't know who started it, but I have to admit it fit. You know, the little Bambi deer, how deer run around—he was kind of a prancer back there."

For many Bears, the breaking point came in November, when Ditka, perhaps trying to make a point about acceptance, had the Fluties over for Thanksgiving. Instead of taking the hint—Doug is here to stay—most of the players had the following reaction: *Ditka never asked me to his house!* "When Ditka had Flutie over for the holiday, Jim went bananas," Zucker told me. "Hell, they all went bananas."

"Why did they bring in Flutie?" I asked McMahon.

"Nobody could figure it out," he said. "Fuller was here, Tomczak was in his second year. And both of them played. I think Ditka did it to get rid of me. He was hoping Flutie would win big and then he could ship me out."

Flutie never did produce for the Bears and was soon gone.

McMahon took a few snaps in the '86 playoffs, but the Martin hit had changed the trajectory of his career. McMahon shrugs it off, but you can tell it bothers him. When I said it seemed like Martin's hit came five seconds after the whistle, he said, "just over three seconds." Charles Martin knocked McMahon into a parallel universe, where most of his career was spent in rehab or on the bench. In the course of fifteen years in the NFL, McMahon started just ninety-seven regular season games.

"Whatever happened to him?" I asked.

"Who? Martin?"

"Yeah."

"They suspended him for the rest of that season. He ended up going to the Houston Oilers. Then, about five or six years ago, he died."

Five: it was Michael McCaskey. The players never respected him. He was Yale, sports coats and slacks, pleats and paisley. "Mike McCaskey is a new breed of owner who favors blue shirts, red ties, and an uncluttered desk," wrote Singletary. "His piercing blue eyes contrast nicely with his distinguished gray hair and expensive suits. He is a man who enjoys using words like finite and continuum. And the sound of his own voice."

The way McCaskey walked the sidelines at the end of the Super Bowl, the way he hung around the locker room, the way he clung to the trophy—it rubbed players the wrong way. It was as if he was saying, "I did it," while most of the guys considered his contribution less than critical. "I can still see him getting off the team bus back in Chicago, holding up that trophy like, 'I am responsible for this,'" McMichael said. "My ass. It was George Halas, Jim Finks, Jerry Vainisi, and Mike Ditka. Michael McCaskey had no input whatsoever."

At one point or another, every Bear had a run-in with McCaskey. "Finally, I couldn't control myself," wrote Singletary. "'Have you ever played football?' I screamed. It startled him. But he composed himself, saying, 'Why yes, I played when I was in college at Yale. I was a wide receiver.'"

"[My agent] still talks about it to this day, and I swear I don't remember it," McMichael said, "but he says when the negotiations ended on the last contract I signed, I got up, leaned over the desk, and [told McCaskey], 'I'd like to hit you right in the fucking mouth.'"

The players thought McCaskey was cheap—that was the complaint. You saw it in the Super Bowl rings the president ordered for his team. Compare the Fridge's ring, on display at the NFL Hall of Fame, to those purchased for players on other championship teams: Bears rings are flimsy and jewel-deficient in comparison. Asked about it, McCaskey offered the sort of explanation that made McMichael want to hit him right in the fucking mouth: "Oh, we plan on going and getting a lot more of them, so we want to have money to buy more."

At times, it seemed as if McCaskey had made a calculation not uncommon to the descendants of great men: mediocrity is better for business. If you win, everyone wants more money—you have to buy rings and get tickets and give bonuses. And the egos! And the head-aches! Who can afford it? Nine players in the Pro Bowl means nine guys who expect to be paid like All-Stars. McCaskey began to balk at the demands. "The team is the only asset our family has," he told Singletary. "It's a fact of life that the Bears cannot reach into other pockets. We have to take a finite pile of resources and be fair in meeting our obligations."

The McCaskeys are in fact an anomaly in the modern NFL. Unlike for most other owners, billionaires who purchased their clubs as a kind of lark or fantasy league hobby, the McCaskeys' wealth is the franchise. If they seem overly careful with money—this has been less the case in recent years; the Bears spent as much as anyone in 2012—it's because they have to be. It's not just the win/loss record at stake but also the financial health of the family.

Of course, most fans could not care less about the fiscal state of the McCaskeys. To them, the truth seemed plain: the Bears would not pay, the players left, the team collapsed, not quickly, but in the glacial way of the Ottoman Empire. It started with Willie Gault, who went to the Raiders after the 1987 season. He was twenty-seven and had years of big plays left. Just like that, the Bears lost their deep threat. Next came Wilber Marshall, an outside linebacker many considered the Bears' most physically gifted player. He went to the Redskins when he was twenty-six. Otis Wilson went to the Raiders. Jay Hilgenberg went to the Browns in 1992. McMichael went to the Packers in 1994. "We started getting real smart," Ditka told me. "We were going to get rid of the people we brought in. Gault left, McMichael left, Marshall left. We lost these guys because we chose not to sign them."

"They didn't trade them," Zucker explained. "They just let them go."

When I asked if it was about money, Zucker laughed and said, "That might've had something to do with it."

For the Bears, McMahon had been the crucial piece, the trickster soul. They didn't win before he turned up with his six-pack, and they have not won since. But McCaskey didn't like Jim McMahon, and, in the end, he would not live with Jim McMahon. No doubt, it was the quarterback's fault. He could not help but rebel. In 1986, when asked what position his team should draft for, McMahon went on TV and said, "owner." Then, a few weeks later, he published his autobiography, *McMahon!*, in which he mocked McCaskey. "If he had his choice, he'd have 45 players with no personality, no individuality at all," wrote the quarterback. "Michael McCaskey would like a bunch of robots. Then, everything would go along peacefully. You might not win many games, but at least there wouldn't be any headbands . . ."

"I think I might rather retire early than play the rest of my career for the current president of the Bears," McMahon writes later in the book. "He doesn't have any qualifications to operate the Bears, except his name. He went from Yale to Harvard to running his own consulting firm to running the Bears. He took over as president and chief executive officer in November 1983, and before he got his feet wet, he was jumping around our locker room in January of 1986, with a Super Bowl trophy."

When McMahon showed the manuscript to his friend the Bears kicker Kevin Butler, Butler begged him to cut the stuff about McCaskey: "Dude, it's your boss. And your boss may be a lot of things, but he's still your boss."

"I love Jim to death," Kurt Becker told me. "Him and I are very good friends. We were roommates and everything. But, I mean, some people try to be crazy, but that son of a bitch actually *is* crazy. He really is. He's nuts. Who trashes the company they work for?"

In 1987, the Bears drafted Jim Harbaugh, a quarterback from Michigan, in the first round. That's when McMahon knew his days in Chicago were numbered. "They never liked Jim," Zucker told me. "They couldn't control him. When I saw that the Bears drafted Harbaugh, I knew what it meant. I went over to camp. It was ten o'clock at night. Ditka was there. He took me aside and said, 'I was so mad with that pick, I quit the Bears for twenty minutes, but then asked myself, "What do you really want to do?" And that's coach the Bears, so I unquit.'" McMahon was traded to San Diego in 1989. "At first, he was happy," Zucker told me. "He wanted a trade. But it was the worst thing for the Bears, and it was the worst thing for McMahon. He was made for that team, and the Bears were never the same."

"They called me at my house in the morning and said they traded me," McMahon said. "I hadn't even gone to work yet. They just said it on the phone: Hey, we're going in a different direction. I said, Yeah? Fine. So I drove in, got all my shit, and left. That was it. I didn't see Ditka in person. Those last couple years, it wasn't good anyway. We hardly talked. I wasn't going to press the issue. I had nothing to say to him. I just got my shit and drove away. That was it."

"Gault was gone, Marshall was gone, McMichael was gone, McMahon was gone," Ditka told me. "I will coach whoever is there. I'll play the hand I'm dealt. But one thing I know for sure, you can't win by subtracting. We brought those people in for a purpose, and you defeat that purpose when you let them go. In most of the cases it was about money. With McMahon, it was about conflicts and personalities with the owner. Well, if you don't understand the game, and how to keep people happy, and how to keep a championship team intact, you got a problem."

This moment—the news that McMahon was packing for San Diego reached me by radio—marked the end of the era. I continued to watch the Bears, but I no longer cared in the same way. My father says the key to life is "to care, but not that much." Well, for me, this was the beginning of *not that much*, which marks the beginning of adulthood, the place where the coastal shelf falls away and the water turns dark blue. McMahon played another eight seasons in the NFL—in San Diego, in Philadelphia, in Minnesota, in Arizona, in Green Bay—but it was never the same. The days of his wandering had begun. It was never the same for us either. You can root for a team, but you can love only a player.

Six: it was Ditka. He was too intense, pushed too hard, chewed up his players like he chewed up his gum. As for the quarterbacks, only McMahon had been able to perform for Ditka, because McMahon didn't take it personally. The rest—Tomczak, Harbaugh—were driven to a breaking point, a crisis in which they either imploded in a dark room or exploded on national television.

You can build a team with the whip, but after a time, especially after they've won, you need to find another motivation. This goes back to what Plank told me about the three kinds of coaches: the aspirin coach, the penicillin coach, the chemo coach. Ditka was a chemo coach, which is what you need for a team with cancer. But after the chemo coach cures the cancer, and the team wins, what does he do? Delivers more chemo, because that's who he is—the guy with the chemo machine— which, in the absence of cancer, kills healthy tissue: first the quarterbacks, then everyone else. "If you're a chemo coach, once a team gets on track and starts winning, don't keep choking it out," Plank explained. "You got the right guys—let them do their thing. You don't even need discipline because they're self-disciplined. But Mike continued to be strong willed, determined—all the things that made him great in creating the Bears led to his downfall."

Ditka never transitioned from building to sustaining, never figured out how to sit back and ride. Everything was life or death and *Stop being such a fucking pussy* and *move, move, move!* Even when the core players got older, he kept running them till they puked. The Bears had the hardest practices in the league, which several veterans told me played a role in their shortcomings: they'd been overworked, had nothing left for the playoffs. "We could've had a dynasty, but Ditka cared more about power than about winning," Otis Wilson told me. "My way or the highway, that was his mentality. He wanted to make people submissive. We were playing football. I'm going to do my job. You don't have to worry about me. But I'm not going to kiss your ass."

Ditka was wearing himself down, too. You can grind the gears for only so long before the clutch burns. He couldn't control his temper. One screwup or mistake, one wiseass comment from the press, and it was asterisks and lightning bolts. "Ditka was a guy who broke racquets in rage when he played racquetball against Cowboy staff members," wrote Rick Telander. He made his receivers "run, and when they didn't run right, he swore at them. He challenged them to fight . . . He turned red. He turned purple."

After a particularly vigorous racquetball game at Halas Hall in 1988, Ditka lay on a bench in the locker room. He couldn't breathe. He was having a heart attack. He was forty-nine. Ed McCaskey seemed almost gleeful. "He was a prime candidate," he explained. "He eats what he wants, drinks what he wants, smokes what he wants, sleeps when he wants." Ditka was back on the sideline in two weeks; he promised to control his temper, said he was done with yelling. That lasted until the first stupid audible. He'd coach for several more years, but now everyone realized that Iron Mike could die. "You knew he was going to flare out at some point," Danny White told me. "Nobody can go on at that pace. He's either going to have a breakdown, or he's got to get out of the game. Landry coached for twenty-nine years, but you can only do that if you have a calm demeanor and a balance in your life, something other than football. But to Mike, football was life. And it's not something to base a life on. It's not dependable. That's what Walter [Payton] said about the fame and fortune of football: it's vapor. When it's gone, it's gone. Somebody breaks the records, the money gets spent, and it's over before you know it."

18

MUCH LATER

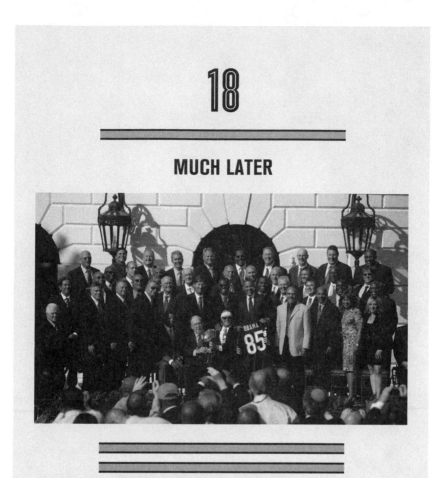

The '85 Bears and the First Fan. Obama called it the best day of his presidency.
(Obama with the jersey. Buddy and McMahon holding the Super Bowl trophy.
Ditka standing, with shades, still looking like a Bear. Kevin Butler and
Emery Moorehead behind the coach and to his left. Richard Dent in the
back row, eleven o'clock from the president.) October 7, 2011

The '85 Bears never got their White House visit. Shortly before the team was to meet President Reagan, the space shuttle *Challenger* exploded. January 28, 1986: the first disaster we watched again and again on cable. It goes up, curves as the sky changes from blue to black, sends out a plume of smoke, then blows apart. It was the day after I'd returned from New Orleans, but the game suddenly seemed like it had happened a million years before. The White House visit was canceled and never rescheduled. It was just one of those things. In 1997, when the Super Bowl champion Green Bay Packers visited Bill Clinton in the White House, McMahon, that team's backup quarterback, wore his Bears jersey. "I talked to my coaches and teammates before we went and told them, 'Look, [the Bears] never got to go, so I'm going to represent our guys.' Only Fritz Shurmur had a problem with it," McMahon told me, "but I think that's 'cause he was with that Rams team we destroyed in the playoffs."

Barack Obama moved to Chicago in 1985, where, just a few years out of college, he fell for the Bears. How could he not? The team, its coach and its ethos, was everywhere. He became a fan and even got to know Dent and Wilson—they worked out together at the East Bank Club. When Obama ran for the Democratic nomination in Illinois's First Congressional District—he was defeated by incumbent Bobby Rush—Dent and Wilson publicly supported him.

In 2011, shortly after the twenty-fifth anniversary of Super Bowl XX, President Obama—"First you're working out, goofing with a guy, then, a minute later, he's the president of the United States," Wilson told me—invited the '85 Bears to finally make their visit to the White House. It took Brian McCaskey several weeks to track everyone down, but that spring fifty or so players, coaches, and executives converged on O'Hare, where they boarded the team plane for Washington.

So here they came: Gault and Dent, Otis and McMichael, Suhey and Ditka and Buddy, some huge and fat, others fit and fine, stalwarts together again. McMahon was bald, concussed, ancient, dazed but exactly the same. "It was a time warp to twenty-six years ago," Tim Wrightman told me. "Nothing had changed. The Bears don't have alcohol on team flights anymore. I don't know if that's because of Ditka's incident or what. They just don't. So McMahon showed up with three cases of beer. I love Jim. He can get away with stuff the rest of us can't. He was wearing this T-shirt—I have a picture of me with him in it—and printed on it was an erect penis that looked like it was coming out the top of his pants. That's what he was wearing to the White House under his button-down. He was going up and down the aisle of the plane, pulling people aside and showing them, and the stewardess is going, ah-ha-ha, so funny. If you or I were to do that, they'd have the sky marshals waiting to arrest us in Washington."

A bus took the team first to a hotel, then from the hotel to the White House with police cruisers leading the way. "I had so much fun," Baschnagel said. "To be with those guys again, to get pampered again. The chartered flight, the escort. It was incredible."

Baschnagel was hinting at one of the difficulties of NFL life: the danger and misery of reentry, the way you go from a world of hotels and motorcades and never having to plan or think, because it's all been taken care of, to the world occupied by the rest of us. Just like that, you've passed through the tunnel and find yourself back on the street in a crowd of nobodies, and it's 5:00 p.m., and it's Sunday, and it's November, and it looks like rain.

The president met with Ditka—Ditka, a Republican, who, once upon a time, toyed with running for the open Senate seat that made everything else possible for Obama. In the end, even Ditka seemed to realize he did not have a senatorial temperament—perhaps if he'd run in the 1850s, when politicians filled spittoons and beat each other with canes.

The players were taken on a White House tour, through checkpoints, in and out of libraries and storied rooms. "I actually had one of the cops cuff me as we were going through," said McMahon. "I said, 'Dude, cuff me. They'll think it's old times.' It was just like we were back in the locker room, and it was yesterday. But a couple guys looked like they're getting around a little slower than they used to. Shit, we're all . . . if we're not over fifty, we're damn near close!"

President Obama came out of a meeting to talk to the players, joke with his friends, tell stories. He was a fan. It was real. You could tell. He grabbed a defensive end by the cuff and said, *Remember how . . .* , his eyes wide as he listened. "He couldn't have been more welcoming," Baschnagel said. "He was genuinely excited." Obama later said it was "as much fun as I will have as president of the United States."

As soon as the White House visit was announced, I started making plans. How often do you get to see the team of teams together again a quarter of a century later? I stood behind a rope line amid reporters, most of them from Chicago newspapers. There were a few national television correspondents. Several Bears fans who worked on Capitol Hill had bluffed their way in. I got my pass with the help of Jake Tapper, a friend, who was covering the event for ABC. The back steps of the White House were on one side of us, the Mall rolled away on the other. Jake told me that this is where President Kennedy met the survivors of the Bay of Pigs invasion after they were released from Castro's prisons.

There was a flurry of energy, a stir of Secret Service, then the players came out of the White House and filled a riser behind the presidential podium. They arranged themselves as they had been arranged for the team photo before the 1985 season. If you hold that picture beside the one taken at the White House, you see coaches and players but you also see time. McMahon was in front—just as he'd been then. He was bald in a blue sport coat, goateed, grinning, wearing a headband. Once everyone was settled, President Obama walked to the dais, flanked by Ditka and Ryan, who looked especially woebegone. It was said he had cancer; you will probably not read his name again until it's in an obituary. "A great thing happened at the White House," Ken Taylor, who played special teams in 1985, told me. "Despite all that had happened, Mike Ditka made sure Buddy Ryan was with him when we came out with the president. We all came out first, then the president usually comes out with the head coach. I was standing next to Mike and I heard him say, 'No, no, no, I want Buddy with me. We're coming out together.' I was like, holy, holy. It's just perspective. Time. Mike realized he didn't win without Buddy and Buddy didn't win without Mike. But together they were amazing."

Obama gave a short speech. Neither soaring nor elegant, it was authentic, a Bears fan drawing on his honest-to-God memory. "In 1985, I had just moved to Chicago," he said. "So, unlike most Chicagoans, I didn't really know what it was like to be a suffering sports fan. There are a few members of Congress and big Bears fans here from Illinois who knew what that was like. But none of us had ever seen what happened that fall. Nobody had ever seen anything like it. This city was invigorated and brought together by this team. This team ruled the city. It riveted the country. They were everywhere. They were like the Beatles. And this was before SportsCenter and before 24/7 sports news had really taken off. But they just captured the country's imagination.

"We loved this team. Everybody in Chicago knew all these guys' names. We even knew the names of the offensive linemen. Now, you know offensive linemen, they don't get enough love. But these guys had their own poster—'the Black N Blues Brothers.' When is the last time you saw a poster of an offensive line?

"But what made this team so captivating wasn't just that they won," Obama went on, "wasn't just that they dominated—it was the way they did it. Yes, they were punishing. Yes, they were dominant. But they also had a lot of fun. And you could tell they enjoyed playing together. They were, of course, led by the coach who set the tone—Hall of Famer Mike Ditka. In training camp, he said, 'Put a chip on your shoulder in July and keep it there till January.'

"Some of you may remember that back in 2004, when I was running for the Senate, some people were trying to draft Ditka to run against me. I will admit I was a little worried—because he doesn't lose."

Obama stopped and looked at the crowd. The reporters were laughing. "And in a sign that anything is possible, even in Washington, Coach Ditka and Buddy Ryan are here together," Obama said. "Coach Ryan's 46 defense changed football forever. Nobody had ever seen anything like it. Nobody knew what to do with it. And with the talent he had on the defensive side of the ball, there wasn't anything other teams could do about it.

"I mean, there are guys who hit, and there are guys who *hit*. And these guys *hit*. Mike Singletary, Steve McMichael, Otis Wilson, Wilber Marshall, Dan Hampton, Gary Fencik, and Richard Dent, the Super Bowl MVP—a guy I used to actually work out with in the gym and [who] made me feel weak.

"This was the defense that set the standard and it is still the standard . . . More than twenty-five years later, the standard against which all other teams are compared is Coach Ryan's defense.

"These guys lived to wreak havoc. It was like they were competing with each other to see who could get to the quarterback or the running back first. There was one game that season in which the other team's offense had the ball in Bears territory a total of twenty-one seconds.

"Now, of course, this was also the second-ranked offense in the league that season."

Turning, Obama said, "Jim McMahon—where's Jim?"

"Just right here," said Mac. "Do you need me to speak?"

"No, we're not going to let Jim have the mic," Obama said. "I'm just going to say nice things about you.

"Jim played quarterback with no fear and lived life with very few rules—a rock-and-roll quarterback who was on the cover of *Rolling Stone*. And he had kids wearing headbands and shades to school . . .

"This team had nine Pro-Bowlers, four future Hall of Famers—five counting Coach Ditka. They won one three-game stretch by a combined score of 104 to 3 . . . They were so confident that the day after they lost their only game of the season, they recorded 'The Super Bowl Shuffle.' They were suggesting I should dance 'The Super Bowl Shuffle' . . . Can't do it. But I do remember it. And in Chicago, you could not get away from this song even if you wanted to. I think it's safe to say that this is the only team in NFL history with a gold record and a Grammy nomination.

"So this team changed everything for every team that came on after . . . They changed the laws of football. They were gritty; they were gutsy; they were hardworking; they were fun-loving—sort of how Chicagoans think of themselves."

Facing the players, Obama smiled and said, "Congratulations to all of you. Thank you for helping to bring our city together. Thank you for the incredible fun that you gave to all of us. Stick around, guys, and enjoy yourselves," he added, moving away, "but as I mentioned back there, don't break anything and keep your eyes on McMahon."

Ditka dropped a big arm across the president's shoulder, snagging him before he could escape. "Wait, wait, one second, one second," said the coach. "We want to give the president something on behalf of the 1985 Chicago Bears"—a jersey, number 85, which Ditka presented in the way of a chalice. "We consider him one of us," said Ditka. "It was a great group of guys. We're very proud that you honored us by bringing us here. It's only twenty-six years after the fact, and five administrations, but thank you."

The players came out of the riser and went down the steps. The sun blazed, the wind blew. It was fall but felt like summer. Even more telling than the Bears mingling on the grass were those not mingling because they had not come. Each had his reasons. Wilber Marshall hadn't come because Marshall, who was said to be ailing—"it's really the hitors that took the worst of it," Mac told me—was squabbling with the team for money he claimed he was still owed from his last contract. The Fridge hadn't come because the Fridge was ailing and preferred to keep close to home in Aiken, South Carolina. "I called him the other day just to see if he was going," Tyrone Keys said. "He told me he has a hard time traveling. He has a wife, and they're just hanging on." Payton hadn't come because Payton was dead. Dave Duerson was dead, too. Dan Hampton skipped the event for personal and political reasons. "He said he didn't want to go because, one, he doesn't like the guy who's in the White House, two, it's been twenty-five years—it's time to let it go—and, three, they didn't invite our wives," Tim Wrightman told me. "So, here's my response, which I posted on Facebook. 'One, I can differentiate between celebrating the president and celebrating the team, although I played on the smarter side of the line. Two, if twenty-five years means it's time to let it go, will you please stop doing those car commercials that say you're a Super Bowl champion? And three, which wife did you want to bring, Dan? The one you had when we won, or the one you have now?'"

The reporters were cleared out, a barrier was erected and, behind that barrier, the '85 Bears drank beer as a band played. It was another characteristic episode in the life of a fan: no matter how close you get, you will never be one of the boys. How close had I come? I could hear the music, but I could not make out the words. They stood us beside a White House driveway, where we were free to buttonhole players who happened to wander past. Taking pity, three old-timers came out:

Dent, Wilson, and Michael McCaskey, who, several years ago, was basically fired by his mom. The team is now headed by another grand-child, George McCaskey, though day-to-day operations are overseen by the Bears' president and CEO, Ted Phillips. According to lore, it was the second Mayor Daley who forced the ouster of Mike McCaskey in 1999. There were many issues in play, including the renovation of Soldier Field, but Daley had resented McCaskey for years—because McCaskey fired Ditka.

The reporters asked fifteen or twenty variations of three questions—"How does it feel?" "Do you miss it?" "How would the '85 team do today?"—but that's not what interested me. What interested me was Richard Dent, not what he said but how he walked. He'd been young and lithe, but while I was living my life he got old, became deliberate, heavy footed, slow. The world weighs on him. The youth has been squeezed from him like water from a sponge.

Something about that walk made me think of how sad it is to play professional sports. First you're fast and strong and everyone cares and it's all you've ever done or wanted to do. Then it's over. If you're lucky, you are like McMahon, who invested his money wisely. But a few years out of the game, most retired players have to struggle to make ends meet—card shows, speaking gigs, whatever comes along. The money came fast and goes faster. In the worst cases, retirement is followed by bankruptcy or destitution. After all, the '85 Bears played before big money. In 1980, when Walter Payton made $475,000, he was the highest-paid man in the game. In the Super Bowl year, McMahon made $100,000. In 1991, playing for the Eagles, he made just over $500,000. According to the website Sports City, Bears quarterback Jay Cutler will make $8.47 million in 2013. The team's wide receiver Brandon Marshall will make over $9 million.

But in the end, it's not the money these players miss. Few of them said a word to me about having arrived a dozen seasons too early. It's the game itself, the big play, the raucous locker room. If you ask a player how his career ended, he never has to think. "It was during training camp," Brian Baschnagel told me. "I was coming off two knee surgeries and had been in the league for ten years. I went into [Ditka's] office on Monday. I said, 'I got to know what you're thinking.' As soon as I said that, he looked down. Mike always looked you in the eye. But he put his head down and hemmed and hawed, then looked up and said, 'Brian, I think you need to think of retiring.' There was an empty feeling. It was early in the morning. I cleaned out my locker before anybody got in. I didn't even say goodbye."

"For me, it happened in '90," said Kurt Becker. "I had nothing left. I finished the season and went in and talked to Mike. I said, 'Mike, man, I'm done.' And he's like, really? I said, 'Yeah, I'm beat up and out of gas.' And he said, 'Well, think about it.' I said, 'I thought about it. I'm done.'"

"It was the body," Emery Moorehead told me. "The off-seasons got shorter and shorter and the pain lingered longer and longer. All of a sudden, that old ankle sprain came back in the second or third week of training camp and you had to play with it all year. It never healed. When you start to break apart, you know it's time. I broke my leg in my last game. It was against the Rams, the first week in December. I got leg whipped by Jimbo. It was strange. I knew I was coming to the end, so when it happened, I thought, That was the last play. I won a Super Bowl my ninth season and I was ready to go, but it's still hard. A lot of guys never figure it out. It's a huge problem: you can't match the excitement of Sunday ever again. It's hard to find a guy who will say okay, I'm going to sell real estate and that will make me happy. Come July, you wish you were back out with the team. It never goes away."

"I didn't want to come back in '87," said Fencik. "I was beat up. Most of my friends were gone. I wanted to leave on a good note. For most players, the end is bitter. You get cut, you feel discarded, un-wanted. I came back in '87 and ended up getting benched. It was a difficult, emotional year. I was glad it was over. I'm glad I got to retire. It would've been humiliating to be cut. It takes about fifteen minutes to clear out your locker. Then I wanted to talk to Mike. I went to his office and he sat me down, had an unlit cigar in his mouth, threw his feet on his desk, and looked at me and said, 'Boy, we really screwed you this year.'

"No matter what you do after, it's never going to be as fun," Fencik went on. "You're used to this tempo of every seven days there's a win or a loss. There's no 'Oh, the meeting got delayed,' or there's no definitive answer. Every week you win or lose. You get used to that pace, you get used to being part of this big thing. Then you walk away. It's over. I actually had a kid in a grocery store come up to me. I could see he was following me and was going to come over at some point and ask for an autograph. He said, 'Excuse me, didn't you used to be Gary Fencik of the Chicago Bears?' For a lot of players losing that identity . . . it's a challenge."

"The morning that I walked out with my bag with all my belongings, I ran into [teammate] Jeff Fisher," said Plank. "I told him I'd been released. There's this line: you're part of the team or not, and I could see him reassessing me. We had a past but there would be no future. We shook hands, but it was empty. I was suddenly aware of all the players who'd gone through it before me. It's the end of a life."

For Dan Hampton, the end came when he realized he was being beaten by players he would once have dominated. "You know that song? 'The old gray mare, she ain't what she used to be'?" he told a reporter. "Well, at some point I realized I was that old gray mare." Near the end of his last game, the Giants had the ball on Chicago's goal line. In the huddle, Hampton implored his teammates: "Guys, don't let them score on the last play of my career." They did, and the Bears lost 31–3.

Steve McMichael was last on the field in 1994. "I was still being hardheaded, thinking I could still play, until Barry Sanders went the distance on me in Detroit," he wrote. "[Barry] cut inside, then went into the gap where the defensive end should've been, but wasn't. The play I'd always made, to come back out and make the tackle, the knee wasn't there, it gave. He was gone. That's when I knew it was over."

"You know what I miss?" McMichael told Mark Bazer. "I miss walking out of that tunnel to the roar of the crowd. Here's some poetry: 'It didn't matter anymore, life and death the same. Only that the crowd would be there to greet him with howls of lust and fury. He started to understand his sense of worth. He mattered.' That was from *Conan the Barbarian*, 'cause I fucking plagiarize."

"I miss being twenty-five years old and playing with my friends," said Plank. "Now we're scattered across the country and it's all in the past. If you're lucky enough to experience something that intense when you're young, you pay for it the rest of your life."

I came to realize that the various fates of these men, taken together, formed a picture of a generation: among them, they've experienced the best and the worst of America. After he retired, Emery Moorehead got a job in the Northbrook office of Koenig & Strey, a real estate firm. He showed houses on the North Shore, a touch of the Super Bowl, a glint of ring to close the deal. He began his new life before his career was over, experiencing what the rocket boys call a hard reentry. "One of my buddies from the team, Reggie Phillips, gave me my first listing up in Mundelein," Moorehead told me. "The season had ended and I'd been out with a friend and our wives. The phone was ringing when I got home. It was 9:30. January or February. Bitter cold. It was another agent from Koenig & Strey. She lived across the street from the Mundelein house and said, 'I see the sign with your name on it and just want to tell you there's a stream of water running out of the garage and turning to ice outside.' A pipe had burst and there was two or three inches of water in the first floor. I had to run out, and now it felt like the middle of the night, and rent a shop vac at a grocery store—it was the only place open. I was on my hands and knees till three or four in the morning. When the football season ended, Reggie had turned off the heat and just left. He was from Texas. He didn't know. All the pipes had burst. When I called him, I was like, 'Dude!' "

When I met Emery, he was in the same office in Northbrook where he answers the phone, "This is Emery." We sat in the conference room and talked about marriage, divorce, family, Ditka, Super Bowl, and high school. The son of a garbage collector, Emery has sent two kids to college and lives a quiet life on the North Shore. It's a long way from third and two with a season on the line, but it's the American dream.

Standing up and jingling his keys, he said, "Let's go."

I'd asked him to show me houses. Partly because I had seen Emery block and catch and now wanted to see him sell, partly because, now and then, something in me says, "It's time to go home." We looked in Evanston and Wilmette, talking football as we drove. When we arrived at a house, he'd shut off his car, say, "Here it is," then lead me up the cobblestone as the robins sang. Little of the athlete remains in Emery. He was shaped like a lifeguard, but the lines have blurred. If he walks into the next world like this, they'll never recognize him.

Doug Plank played his last game for the Bears in 1982: missed tackle, head-to-head, lightning flash. He played part of another season in the USFL but the old zipperoo was gone. When he should've been accelerating, he was bracing for impact. A body wants to learn from its disasters. He'd been working all along, taking whatever jobs he could find

in the off-season. "I sold Culligan water softeners," he told me. "I reha-
bilitated houses. I was a realtor. That was life as a professional athlete.
My salary my first year was $18,000."

He went back to Columbus, Ohio, after he retired and bought into a
Burger King. He was not a celebrity owner, standing out front meeting
and greeting—he worked in back, standing over the grill. In 1985,
when the Bears made their run, he was too busy to feel like he'd missed
out. "Here's what I recommend for former athletes," he told me. "If you
want to get past it and stop feeling bad, run a restaurant. We opened at
six a.m. and closed at two a.m. Bury yourself in work. You'll never have
time to feel sorry for yourself."

"What's the hardest part of making that transition?" I asked.

"What transition?"

"From Soldier Field to Burger King?"

He laughed, then said, "Well, when I made a great Whopper, nobody was clapping as I wrapped it up and put it down the chute. And
you know, you really do miss getting that adoration on a consistent
basis. We're driven toward it. As kids, we all want to get a pat on the
back. That's what you miss: the adult version of a pat on the back. We
just don't get it. That's why I'm cheesy. I make a big deal of little things.
Doing things the right way, giving guys accolades for that. It's important. In Burger King we used to call it taking a walk. Taking a walk
means you get out of your office and walk around the restaurant. You
walk outside and look for trash. Is the dining room clean? Are your
employees dressed properly? Are they smiling? Are the lights on? We
all need to take a walk more often. Just look around and say, 'Is everything right? Is everything the way it should be? Are we giving ourselves
the best chance to have success?' And if we are, then what's wrong with
going up to that person that has that area cleaned up, and is focused,
with a smile on their face, and saying, 'Hey, I want you to know I ap-
preciate it.' If there's one thing I learned as an owner, it's that the players, people that work for you, they're the ones that are going to make
you successful."

Plank bought another Burger King, then another. By 1992, he owned
several franchises. The national corporation asked him to take over its
operations in the Southwest, which meant a move to Arizona. He later
sold his restaurants back to the corporation but stayed in Scottsdale,
where the climate is kinder to men with titanium shoulders.

Plank's life changed again about twenty years ago. "I'm driving to a Burger King I own down in Tempe and on the radio I hear that Buddy Ryan has just been announced as the general manager and head coach of the [Arizona] Cardinals," Plank told me. "And I'm thinking, gosh, they need me for lunch if they're making combo meals. But Buddy was the guy that named the defense after me. I figured I owed him a visit. So I went down and congratulated him. Then we're talking. And you can imagine all the media types. It was after a press conference. And someone says, 'Who's this guy, Buddy?' And Buddy goes, 'This is Doug Plank, number 46. The 46 defense.' Within five minutes somebody from the Cardinals walked up and said, 'Hey Doug, would you like to do our pre- and postgame radio show?' "

Plank works as a broadcaster and is now head coach of the Orlando Predators of the Arena Football League. He's coached at Ohio State and for the New York Jets, where he worked for Buddy's son, Rex. "Looking back, I'd much rather have a defense named after me than have gone to the Super Bowl," he said. "I say that with all honesty. Two years ago, while I was working with the Jets in the weight room, the NFL commissioner, Roger Goodell, walked through, introducing himself to players and coaches. He comes over to me and I put down the dumbbells and say, 'It's a pleasure meeting you, Commissioner. I'm Doug Plank.' And once again, it's one of those Joe Paterno moments: he's just looking at me, shaking my hand, remembering. Doug Plank. The 46 defense. And he says, 'You were a great player.' What's that worth? Wouldn't somebody pay a lot of money to have the NFL commissioner say that?"

Willie Gault played through 1993, finishing with the Raiders, then dedicated himself to his real dream: Hollywood. If you want to reach Willie, it's via his agent. If you want to see Willie, it's via his head shot. He looks like a romantic in his publicity photos, suave with an open shirt and a white-toothed smile, his chest accented by a necklace of coral shells. His television and film credits, scattered across the twenty years, include *Hangin' with Mr. Cooper* (Clifford), *Baywatch* (Willa's dad), *Night Vision* (FBI Agent Coleman), *Holy Man* (NordicTrack Guy), *Millennium Man* (Lieutenant Dunn), *The Pretender* (Willie the Sweeper, nineteen episodes), *Grounded for Life* (Hugh), *The West Wing* (Agent, four episodes), *Deuce Bigalow: European Gigolo* (Black Man in

Airport). Of all the Bears at the White House, only Gault looked like he could still get up and down the field. When Willie was a Bear, Ditka designed a play to take advantage of his speed. It was called Big Ben. Willie took off. Mac waited three beats, then threw the football as far as he possibly could.

Mike Richardson was known as L.A. As fans, we assumed it stood for Los Angeles, as Richardson grew up in Compton, but it actually stood for Lazy Ass. Almost everything he did well came naturally. He was fast, hard-hitting, and had great hands—but if he had to work for it, it wasn't going to happen. Richardson spent seven years in the NFL, finishing in San Francisco in 1989. At twenty-eight, he was done with everything that came easy. He moved back to L.A., where he bounced from job to job, losing touch with teammates along the way. He was the blip that suddenly vanishes from the radar screen. His drug habit began to swallow his life, and he aged quickly. He got in trouble with the police. He was arrested. In the course of sixteen years, he was convicted twenty-one times. Five of the convictions were for felonies.

Following a routine traffic stop in 2006, the police found twenty-eight grams of rock cocaine and ten grams of amphetamine in his car. He was sentenced to one year in prison. Did that, got out, violated his parole and was sent back for thirteen more years. He was given a second shot at parole after just three. Ditka and Dent sent letters to the judge, begging for leniency. "I will help in any way necessary to try and find a way to help him through this tough time," Ditka wrote. "I believe his life is worth trying to save." "I know that Mike is troubled, but is a good man to his soul," wrote Dent. "I would deeply beg the court to give Mike one last chance."

"You reached heights in your career, in your life," Judge Kelly told Richardson before he was released. "You attained goals that few people in the world can ever attain. You were a Super Bowl champion. You tasted greatness. You have it inside of you . . . But the drugs are going to crush it all. And it has already crushed a substantial portion of your life."

Steve McMichael, the defensive tackle known variously as Ming the Merciless and Mongo, never stopped being Steve McMichael. Soon after his last football game, he was on the road with the World Wrestling Federation. He took part in WrestleMania, fought Bam Bam Bigelow and Kama Mustafa, aka Papa Shango, aka the Godfather. Later, when McMichael moved to World Championship Wrestling, he worked as hero and heel, commentator, instigator, dispute settler, tag teamer, big talker, clown killer. He fought Ric Flair and Bill Goldberg and was involved in every plot and subplot of that impossible-to-follow netherworld. "It was fun for a couple of years," he said. "But the road . . . I'd be home two days out of the month just to get clean clothes. You start to smell like a carny in the midway." The hardest thing, he said, was "learning how to whip my own ass."

McMichael has remained a fixture on the Chicago sports scene, an aging giant with a bowl haircut, singing "Take Me Out to the Ball Game" during the seventh-inning stretch at Wrigley Field. He coaches the Chicago Slaughter of the indoor football league. He recently ran for mayor of Romeoville, a southwest suburb of Chicago. And lost. He was married, then divorced, then married again. His second wife is named Misty. He has a child. "I'll be sixty-five when she's fifteen," he said. "That's when I'm going to start letting her date. You know what I'm going to tell the little boys? I'm going to tell them, 'I'm so old now I ain't got no problem going to jail. Killing your little ass just helps support my free jailhouse nursing care. That way, I'm not a burden on my family.'"

Shaun Gayle was a special teams standout and a second-string defensive back on the '85 Bears. He recovered the ball Giants punter Sean Landeta whiffed on in the playoffs and ran it for a touchdown. He later replaced Fencik at safety. He spent a dozen years in the league and made the Pro Bowl in 1991. He was handsome—too handsome. A little is helpful; very presents problems. He became a television broadcaster and worked as a commentator on Sky Sports in the United Kingdom. You'd be flipping through the channels on a trip to London and there was Shaun Gayle explaining some intricacy of American football.

He lived in Deerfield, in one of those big houses on one of those flat streets that just go round and round. On October 4, 2007, an intruder broke into his house and shot and killed his girlfriend, Rhoni Reuter— she was seven months pregnant. In March 2009, the police arrested Marni Yang, described as Gayle's business associate. When the case went to trial in 2011, Gayle admitted he'd slept with Yang the night before the murder. Asked how often they had sex, Gayle said, "It was, on average, roughly two to three times in the course of a year." Yang was sentenced to life in prison.

Gary Fencik was attending Northwestern's Kellogg School of Business while the '85 Bears were making their run. It gave him a stunning résumé: Barrington High School, Yale University (BA), Kellogg School of Business (MBA), Chicago Bears (twelve years, two Pro Bowls, one Super Bowl, career interception leader). In negotiations for his last contract, he inserted a clause that guaranteed him the right to purchase four season tickets if the team ever built a new stadium. The seats had to be between the 40-yard lines. Those tickets, which Fencik got after the renovation of Soldier Field, are probably worth more than Doug Plank made in his entire career.

These days, Fencik sounds less like a football player than a banker, which he is: "As soon as I retired, I joined the firm I'm still with," he told me. "We manage pension assets with a focus on private equity. We have a venture capital group and our primary strategy is a fund of funds. We'll take ten, twenty million and put it into various ventures around the world."

Of course, the football thing—it never goes way. A few years back, Fencik served as head coach of his daughter's flag football team. What do you think happened? He went insane. Drills, meetings, options; reverses, tricks, flea flickers, the flying wedge—an arrow of adolescent girls blazing up the field. In the end, he had thirty plays, too many to remember, so he had them printed on armbands, which the quarterback could check as she took a knee in the huddle—just like the kind worn by the pros. When the team won it all, Fencik had a mini–Super Bowl trophy made for each player.

Buddy Ryan turned the Philadelphia Eagles into a power but never could win the big game. He was zero and three in the playoffs. Perhaps he was too defensive minded, overly attuned to just one side of the ball. After going ten and six in 1990, he was fired. He took the defensive coordinator position with Houston but was fired again, this time after he punched his own team's offensive coordinator on the sideline. When he arrived in Arizona in 1994, he told the press, "You've got a winner in town!" He lost half his games in 1994, more in 1995, and was fired before the '96 season. He suddenly seemed very old. His method—beat 'em down, build 'em up—was of an earlier era. You grab a kid by the face mask or call him fat Jap today, he'll call his lawyer. Buddy Ryan didn't change; the country did. He retired to a farm in Kentucky, where he trains horses. He has one named 46 Blitz, and another named FiredForWinning.

The decision came from the Bears front office: 1987 would be Walter Payton's last season. At thirty-three, he was no longer a broken field runner who could weave through traffic. On his best plays, he was good for three or four yards up the middle. "He [didn't] embarrass himself, but he had lost the stuff, no question," Ditka said. Payton played his last game in the playoffs against the Redskins. The Bears were down 21–17 with time running out. They had the ball on their own 36. "Fourth down and a season to go," said the announcer. Mc-Mahon was in the shotgun, Payton and Suhey behind. Mac licked his fingers, took the snap, got away from the rush, faked the bomb, then tossed a soft screen to Payton, who had nothing but open field ahead. Years before, Walter described this as his dream situation: give me the ball with everything on the line and ten to go. He went upfield, turned from a tackler, and raced toward the sideline, trying to beat his man around the end, but he no longer had the speed. He was driven out-of-bounds a yard short of the first down.

A second later, the game was over. A second after that, the stadium was empty. Darkness washed over the grounds. Only Payton remained, in his equipment, his chin strap buckled, waiting to be sent into a game that would never be played. He had his feet out, head down. "I'll always remember Walter, when we got beat by Washington, that last game, sitting on the bench till the stadium was just about empty," McMichael wrote. "He sat on the end of the bench like he was trying to suck it all in and remember where he was right then in his life. Just sitting with his head down, reflecting, like [Rodin's] statue of the Thinker."

"They paid me for football," Payton said, "but I would have played for nothing." Payton was never going to be satisfied showing apartments, or making combo meals. He was an adrenaline junkie. He might've been too old for football, but he was still a young man, and, when he left the game, he lost everything that made life fun. "It's like being a Vietnam vet," he said. "You go in and it's such a different world, and all of a sudden you come home and you're expected to just be normal and you're not normal." He spent years searching for ways to get the blood moving. He had affairs. He fired weapons. He raced for Paul Newman's stock car team. He toyed with a return to the game. With the failure of each attempt, his mood blackened—he treated himself with drugs. It's the typical experience of an NFL star trying to adjust to the blandness of civilian life.

As I read Jeff Pearlman's book *Sweetness*, I jotted down some of the symptoms said to characterize Payton at loose ends:

Took a lot of pills
Avoided old friends
Missed appointments
Gained weight
Was a lunatic for Brach's candy
Stopped working out
Cheated on his wife
Accidentally shot an employee
Made speculative investments, lost money
Worked as assistant coach for a high school basketball team
Lent his Super Bowl ring to a kid who lost it in a couch

"Walter Payton often found himself suffocated by darkness," wrote Pearlman. "Oh, he wouldn't let on as such. He smiled and laughed and told jokes and pinched rear ends and tried his absolute best to come across as the life of the party. Inside, however, happiness eluded Payton in the same manner he had once eluded opposing linebackers."

"I was definitely lost those first few years," Payton wrote. "I went through withdrawal when it was game time. It was the biological clock kicking in."

"It sounds like just about every other guy who ever had to adjust to normal life after the NFL," Kurt Becker told me.

As Pearlman wrote, Walter was a nut for Brach's. A piece of candy was like a plug of tobacco. His pockets were filled with wrappers. He sucked on them from morning till night, which is why he was annoyed, then alarmed, when he came upon one bum piece of candy, then another, then another. Then the stomachaches started, mild at first, then like knives. He tired easily, had to lie down in the afternoon. Smells began to bother him. Then everything lost its taste. The whites of his eyes turned yellow. He went to a doctor, who sent him to the Mayo Clinic. In December 1998, he was diagnosed with primary sclerosing cholangitis, a rare liver disease. The bile ducts stop working, the poisons build up, you start to die.

No one can say what had caused the disease. I wondered if it could have been all those years of punishment. He had not missed a start in thirteen seasons and now, still young, he was being erased from life. The doctors gave him a year, maybe two—he was put on the list for a liver transplant. He told few people about his illness, but it was hard to keep the secret. Payton's son Jarrett, a star high school running back, held a press conference to announce what college he would attend. A camera lingered on Walter, standing behind his son. He had lost fifty pounds in a few months. A reporter named Mark Giangreco blanched. "The man there who looks like Gandhi is the former Walter Payton," he said. "I think I could take him on."

The rumors that spread around the city—Payton is gay, Payton has AIDS—convinced him to go public with his disease. He appeared on Oprah and Larry King. He needed help finding a liver. He broke down at a press conference, hugging his son as the tears flowed. When a reporter asked if he was scared, Payton said, "Hell yes, I'm scared." A follow-up appointment at the Mayo Clinic found cancer. It had spread to Walter's liver, making him ineligible for a transplant.

Payton had always liked fullback Matt Suhey, but the illness made them even closer. "It's like the movie *Brian's Song*," said Payton, "only, in this version, it's the brother that dies." Suhey took Walter to the doctor, gave him medicine, drove him around. Payton was a joker. "Two weeks before he died, he told me he wanted me to take him to Mike Singletary's house," Suhey said. "We were driving around and Walter would say, 'That's his house.' So I'd go to the door and it would be someone who never heard of Mike Singletary. I'd look back and there was Walter sitting in the car laughing at me." Payton fought with Singletary when they played but wanted to see him before he died. He respected Singletary and needed his blessing. "I went in and got on my knees and began to pray as I held his hand," Singletary wrote. "When I finished praying, I got up . . . and looked at him and I couldn't believe the peace on his face. There was such peace, it was unbelievable. I didn't know that was the last time I would see him alive."

Payton died on November 1, 1999. He was forty-five years old. "He must have weighed 90 pounds," McMahon said. "Here's a guy that did everything to his body, he couldn't break it in thirteen years on the field. It was devastating. It sucks. Life's unfair sometimes, you know?"

"I will always remember Walter the great football player and Walter the champion for life," said Singletary, "but there's something that I realized, and something that I always knew but I had never really seen—a man who is created by God and was given a message to deliver. All of us are vulnerable at any moment, and as I looked at Walter in those final days, the glory of God was never more apparent to me. When I say that Walter was courageous, I mean courageous in coming to a realization that life is more than touchdowns. Life is more than all the great runs and everything. Life is to be lived at every moment, and you have to be courageous in life and death and he was. He made a difference. We all should be so lucky."

Speaking at the memorial a few weeks later, Singletary said, "Walter made one last great run. Fourth down, no time-outs, and he looked across the line of scrimmage and they were all there. He didn't have any blocking whatsoever. And as he looked, he saw they were there to take him out. Hate, fear, unforgiveness, selfishness, everything else you can imagine, they were there. And Walter was asking the question, How do I get past this? And as he looked forward, he just looked up and Christ was there saying, Walter touch my hand. Grace is yours today. And Walter took His hand. He didn't have to run, he didn't have to jump, he didn't have to earn it. It was free."

Ditka spoke next: "I think Coach Halas has finally got the greatest Bear of them all on his heavenly team. You know, when you think about all the guys who have gone before us, Nagurski, Luckman, Piccolo, Stydahar, Galimore, Farrington, Osmanski, George, Lee, Marconi, Dave Whitsell . . . all those great Bears have joined George Halas. He's saying, Hey, I've finally got the last piece of the puzzle, I've got the greatest Bear of all.

"Now, the Bible tells us very simply that all men are like grass and their deeds are like the wildflowers. Now, the grass will wither and the flowers will fall, but the word of the Lord will live forever. And I believe this in the bottom of my heart, I really do, and I've believed it for a long time. I know the two great commandments we are given. I know that Walter loved God. He honored God with his whole heart . . . and soul. He always kept God in front of him.

"The game is greater than the athletes who play it. It always has been that way and it always will be. Walter knew it, too. So when they make a mark against his name, it's not going to be whether he won or lost, but how did he play that game, and man, did he play that game. Walter Payton really played the game."

For most veterans, retirement is the story of their bodies: surgeries and pain; the saga of knees, the hymn of shoulders.

Wilber Marshall is bad knees and bad back and paying for every big hit. William Perry is stay-at-home, a man who got everything from the game, then had most of it taken away. But Dave Duerson's story is the most tragic of all.

Duerson was a great player, one of the All-Pros the Bears let walk away. He played for the Giants, then ended his career in Arizona in 1993. He made the reentry into civilian life look easy. He succeeded in business, worked for the players' union. He was a family man. He was loved by many people. Then, as he got into his forties, something changed. He began to forget, got lost in his own neighborhood. His mind became disordered. He had trouble making decisions. He had headaches. He was beset by inexplicable rage. His mood turned dark. He was sad. He was mean to the people he loved. He was confused, and sick, and hurt, and angry, and tired.

On February 17, 2011, Duerson was found dead in his house in Sunny Isles Beach, Florida. He'd shot himself in the chest. He had sent a text to his family saying he was going to shoot himself in the chest because he wanted his brain preserved and studied by the doctors at the Brain Bank in Boston. "It took everybody by surprise 'cause we'd seen him a month before that happened," McMahon told me. "He was a little quieter than usual but you couldn't have told me he was going to shoot himself. I wouldn't have believed that. I guess in his note he said he was tired of not being able to make a decision. He was always a bright guy. At the end, he couldn't find his way home and stuff like that. And when you have a guy with that kind of pride, it was like, well, what else can I do?"

Duerson was convinced he was suffering from chronic traumatic encephalopathy (CTE), an Alzheimer's-like disease that's been found in an increasing number of dead football players. CTE, which results from repeated head trauma, causes memory loss, mood swings, depression. It can be diagnosed only in an autopsy. After the Brain Bank issued its Duerson report—he was indeed suffering from CTE—his death, along with the deaths of, among others, Mike Webster of the Steelers, Andre Waters of the Eagles, and Junior Seau of the Chargers, fueled a crisis that is threatening the future of football. Does the game give its own players brain damage? When you cheer a big hit, are you cheering the onset of a disease that will eventually rob a person of everything?

I interviewed Chris Nowinski, who, according to his website, is "the co-founder and president of the Sports Legacy Institute, a non-profit organization dedicated to solve the sports concussion crisis, and serves as a co-director of the Center for the Study of Traumatic Encephalopathy at Boston University School of Medicine." At the center, also known as the Brain Bank, doctors study deceased athletes who'd been showing symptoms of the disease. It's usually Nowinski who gets in touch with the families, asks them to tell their stories and donate the brains of their loved ones. He grew up in Chicagoland, where he was a standout high school football player. He went on to play at Harvard, before becoming a pro wrestler. He was the WWE's first Harvard alum, but his career was cut short by a concussion. He grew alarmed when his symptoms—dizziness, nausea—did not go away. He began talking to doctors, asking questions. He eventually published his findings in the book *Head Games: Football's Concussion Crisis*. It's this work that led him to the Brain Bank.

When I asked about the symptoms of CTE, he said, "We know it must start while you're still an active athlete, so the deterioration is happening from the teens or twenties or even earlier, but there's no defined time when symptoms appear. It depends on a number of factors, from genetics to trauma to how concussions were treated. The most common symptoms include cognitive disorders, short-term memory problems, depression. These behavior disorders are often highlighted by impulse control problems, which appears to have been a problem for Mr. Duerson."

When Nowinski was seventeen, he won an award honoring the best high school linebacker in the Chicago area. It was presented by Duerson, who was twenty-nine. They chatted on stage, posed for a picture. The next time Nowinski saw Duerson was on a surgical table in Boston, where his brain was being removed from his skull.

"How bad was Duerson's disease?" I asked.

"Dr. Ann McKee described it as moderately severe," he told me. "In other words, it wasn't in an early stage."

"How many pro football players do you think have it?"

"We ran the numbers on NFL players who died over a one-year period. We had gotten fifteen or so of those brains and they all had it. That meant three or four percent. But it's only that low if every person we did not look at did not have it, and that's unlikely. I believe we're going to find an actual number eventually and it's going to be very significant."

"Should parents let their kids play football?"

"I'm uncomfortable with children playing football the way it's played today," he said. "We've proven that we have this in teenagers who are getting it in high school football or youth football. The day we can diagnose it while people are still alive will be the day we'll have to ask the world, 'What percentage of kids is allowable to have this disease from playing a sport?' I challenge anyone to make that number higher than zero."

I sometimes wonder about the legacy of big hits—not just the damage they do to the body and brain but the way they affect the psyche. Once, in a hockey game, when I was about sixteen, I got caught behind the net with my head down and a kid named Oscar hit me so hard it did not even hurt. I found myself a few seconds later sitting ten feet from the puck, thinking about a spiderweb I had seen the previous summer in Eagle River, Wisconsin. I was in a daze and I stayed that way for a week. I kept playing hockey but never again played the same way. I had realized that I could break.

"I recently had the opportunity to meet a player that I forced out of the National Football League," Doug Plank said as we drank coffee beneath an acacia tree. "And I have to tell you, it isn't a good memory. This was a receiver running a deep end route, a dig route—he dashes fifteen or twenty yards down the field and crosses the middle. I remember this once—don't ask me why—I made a decision to hit him low. I tore his cartilage, his ACL, his MCL. It was over for him in an instant. He lay on the ground in agonizing pain. And I could hear this groan—it came from the deepest part of his person. I remember not feeling good about that. Then, about two months ago, I ran into that person. Here, in town. It was so hard. It would have been easy to duck in a corner. I knew he was there. But I thought, You know what? I want him to know how I felt that day. I never hit a person low again. If I hit a guy from waist up, okay, they might get a hip pointer, break a rib, get knocked out. But they're coming back. You're not tearing up their career. I walked over to him and said, 'I want to tell you how sorry I am.' Well, I got to tell you, two grown men broke out in tears right there. He goes, 'You don't know how much I thought about you over the years, wondered who you were, what kind of person, and why you did this to me.' And I told him I felt the same way and often thought of him. It's not one-sided. You do something, you walk away and forget it. It's not like that. You live with these things for a very long time."

19

ROAD TRIP TO CANTON

Last summer, I got in my car and drove west. I had been working on nothing but the Bears for a year, and all of a sudden I was overwhelmed by the desire to see some of the places that gave birth to professional football, the coal towns that, once upon a time, turned out quarterbacks as they had also turned out car parts and steel.

Starting in Connecticut, I followed Interstate 87 across the Tappan Zee Bridge, then headed into New Jersey, Springsteen country, warehouses and weeds. If you listen to early, then middle Springsteen, you will notice how the amusement parks of youth turn into the factories where you spend the rest of your life; how, like a trick in an old movie, the Ferris wheel dissolves into "the machines and the spires," the foundry's fiery dynamo. You might imagine sports being developed on farms or in country towns, but pro football was popular in big towns from the start, its field following the contours of two things that define modern life: the city block and the TV screen.

The Pennsylvania Turnpike goes right by Carlisle, but the tollbooth lady had never heard of Jim Thorpe or the school he made famous early last century. Thorpe was sixteen when he enrolled at the Indian Industrial School, a Dickensian institution meant to prepare Native Americans for a life in the machine trades. It's where Thorpe carried his first football. Many consider him the best athlete the United States has ever produced. The school is a military base now. At the entrance to the gym, I stood before a statue of Thorpe, Greek in style, the athlete holding a discus as a lesser man might hold a remote control. He was ruddy, with a pocked face and coarse hair and a body that went to seed in his middle years, but pictures at Carlisle show him in his youth: dark eyed and strong. The stadium where Thorpe played survives, the field overlooked by an old-fashioned grandstand—you half expect to see a rubber tycoon in spats sitting by the rail. White men filled the bleachers on Saturdays, excited to watch Indian teams fight, a spectacle that, a few decades before, could have been enjoyed only at a Wild West Show. As the star of the first great professional team and the NFL's first commissioner, Thorpe gave football its uniquely American identity.

The road to Pittsburgh leads through tunnels and past towns, through Appalachian Mountain hollers where the sons of miners have yet to hear of George Halas's modern T-formation. The city appears all at once, a scrim of bridges and buildings stained to a deep mottled rust. The first pro leagues began around here, in sooty towns that stud the bituminous mountains, first as a recreation for workers, a diversion between shift whistles, then as a real competition with paid ringers playing under assumed names. The Packers, who joined the NFL in its second season, are the last of the factory town teams, preserved as a reminder of origins. In this sense, the NFL is not unlike *Don Quixote*: a parody of a library of romantic literature that's ceased to exist. The books are gone, but the joke remains.

I made two stops on my way out of Pittsburgh: Beaver Falls, the birthplace of Joe Namath, and Aliquippa, the hometown of Mike Ditka. Johnny Unitas worked on a road crew in Aliquippa. It might be the bleakest place I've ever been. Once the booming home of J & L Steel, it began its decline when the mill closed in the 1980s. Just about every store on Main Street was boarded. The people who remain appear trapped. The high school is on a hill above town. The football field is in a valley, ratty, rocky, surrounded by row houses built for workers who died a generation ago. In such places, it can seem the people have just one thing to offer: their bodies, which they fed to the factories as they feed to the game.

What happens to such a place when the world changes? When an economy that had been about bodies and brains gives way to an economy about brains alone? In Aliquippa, you realize that violence was a crucial aspect of the game from the beginning, the hitting a cure for every kind of mood, the way that, when you are so low you have to reach up to touch bottom, nothing beats getting drunk, going to town, and picking a fight with a man twice your size. For some, pro football's appeal is the aerial assault, the ballet of receivers getting both feet inbounds, but for others it's the Stone Age pleasure of watching large men battle to the point of exhaustion. There are moments when the game is able to capture what it's like to be alive in a world filled with friends and enemies, and some help you, and some hurt you, and there is a place for teamwork and intelligence, but the winner is usually the person who can stand the most and take it the longest and get back on his feet just once more than he's been knocked down.

The country opens up as you cross into Ohio, the gloomy mill towns giving way to corn and silos, farms that stretch to the horizon. The Pro Football Hall of Fame had my car in its tractor beam. Why Canton? Because that's where the league was founded, in Ralph Hay's Hupmobile showroom. The exhibit begins with a statue of Thorpe and continues through displays of old equipment: cleats, jerseys, football pants, and, most tellingly, helmets, which evolved from none at all to leather, plastic, then whatever space-age material they're made of now. The museum's holy of holies is a dimly lit circular room lined with busts of the anointed, starting with George Halas and Curly Lambeau and ending, for now, with Cortez Kennedy and Curtis Martin. I compare the mood in this room, where grown men, in their jerseys, wander among iron heads, somber, serious, even a little sad, to the mood at national memorials, where we bear witness to some crucial American moment. Football is a religion, a shared history of victories and defeats.

When I talked to old gridiron men like Dick Stanfel, an offensive lineman who went All-Pro for the Washington Redskins in 1952 and 1953, or Bill Tobin, who played running back for the Houston Oilers in 1963, they spoke of football as "already gone," the sport having evolved from the ball control game of their youth into a kind of "basketball on grass." According to these men, football is violent by design. It became a sensation because of television but also because it expressed certain truths about American life: the dangers of the mines and mills; dirt, struggle, blood, grime; the division of labor; the all-importance of the clock. Football was not a reprieve from working life, it was that life translated into another language.

The phrase "already gone" was especially striking, as it seemed to suggest not just changes in the game but also the death of the hard-scrabble towns that gave pro football its ethos. These men were dismissive of rules meant to protect quarterbacks and wide receivers. The forearm shiver, the clothesline, the head slap that sent stars turning not unpleasantly around your helmet: getting hurt's always been part of it. Have the injuries gotten so much worse? No one really knows because no one bothered to examine the veterans of the '33 Giants or '46 Bears or '64 Packers who became bewildered or angry in retirement, or made a spectacle of themselves at alumni dinners. They did not count them because they did not know, and they did not know because they did not care. Football was just another risky job in a nation filled with them, and a better, more interesting life than that of railroad welder (Ditka's father) or coal deliveryman (Unitas's father). Danger was the not unreasonable cost of playing the game. Why do you think both sidelines go ghostly when a man stays down? Because each player knows it can all be over in a moment: not just the game, or the season, but everything. It's one of the truths that make football more tense than other sports. The stakes are high and the pain is real.

I used to hope the Bears would lose the coin toss so the 46 defense would come out first. I wanted to see the other team not just beaten but annihilated, their quarterback too intimidated to look downfield. In your mind, the opposition becomes the enemy, and there's nothing more satisfying than seeing your enemy humiliated. Yes, it's just a game, but for a few hours, it feels like justice.

But I've come to rethink some of my taste for the knockout blow. It's impossible to watch the player who stays on the ground without guilt. What have you just seen? A ten-yard loss, or the beginning of a trauma that will define a man's life? The release experienced by a fan watching in 2013 is the same as it was for a fan watching in 1933, but the game itself is not the same. The players have gotten so big, so athletic, and so fast—it's as if football has outgrown its skin, as if the stars have become too powerful for their own good. In the early days, when the iron cities of the Midwest were booming and an upper-deck seat could be had for around five bucks, the stands were filled with the same sort of men who filled the rosters. A blue-collar league for a blue-collar crowd: pipe fitters and burners, men who worked with their hands and gave up their bodies. The hardship of the game was more than just a spectacle. It echoed the physical and mental challenges these people faced every day. Seeing your own struggle at a remove is a kind of transcendence.

But the players and fans parted company long ago. An NFL game, where bad seats can cost over a hundred bucks, has too often become a rich man's diversion. It's one reason Gary Fencik was a hero in Chicago: he connected the gridiron to the skybox. But when we watch from home, as if from a million miles away, we witness a surreal drama: a Sunday afternoon passion play, the quarterback on the road to Calvary. It's only when a player goes down that we remember it's a contest of actual human beings, many of whom begin to fall apart before they retire. And so even the most gung ho of us cannot help but feel conflicted. On the one hand, there's no better, faster, more exciting sport. On the other, the consequences are real; the hit lasts a moment but the effects linger. Like the man in the Hitchcock movie, we know too much.

Is there a way to protect athletes, to reform the sport without losing the old zipperoo? That's what the owners, players, and everyone who cares about it is searching for: the fixes that can change everything yet preserve what's important. If we fail, some worry that football will go the way of boxing. Not because people won't watch, but because parents won't let their children play. (I don't know if I'll let my sons play.) Those who love it know it has to change, as it has changed in the past. It was a scrum that took to the air. It was checkers that turned into chess. Here's what I tell my friends: don't fear, as every reform has eventually resulted in a better game. I only hope that, no matter what shape these regulations take, there will be some George Halas on the Chicago sideline to spot the loophole that turns the new rule into an explosion of points. As you follow a team but only love a player, I find that as much as I love big hits, I love Dave Duerson more.

20

I DID IT MY (FUCKING) WAY

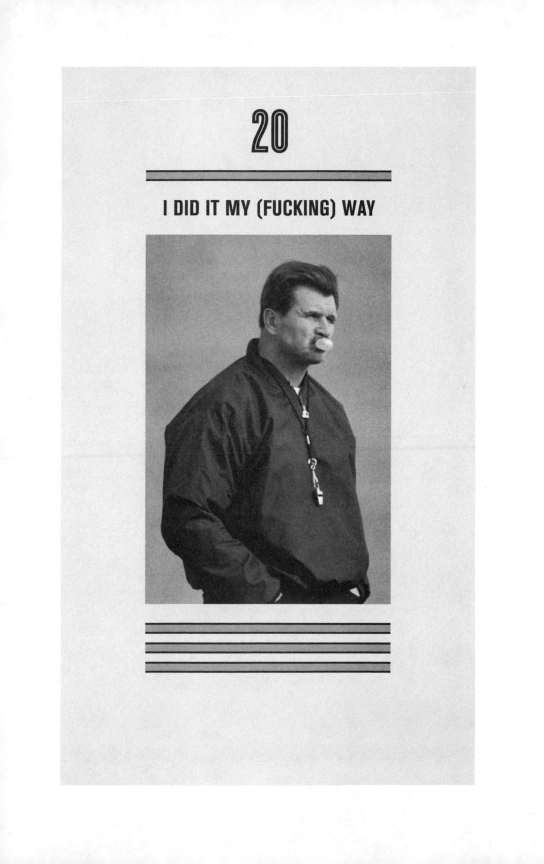

I met Mike Ditka on the second floor of his restaurant— Ditka's—on East Chestnut Street in Chicago. He was wearing black— all black, nothing but black, in the way of Johnny Cash. He was as big as a bear and looked like a bear and it was clearly a struggle when he got up to shake my hand and look me over. He has an artificial hip, fake everything. Jim Morrissey had warned me about Ditka. He said he was tough and mean and would give me a hard time.

"Tough and mean," I said, "but with a heart of gold?"

"No heart of gold," said Morrissey.

Ditka held my hand, looking down at me as a man looks down at something from a great height. The room was packed. I felt every eye, the eyes of a thousand fans. The walls were covered with murals. Halas, Grange, McMahon, Payton—they were there, too, looking down on him looking down on me. "Why the hell would you want to write about the '85 Bears?" Ditka asked. "Do you know how many people have written about that team?" He was still holding my hand, enveloping it in his giant paw, challenging me.

"Why did you run that same offense all those years?" I asked. "Presumably you believed you could win with it and could do it better than it had ever been done."

He thought for a moment, grunted, said, "Good answer," and invited me to sit down.

I asked him everything I had ever wanted to ask: about McMahon in Minnesota, and Sweetness, and the 46, and Plank, and Halas, and

Luckman, and Aliquippa, and the steel towns, and the work ethic, and America, and my own life, and what should I do? And is it better to accept the world as it is and be happy or to struggle and be miserable? In a sense, life is nothing but a search for a coach: Ditka found his in Halas and I found mine in Ditka.

He would never make it to the Hall of Fame as a coach. He's too idiosyncratic, too particular to one moment and one team, but he was a great leader, not just for a group of players but for an entire city. For many years, I continued to follow the Bears mostly because I wanted to see Ditka succeed. By 1992, he seemed like the last survivor of an ancient order: all the old players had left or retired. It seemed McCaskey was merely waiting for the right occasion to get rid of Ditka, too. As long as Iron Mike was at the helm, the Bears would be Halas's team.

It happened in 1993. Playing in Minnesota, Jim Harbaugh called an audible that led to an interception. Ditka gave his quarterback the business on the sideline. He'd done the same with Avellini and Lisch, but it was a different age. McCaskey fixed on the incident: *Who, after seeing that, would want to play for this team?* A few days later, while participating in a call-in radio show, Ditka got in an argument with "Neil from Northlake." Driven to the edge of his temper—he never could control his temper—Ditka told Neil from Northlake, "My office is at 250 Washington Street in Lake Forest, and if you care to come up there, I will kick your ass."

The Bears finished the season 5 and 11, Ditka's worst since his first years with the club. Mike McCaskey took the coach aside, told him to pack his stuff, clear out. It was over. Ditka had another year on his contract. He asked if he could finish it. McCaskey said no. The next day, the decision was announced at a press conference in Lake Forest. Extra police were on hand. The front office feared a violent reaction from fans. You don't cashier General Patton. Ditka stood before reporters. His hair was combed flat, his knuckles were huge, his mustache perfect. His voice broke. "'Regrets . . . just a few,'" he said, "'but too few to remember.'" He paused. "I can't sing it as good as Sinatra." Even in the final moment, Ditka botched the line. He walked out the front door of Halas Hall, where fans stood, heads down, crying. He scanned the crowd. Was he looking for Neil from Northlake?

When the news reached Aliquippa, the town went into mourning. People said the mood was the same as it had been the day that President

Kennedy was shot. I was in Manhattan, in a meeting at *Rolling Stone*. An old reporter told me in that gleeful way of old reporters: "Did you hear about your buddy, Ditka? They fired his ass." The blood rushed into my face. I asked to be excused and went down into the street, veins pounding in my head. I sat on a curb at 51st Street and Sixth Avenue, dropped my chin in my hand, and cried. Never had I felt so far from home.

NOTES

1: THE SUPER BOWL SHUFFLE

In addition to my memory, sources for this chapter include interviews, DVDs of old Bears games, and several books, including *Chicago Bears: The Complete Illustrated History* by Lew Freedman; *Da Bears: How the 1985 Monsters of the Midway Became the Greatest Team in NFL History* by Steve Delsohn; and *The Chicago Bears and Super Bowl XX: The Rise and Self-Destruction of the Greatest Football Team in History* by John Mullin. I interviewed many players and coaches from the Bears and other teams. The Steve McMichael quotes here and elsewhere come from his book—*Steve McMichael's Tales from the Chicago Bears Sideline*—as well as newspaper stories and books. Especially helpful was an interview McMichael did with my friend Mark Bazer, whose monthly live interview show at the beloved Chicago club The Hideout airs online at *The Huffington Post*. I spoke to McMichael on the phone, but he would not sit for an interview. He told me he was done with reporters, his gripe being Jeff Pearlman, whose *Sweetness: The Enigmatic Life of Walter Payton* had just been published. Its portrait of a depressed, suicidal Payton infuriated the running back's teammates. Asked what he'd do if he met Pearlman, Ditka said, "spit on him." In addition to my interview with Ditka, I made use of both his autobiographies, *Ditka: An Autobiography*, as well as its follow-up, *In Life, First You Kick Ass: Reflections on the 1985 Bears and Wisdom from Da Coach* by Mike Ditka with Rick Telander (Champaign, IL: Sports Publishing, 2005). Ditka's version of the Lord's Prayer is recounted in *Ditka*. I did visit Tulane during Super Bowl weekend and wound up going there—another way the Bears shaped my life. I've not spoken to Matt Lederer in twenty-five years. We had a falling-out in college. I'm sure it was my fault.

2: THE WAR ROOM

Ditka's press conferences can be seen on YouTube. I've watched them over and over, and they only get better. I suggest you make a weekend of it. On Ditka and the gum throwing, see Mike Royko, "In California, It's a Sticky Situation," *Chicago Tribune*, December 17, 1987. The victim's attorney told Royko, "We're not attempting to turn it into a mountain. But you have to understand that my client has been going to games for years, and this kind of thing has never happened to her before." I got the inside story from several Bears. Emery Moorehead's version was the most colorful. He laughed as he remembered the police showing up at the hotel in San Francisco. I interviewed Ron Jaworski at the offices of NFL Films in Cherry Hill, New Jersey, where I also interviewed several producers and broadcasters. NFL Films, started by Ed and Steve Sabol, is the house organ of the league. George Halas called the Sabols "the keepers of the flame." The Sabols are partly responsible for how the game is watched today. For more on this, see my article "They Taught America to Watch Football," *The Atlantic*, October 2010. The rest of the material in this chapter comes largely from interviews. I interviewed many of the '85 Bears in greater Chicago, including Otis Wilson, whom I met at a Park District office on the North Side. He wore a silky track suit and was supercool. I interviewed Plank on numerous occasions, first by phone, then in Scottsdale. It was these interviews that convinced me to write this book. In describing his experiences, Plank made me understand football in a new way.

3: THE OLD ZIPPEROO

I've drawn on many sources for my portrait of Halas, including obituaries, newspaper and magazine profiles, and my own interviews. Especially helpful was the coach's autobiography, *Halas by Halas*, as well as *Papa Bear: The Life and Legacy of George Halas* by Jeff Davis (New York: McGraw-Hill, 2004). See also Patrick McCaskey's memoir, *Bear With Me: A Family History of George Halas and the Chicago Bears*. Patrick McCaskey is a Chicago Bears board member and the team's senior director of special projects. On Pilsen and other Chicago neighborhoods, see *The Encyclopedia of Chicago* by James Grossman, Ann Durkin Keating, and Janice L. Reiff. On Mayor Daley, see *American Pharaoh: Mayor Richard J. Daley—His Battle for Chicago and the Nation* by Adam Cohen and Elizabeth Taylor. A great book. Also see Mike Royko's portrait of political power, *Boss: Richard J. Daley of Chicago*.

On the history of football, see *Pigskin: The Early Years of Pro Football* by Robert W. Peterson; *A Brief History of American Sports* by Elliott J. Gorn and Warren Goldstein; and *What a Game They Played: An Inside Look at the Golden Era of Pro Football* by Richard Whittingham. An excellent primer on all this is *How Football Explains America* by Sal Paolantonio. Crane Tech: sadly, this is one of the schools Mayor Rahm Emanuel decided to close in 2012. See Noreen Ahmed-Ullah and Joel Hood, "CPS Planning New Neighborhood School to Replace Crane Tech," *Chicago Tribune*, February 21, 2012. The school had been plagued by violence in recent years. Coach Robert Zuppke: in addition to books mentioned above, see *The Galloping Ghost: Red Grange, an American Football Legend* by Gary Andrew Poole. Before taking the job at the University of Illinois, Zuppke coached at Oak Park High School, where one of his players was Ernest Hemingway. After Zuppke was fired in 1941, he went to Cuba and spent quite a long time living in Hemingway's house, the Finca Vigía. On Halas's season with the New York Yankees, see *The Baseball Encyclopedia: The Complete and Definitive Record of Major League Baseball.* Wally Pipp took himself out of the lineup, complaining of a headache. The Brooklyn Robins would later change their name, first to the Trolley Dodgers, then just the Dodgers. Bill Belichick and Wes Welker: Belichick's Wally Pipp comment was captured on *Hard Knocks*, the NFL Films reality show, coproduced with HBO, where it airs. Iron Man Joe McGinnity: born in Decatur, he had several outstanding seasons with the Baltimore Orioles and New York Giants. Pitching for the Giants in 1904, he went 35–8 with a 1.61 ERA. Ralph Hay and the early history of the NFL: see *Old Leather: An Oral History of Early Pro Football in Ohio, 1920–1935* by Chris Willis (Lanham, MD: Scarecrow Press, 2005), in addition to the books mentioned above.

4: LEATHER HEADS

The history of the NFL and the Oorang Indians: see *Pigskin: The Early Years of Pro Football* by Robert W. Peterson, as well as the books mentioned above. See also *Passing Game: Benny Friedman and the Transformation of Football* by Murray Greenberg (I love this book). On racism, George Preston Marshall, and the Washington Redskins, see *Showdown: JFK and the Integration of the Washington Redskins* by Thomas G. Smith. On Jim Thorpe, *Jim Thorpe: Original All-American* by Joseph Bruchac; *Native American Son: The Life and Sporting Legend of Jim Thorpe* by Kate Buford; and *Jim Thorpe: World's Greatest Athlete* by Robert W. Wheeler. Some of this history is told at the NFL Hall of Fame in Canton, Ohio. Some more is told at the Heinz Museum in Pittsburgh, which has a wing dedicated to the sporting life of western Pennsylvania. It opens with a life-size statue of Franco Harris making "the immaculate reception," which was probably a blown call by the referee.

5: THE EYE IN THE SKY

On Halas and the move back to Chicago, see the books above, as well as *"Then Ditka Said to Payton . . ." The Best Chicago Bears Stories Ever Told* by Dan Jiggets; *Chicago Bears: The Complete Illustrated History* by Lew Freedman; *Halas by Halas*; *Papa Bear* by Jeff Davis; *Pigskin: The Early Years of Pro Football* by Robert W. Peterson; and *Bear With Me* by Patrick McCaskey. The story of Bronko Nagurski and the brick wall appears in many places, including *What a Game They Played: An Inside Look at the Golden Era of Pro Football* by Richard Whittingham. For more on Nagurski, see *Monster of the Midway: Bronko Nagurski, the 1943 Chicago Bears, and the Greatest Comeback Ever* by Jim Dent. For more on Wrigley, see *Wrigley Field: The Unauthorized Biography* by Stuart Shea. (Funny that a guy named Shea wrote a book about Wrigley.) Buffone's comment on Halas's coaching styles appears in *Papa Bear* by Jeff

Davis. For the history of gridiron innovations, including the modern T-formation, see *Luckman at Quarterback: Football as a Sport and a Career* by Sid Luckman; *Halas by Halas*; and *Papa Bear*. Also *Return to Glory: The Story of the 1985 Chicago Bears* compiled by the *Chicago Sun-Times*. On George Wilson: he was the head coach of the Detroit Lions when George Plimpton went undercover to train with the team, the result being his phenomenal book, *Paper Lion*. Plimpton described Wilson and the famous block. Great resources on Sid Luckman are the sports reports that appeared in the New York papers after most of his high school and college games, including the *New York Times*. See the *Times* obituary, William N. Wallace, "Sid Luckman, Star for the Bears, Dies at 81," July 6, 1998. On Luckman's college accomplishments, see the Columbia Lions website: gocolumbialions.com. I went to summer camp with Sid's grandson. We had an epic fistfight in the rain—it's still talked about in Eagle River, Wisconsin. Before Luckman died, a member of his family asked me to write a book about him. Stupidly, I said no; I worried I could not do him justice. I wrote an essay on Luckman in the recent anthology *Jewish Jocks: An Unorthodox Hall of Fame* edited by Franklin Foer and Marc Tracy. My chapter is "Sid Luckman: Hebrew Mind, Cossack Body."

6: THE QUARTERBACK

I relied on many books for this chapter. On the emergence of the modern NFL, I found a handful especially helpful, including *America's Game: The Epic Story of How Pro Football Captured a Nation* by Michael MacCambridge (New York: Random House, 2004); *Brand NFL: Making and Selling America's Favorite Sport* by Michael Oriard (Chapel Hill: University of North Carolina Press, 2007); *Blood, Sweat, and Chalk: The Ultimate Football Playbook* by Tim Layden; and *How Football Explains America* by Sal Paolantonio. Bob Snyder, who came back to play QB for the Bears during the war, told his story in *Pigskin*. On George Preston Marshall, the Redksins, and race in the NFL, see *Showdown: JFK and the Integration of the Washington Redskins* by Thomas G. Smith. On Halas in the war years, see *Halas by Halas* and *Papa Bear*, as well as the official biography on the Bears' website, according to which Halas "spent three years in the South Pacific with the Navy, mainly organizing R&R and entertainment for weary troops." On Lombardi, see David Maraniss's *When Pride Still Mattered: A Life of Vince Lombardi*. Lombardi said, "Winning isn't everything, it's the only thing." The history of this phrase is fascinating. Reported in various forms over the years, it apparently comes from a football movie in which John Wayne played a broken-down football coach in need of a second chance. Lombardi was a big moviegoer. Ditka: "The past is for cowards and losers." This quote is reported in *"Then Ditka Said to Payton . . ." The Best Chicago Bears Stories Ever Told* by Dan Jiggetts. On Namath, there is more ink than there is water in the Caspian. You might start with *Namath: A Biography* by Mark Kriegel. For the title alone, I recommend Namath's autobiography, *I Can't Wait Until Tomorrow . . .'Cause I Get Better-Looking Every Day*. I made use of these books, as well as the profiles that *Sports*

Illustrated published about the quarterback in the '60s and '70s, testaments to the New Journalism. Raiders v. Bears, 1984: this was featured as NFL Game of the Week in 1984, and a beautifully produced recap can be seen online at NFL Films.com. Mac's kidney injury: my best sources on this were interviews with Jim McMahon, Kurt Becker, and Emery Moorehead. Peter Gent's *North Dallas Forty* was published a few years after he retired from the Dallas Cowboys, where he'd been a wide receiver. It's probably the best book written about life in the NFL. Gent died in 2011; he was sixty-nine. On Cutler's injury, see Sean Leahy, "Jay Cutler Under Attack for Leaving Bears' Loss with Knee Injury," *USA Today*, January 23, 2011. Cutler's injury was given a different resonance when an MRI showed he had seriously hurt his knee. Still more doubt came the following season when Redskins QB Robert Griffin III played on a wounded knee, the result being a perhaps career-altering injury in the playoffs. For a wild take on all this, see the website SB Nation skewer ESPN's theory that "Jay Cutler is responsible for RGIII's knee injury," www.sbnation.com/nfl/2013/1/10/3861430/jay -cutler-is-at-fault-for-rg3s-knee-injury.

7: MIKE DISCO

On Ditka's life and biography, I relied on the books mentioned above, that is, Ditka's autobiographies as well as the biographies of Halas and the histories of the Bears. Each of these books takes a stab at Iron Mike's story. I also drew on the interviews that I did with men who played with Ditka and those who played for him at varying points in his career, including Danny White in Dallas, and Jim McMahon, Jim Morrissey, and Tim Wrightman in Chicago. Then the coaches and football executives who worked for and with Ditka: Dick Stanfel, Johnny Roland, Vince and Bill Tobin. Also Brian McCaskey. And then, of course, Ditka himself. To get a sense of the terrain, I visited Aliquippa, Ditka's hometown, and the country around it. I ate at Ditka's restaurant in Chicago and visited Ditka's resort in Florida. This turned into my story "Waiting for Ditka: Thirty Years After He Saved Chicago, the Fabled Bears Coach Is Everywhere—and Nowhere," *The Atlantic*, December 2011. On Ditka as a new kind of tight end, see Cooper Hollow, "Ditka: A Hall of Fame Career: Desire Helped Him Break the Mold at Tight End Position," *Chicago Tribune*, July 29, 1988. Teaching Ditka to catch: the numbers on the balls anecdote appears in *Papa Bear* by Jeff Davis: "Sid taught me to catch the ball and look at the number," Ditka told Davis. "He wrote numbers on the ball. I had to catch it and call out the number. I had to look at it all the way in and put it away before I started to run with it."

8: SUCKING IN THE SEVENTIES

A lot of the Chicago stuff in this chapter comes from my memory, which I corroborated or corrected by searching the archives of the *Chicago Tribune* and *Sun-Times*, as well as various books, including *The Encyclopedia of Chicago* and *Chicago: A Biography* by Dominic Pacyga. On Jimmy Piersall, see Jim O'Donnell, "Jimmy Piersall Covers All Bases: No. 37 Is Still Fired Up About His Field," *Chicago Tribune*, October 25, 1992. See also Frank Corkin's column, "Frank's Corner," which appeared in the *Meriden Record-Journal*, October 8, 1981, and included Piersall's entire comment, made during that interview with Mike Royko: "I think every ball club should have a clinic once a week for the wives because I don't think they know what the hell baseball is. First of all they were horny broads who wanted to get married, have a little security and a big, strong baseball player." Other sources include the NFL archives. On Sayers, see his autobiography, *I Am Third*. It was a basis of the movie *Brian's Song*. (He's third because God is first and family is second.) Also see *My Life and Times* by Gale Sayers. The jacket shows Sayers leaping over Ditka. On Butkus, see *Stop-Action* by Dick Butkus. This is the book that was treasured by McMichael and Singletary. Also *Butkus: Flesh and Blood* by Dick Butkus. On Butkus's retirement see "Butkus Wins $600,000 Lawsuit Against Bears," Associated Press, September 14, 1976. Sayers as a deer: it reminds me of what Coach Zuppke said about his running back Red Grange: "Red had that indefinable something that the haunted wild animal has—uncanny timing and the big brown eyes of a royal buck." Payton was the star of my childhood, so it was a pleasure to reread the old profiles. I found the following books useful: *Never Die Easy: The Autobiography of Walter Payton*, and *Sweetness: The Enigmatic Life of Walter Payton* by Jeff Pearlman. On Ed McCaskey, see *Papa Bear* by Jeff Davis; *Bear With Me* by Patrick McCaskey; *In Life, First You Kick Ass* by Mike Ditka; and *Chicago Bears: The Complete Illustrated History* by Lew Freedman. Other details come from discussions with players as well as Brian McCaskey. Also *It's Been a Pleasure: The Jim Finks Story: One Man's Football Journey* with contributions from seven award-winning sportswriters. Finks was the Bears' general manager from the mid-'70s to the early '80s. To further my argument about the sadness of big brothers whose little brothers surpass them, see *Walter & Me: Standing in the Shadow of Sweetness* by Eddie Payton. Jim Brown on Walter: "What kind of animal . . . ?" This quote comes from an NFL Films documentary on Payton, which was part of its *A Football Life* series.

9: READY, FIRE, AIM

Personal interviews were hugely helpful assembling these pages, especially those with Danny White, who played with Ditka in Dallas, and with Ditka himself. Other details come from books mentioned above on Ditka and the Bears. Ditka to the Eagles: the Eagles were actually coming off a decent season when Ditka showed up. They had gone 9–5 in 1966 but would finish 6–7–1 in Mike's first season with the club, and 2–12 in his second. On player statistics and team standings, see *The Football Encyclopedia* as well as pro-footballreference.com. Ditka's comments on his coaching tactics, specifically his instruction about hitting in the solar plexus, appear in his autobiography *Ditka*. He made similar comments to *Sports Illustrated* at the time. On Ditka's letter: I interviewed Neill Armstrong and got the sense that he felt Ditka had done him dirty with the letter. His anger at Halas is evident. When I asked him if Halas was tough, he said, "I'd say so. He fired me." On Mugs, see "George Halas Jr. 54, Dies in Chicago," *New York Times*, December 17, 1979. A legal battle followed the death. Halas's first wife suggested the death might have resulted from foul play, or else negligent medical care. Mugs's body was exhumed for a second autopsy in 1987, which showed nothing. (See Charles Mount and Rudolph Unger, "Judge OKs Halas Jr. Autopsy," *Chicago Tribune*, August 6, 1987.) Jerry Vainisi was the team's treasurer from 1972 to 1982. When Jim Finks left the team after Mugs died, Vainisi took over as general manager. Vainisi left the team after 1986 and later worked for the Detroit Lions. He retired from football altogether in 1995 and works as a lawyer in Chicago. He's known to many as the man who got rid of the Bears' cheerleading squad, the Honey Bears. (See Rich Lorenz, "Bears Say Cheerio to Cheerleaders," *Chicago Tribune*, November 16, 1985.) Vainisi's comments on Halas's plans appear in *Papa Bear* by Jeff Davis. On Ditka's first practices as the Bears coach: every player I spoke to told me his own version of the story. Especially helpful were Brian Baschnagel, Doug Plank, and Bob Avellini. The letter sent to Halas by "The Chicago Bears Defensive Team" was reprinted in *The Daily Herald* on Sunday, December 27, 1981 ("Halas Rewards Defensive Staff; Ryan Stock Grows"), as was the old man's response. In addition to books mentioned above, details in this section—the garbage bags and so on—come from interviews. Ditka versus Avellini: these stories appear in Ditka's book *In Life, First You Kick Ass*. I got more from interviews with Ditka and Avellini. On the last days of Halas, see *Papa Bear* and *Bear With Me*, as well as tributes and obits that filled the newspapers. (See Dave Anderson, "The Bear Who Really Was One," *New York Times*, November 2, 1983.) "Anybody but Michael": it sounds like a line from *The Godfather*. It's reported by Jeff Davis in *Papa Bear* and in several other books, including *The Best Chicago Sports Arguments: The 100 Most Controversial Questions for Die-Hard Chicago Fans* by John "Moon" Mullin (Naperville, IL: Sourcebooks, 2006), who adds the following: "Whether or not that actually happened has become almost superfluous; those were the sentiments of millions of Bears fans, if not precisely the founders." On Michael McCaskey, see "How the Chicago Bears Fumbled Away a Fortune," *Forbes*, September 13, 2010. On drafting the '85 team, I referred to articles, the book about Finks, and interviews with Ditka and Tobin, the men most responsible. I had dinner with Finks when I was an eighteen-year-old Tulane freshman, a wonderful night during which I plied him with questions, the answers to which have shaped my views. He told me, for example, that fans watching the 1979 draft booed when he took Hampton first, which shows you what people know.

10: THE FRIDGE

Much of the blow-by-blow on the San Francisco and Dallas games comes from interviews with, among others, Danny White, Gary Fencik, and Otis Wilson. When I asked Wilson to name the biggest hit he'd ever delivered, he said it came a season later, when he clotheslined Steelers receiver Louis Lipps, who was coming to make a crackback block: "It's easy to knock somebody out with a helmet," Otis told me, "but to get them with a forearm, that's impressive." I also watched these games. Again and again. Ezra Pound defined literature as news that stays new; to me, the game played by the Bears and the 49ers in 1985 is literature. Rick Telander's roof: Brian McCaskey told me this story, and it's been widely reported. Ditka's drunk driving: the coach writes about it in his first autobiography. McMahon writes about it in his book, too. I also got the story in interviews from McMahon, Moorehead, and others. As for the ticket, I saw it with my own eyes in the hallway at New Trier. Ron Jaworski dedicated a chapter of his book *Games That Changed the Game: The Evolution of the NFL in Seven Sundays* to the 1985 Dallas game, which he describes as the most violent he'd ever seen. See also every other book ever written about the '85 Bears, especially *Calling the Shots* by Mike Singletary. I got still more from interviews with Jaworski and his cowriter Greg Cosell at NFL Films, in New Jersey. The Everson Walls anecdote appears in *Steve McMichael's Tales from the Chicago Bears Sideline*. On Danny White's second knockout: the quarterback recently had surgery on his spine, which, he said, was a direct result of Wilson's hit, delivered almost thirty years ago. Jim Brown's quote—"the Bears beat people up"—appears in *Da Bears! How the 1985 Monsters of the Midway Became the Greatest Team in NFL History* by Steve Delsohn. On Dallas coach Tom Landry, see *Tom Landry: Man of Character* by Donnie Snyder, also *Tom Landry: An Autobiography*. On Bill Walsh, see *The Genius: How Bill Walsh Reinvented Football and Created an NFL Dynasty* by David Harris.

11: A RACE TO THE QUARTERBACK

The bedrock of this chapter is my interview with Gary Fencik. He talked about Buddy Ryan and the workings of the 46 defense. This interview was supplemented by others, especially those with Plank, namesake of the 46. Plank checked over all the formations drawn for this book and sent me his own rendering of the 46 defense. I also spoke to Jim Morrissey, Otis Wilson, Tyrone Keys, and Neill Armstrong, who claims a variation of the 46 was being played in Canada years before. I spoke to several quarterbacks who had to play against the 46, including Joe Theismann, Danny White, and Ron Jaworski. Cris Collinsworth gave me the wide receiver's point of view. See also Rex Ryan's DVD, *Coaching Football's 46 Defense* (Monterey, CA: Coaches Choice, 1999). Two books lay out the 46 better than most others: *Blood, Sweat, and Chalk: The Ultimate Football Playbook* by Tim Layden and *The Games That Changed the Game: The Evolution of the NFL in Seven Sundays* by Ron Jaworski. I interviewed Jaworski and Cosell, and both were extremely helpful. On Buddy's bio, I referred to interviews and the books mentioned above. See also *Play It Like You Mean It: Passion, Laughs, and Leadership in the World's Most Beautiful Game* by Rex Ryan. Jeff Fisher's quote—"Buddy had a grading system"— appears in *Da Bears! How the 1985 Monsters of the Midway Became the Greatest Team in NFL History* by Steve Delsohn. Dave Duerson's quotes on Buddy are included in *The '85 Bears: Still Chicago's Team*, compiled by the *Chicago Tribune*. Fencik talked about Al Harris and Todd Bell. Also see Brad Biggs, "Hard-Hitting ex-Bear Bell Dies of Heart Attack at 47," *Chicago Sun-Times*, March 17, 2005. Also *Steve McMichael's Tales from the Chicago Bears Sideline.* Plank told me he met Fencik before practice on the way to Lake Forest. Fencik's car had broken down, and he was hitchhiking. Plank picked him up. Plank believes he inspired Fencik, schooled him in the art of the big hit.

12: SHANE COMES TO THE METRODOME

This chapter is based on repeated watching of the Bears/Vikings game, as well as interviews with Ditka, McMahon, Steve Zucker (Mac's agent), Brian Baschnagel, Gary Fencik, and others. The event was extensively covered in the local papers. I saved a bunch of these stories for years and used them here. See also Ditka's *In Life, First You Kick Ass* and *Ditka.* A key text is Mac's autobiography, *McMahon! The Bare Truth About Chicago's Brashest Bear.* Details on McMahon's childhood come from these books, as well as my interview with the QB. His DUI was covered in the Florida papers ("McMahon 'Wasted' While Driving," Associated Press, November 10, 2003). Also of great help were the series of articles by John Branch in the *New York Times* about Derek Boogaard, the New York Rangers enforcer, who suffered from CTE and died of a drug overdose in 2011. The first piece, "A Boy Learns to Brawl," was published December 3, 2011. See also Alan Schwarz, "Duerson's Brain Trauma Diagnosed," *New York Times,* May 2, 2011. Alan Schwarz did groundbreaking work on CTE for the *Times*—a good place to start for anyone interested. See also Ben McGrath, "Does Football Have a Future? The N.F.L. and the Concussion Crisis," *New Yorker,* January 31, 2011. On Michael Vick's contract, see "Scoop Jackson," "The Meaning of Michael Vick's $100M," ESPN.com, September 7, 2011.

13: STAR-CROSSED IN MIAMI

The stuff on the Miami game comes from interviews and books, all those mentioned above as well as *Everyone's a Coach: Five Secrets for High-Performance Coaching* by Don Shula. Rex Ryan's quote about the aura of the 46 appeared in *The Games That Changed the Game: The Evolution of the NFL in Seven Sundays* by Ron Jaworski. Mercury Morris served three years in prison; his conviction was then overturned on grounds he'd been the victim of entrapment. See "Morris Is Freed," *New York Times,* June 13, 1986. "The Bears did not go with a nickel . . .": Shula's quote appears in Jaworski's *The Games That Changed the Game.* Hampton's comments on the Ditka/Ryan halftime fight appear in *Da Bears! How the 1985 Monsters of the Midway Became the Greatest Team in NFL History* by Steve Delsohn. "The Super Bowl Shuffle": Information on this infectious song and video comes from books listed above, as well as my interviews and experience. On the scandal regarding "The Shuffle," see " 'Super Bowl Shuffle' Accounting Due Soon," *Chicago Tribune,* July 29, 1986. Also Dan Pompei, "Gault Gets Credit for the Super Bowl Shuffle," *Chicago Sun-Times,* January 3, 1986. Deadspin ran an oral history of the Shuffle in the winter of 2012. For more on "The Super Bowl Shuffle," just go to YouTube and watch the thing.

The information in this section comes first and foremost from the game itself, which I watched then, watched now, and watched in between. As noted, I tried and failed to speak to Joe Ferguson, but I did get a great deal of information and insight from Ditka, Fencik, Tyrone Keys, Jim Morrissey, and Doug Plank. Ditka's quote on the Hit—"the lick Wilber put on Joe Ferguson"—comes from an ESPN special on the Bears. Mac's comment on the team plane returning from Detroit comes from *The Rise and Self-Destruction of the Greatest Football Team in History* by John Mullin, and from Tim Wrightman, who told me the same story.

In these chapters, I relied on the broadcasts of the games themselves, the record books, and the play-by-play, as well as interviews with participants. To this, I added details from the sports stories written at the time, as well as the reporting done in books: *In Life, First You Kick Ass* by Mike Ditka; *McMahon!* by Jim McMahon; *Da Bears! How the 1985 Monsters of the Midway Became the Greatest Team in NFL History* by Steve Delsohn; and *The Rise and Self-Destruction of the Greatest Football Team in History* by John Mullin. For a description of Lawrence Taylor's impact, see *The Blind Side: Evolution of a Game* by Michael Lewis. Also on Taylor: *LT: Living on the Edge* by Lawrence Taylor. The crackback block: it seemed to be on the verge of being banned in 2012. See "Requiem for the Crackback?" Deadspin.com, March 23, 2009, and Dan Hanzus, "League Will Consider Changes to Blocking Rules for Safety," NFL.com, November 23, 2012. McMahon and the headband: it was a topic in every interview. See also "Headband Brand Banned? After Drawing $5,000 Fine, McMahon Wears One for Rozelle," *Miami Herald*, January 13, 1986. The stuff on Chicago in the '80s is from my life. The details from New Orleans come from articles and stories published at the time, including the *Rolling Stone* cover story on McMahon. The Super Bowl itself is there for everyone to see. For the misery of Payton, I'm indebted to Payton's own account in *Never Die Easy*, as well as Jeff Pearlman's account in *Sweetness: The Enigmatic Life of Walter Payton* and my own interviews. Bill Murray on the sideline: I know how he got there. Brian McCaskey, known in the Bears' locker room for his Murray imitation—he could do every line from *Caddyshack*—gave Murray his press pass, adding, "Don't say where you got it. We're not supposed to give these away." Later, when a local TV reporter asked Murray how he'd gotten on the field, he said, "Brian McCaskey gave me his pass." Super Bowl controversy: on acupuncture and Mac's butt, see Jackie McMullan, "Acupuncturist Sticking to the Silent Treatment; Shiraishi Arrives, but Chooses to Avoid Prickly Issue," *Boston Globe*, January 23, 1986, and Dan Pompei, "False Story Brings McMahon Threats," *Chicago Sun-Times*, January 24, 1986. On the Packers fan saved by his regalia, see "Cheesehead May Have Been a Lifesaver: Packers Fan Uses Foam to Protect Self During Plane Crash," *Chicago Tribune*, November 29, 1995.

17: WHAT WENT WRONG

In this chapter, I have drawn on every book and every interview already mentioned. There is nothing I do not refer to here, nothing I did not have in mind. Especially helpful were interviews with Vince and Bill Tobin, as well as Ditka, Wilson, Wrightman, and Fencik. On cracking the 46, I was guided by my conversations with Jaworski, Theismann, Ditka, McMahon, and Vince Tobin. Charles Martin: his obit, "The Man Behind the Mean," written by David Haugh, appeared in the *Chicago Tribune* on February 1, 2005: "To Bears fans, Charles Martin will always be recalled for the body slam that ended Jim McMahon's season in 1986. But there was more to the man they buried Monday. Years before he threw quarterback Jim McMahon to the Soldier Field turf to ruin any realistic hopes the Bears had of repeating as Super Bowl champions in 1986, former Green Bay Packers defensive tackle Charles Martin struggled with knowing when to stop." McMichael's quote about punching McCaskey in the mouth comes from his own book, *Steve McMichael's Tales from the Chicacgo Bears Sideline*. McCaskey's explanation for the flimsy Super Bowl rings appears in *The Rise and Self-Destruction of the Greatest Football Team in History* by John Mullin, as does Howie Long's quote about taking a beating from the Bears. The Fridge's ring really is in the Hall of Fame. "He was a prime candidate . . .": This quote about Ditka's heart attack appears in *Chicago Bears: The Complete Illustrated History* by Lew Freedman.

18: MUCH LATER

I was lucky to attend the Bears ceremony at the White House and see those great players together again. The reports on each player were drawn from my interviews, as well as the books cited above. Shaun Gayle's troubles have been widely reported, as have those of Mike Richardson. Fritz Shurmur: the one Packer to disapprove of Mac wearing his Bears jersey to the White House was a defensive coach; he had been with the L.A. Rams in 1985, meaning he was on the sideline when McMahon flashed his Rozelle headband. On Mike McCaskey and Richard Daley, see Fred Mitchell, "McCaskey Returns Daley's Fire," *Chicago Tribune*, February 19, 1993. Here's how the story begins: "Bears President Michael McCaskey was a bit surprised when Mayor Richard Daley held a special press conference to register his displeasure over the firing of Mike Ditka." See also John Kass, "Daley Leads Chorus of City's Grabowskis: Wrong Guy Is Out," *Chicago Tribune*, January 6, 1993. On McCaskey's firing, see "Bears Oust McCaskey as Team President," Associated Press, February 11, 1999. On Mike Richardson, see Larry Welborn, "Prison Sentence for ex-NFL Star Reversed on Appeal," *Orange County Register*, June 3, 2010. On Shaun Gayle, see Dan Rozek, "Ex-Bear Shaun Gayle Says He Had Sex with Marni Yang Night Before Killing," *Chicago Sun-Times*, March 8, 2011. Gary Fencik works at Adams Street Partners. You can view his profile on the firm's website. Buddy Ryan, his ranch, his horses: see Joe Drape, "On Ryan's Farm, Memories Fresh and Fading," *New York Times*, February 3, 2007. Walter Payton's final game: Dave Anderson, "Walter Payton's Last Time," *New York*

Times, January 11, 1988. On Walter's illness and death, see Ditka's autobiography, as well as *Calling the Shots* by Mike Singletary; *Never Die Easy* by Walter Payton; and *Sweetness: The Enigmatic Life of Walter Payton* by Jeff Pearlman. On CTE, see the sources mentioned in the notes for chapter 12, as well as *Head Games: Football's Concussion Crisis from the NFL to Youth Leagues* by Christopher Nowinski.

19: ROAD TRIP TO CANTON

I wrote a story about this trip after I returned: "A Journey to the End of Football," *New Republic,* September 14, 2012. The chapter in this book is a second run at the same monkey, only now with the experience of writing the book behind me. Much of it's the same, some of it is different, this being evidence of just how greatly my own views on football and its future have evolved in the last year. The information was gathered mostly in the cities I visited on the trip: Aliquippa and Beaver Falls, Pennsylvania; Massillon, Ohio. The Hall of Fame in Canton is filled with information. Also of interest was the Heinz Museum in Pittsburgh. All in all, a great trip. On the way home, I stopped in Hershey Park. Additional information comes from books on Thorpe mentioned above, as well as the books by Ditka and Namath. See also *Johnny Unitas: The Best There Ever Was* by Roland Lazenby.

20: I DID IT MY (FUCKING) WAY

The details in this short section come from Ditka's biographies, other books about the Bears, articles from the time, and my own interview with the coach. In his column, Mike Royko said Ditka should have been more true to himself at that last press conference and "punched McCaskey and walked out."

INTERVIEWS

Tom Andrews, guard, Chicago Bears, 1984–1985
Neill Armstrong, coach, Chicago Bears, 1978–1982
Bob Avellini, quarterback, Chicago Bears, 1975–1984
Brian Baschnagel, wide receiver, Chicago Bears, 1976–1984
Kurt Becker, guard, Chicago Bears, 1982–1988; 1990
Cris Collinsworth, wide receiver, Cincinnati Bengals, 1981–1988
Richard Dent, defensive end, Chicago Bears, 1983–1993; 1995, three games (at the White House)
Mike Ditka, coach, Chicago Bears, 1982–1992
Gary Fencik, safety, Chicago Bears, 1976–1987
Ron Jaworski, quarterback, Philadelphia Eagles, 1977–1986
Tyrone Keys, defensive tackle, Chicago Bears, 1983–1985

Brian McCaskey, currently the senior director of business development, Chicago
   Bears
Michael McCaskey, president, Chicago Bears, 1983–1998 (at the White House)
Jim McMahon, quarterback, Chicago Bears, 1982–1988
Emery Moorehead, tight end, Chicago Bears, 1981–1988
Jim Morrissey, linebacker, Chicago Bears, 1985–1993
Chris Nowinski, the Brain Bank, Boston
Doug Plank, safety, Chicago Bears, 1975–1982
Kenny Rodgers, producer, NFL Films
Johnny Roland, running back coach, Chicago Bears, 1983–1992
Rob Ryan, producer, NFL Films
Ed Sabol, president and founder, NFL Films
Steve Sabol, president and producer, NFL Films
Dick Stanfel, offensive line coach, Chicago Bears, 1981–1992
Ken Taylor, defensive back, Chicago Bears, 1985
Joe Theismann, quarterback, Washington Redskins, 1974–1985
Bill Tobin, general manager, Chicago Bears, 1975–1993
Vince Tobin, defensive coordinator, Chicago Bears, 1986–1992
Danny White, quarterback, Dallas Cowboys, 1976–1988
Otis Wilson, linebacker, Chicago Bears, 1980–1987
Tim Wrightman, tight end, Chicago Bears, 1985–1986
Steve Zucker, lawyer, sports agent

BIBLIOGRAPHY

Baseball Encyclopedia: The Complete and Definitive Record of Major League Baseball. 10th ed. New York: Macmillan, 1996.

Blanchard, Ken, and Don Shula. *Everyone's a Coach: Five Business Secrets for High-Performance Coaching.* New York: Harper, 1996.

Bruchac, Joseph. *Jim Thorpe: Original All-American.* New York: Dial Press, 2006.

Buford, Kate. *Native American Son: The Life and Sporting Legend of Jim Thorpe.* New York: Knopf, 2010.

Butkus, Dick, and Robert W. Billings. *Stop-Action.* New York: Dutton, 1972.

Butkus, Dick, and Pat Smith. *Butkus: Flesh and Blood.* New York: Doubleday, 1997.

Chicago Sun-Times. Return to Glory: The Story of the 1985 Chicago Bears. Indianapolis: News Books International, 1986.

Chicago Tribune. The '85 Bears: Still Chicago's Team. Chicago: Triumph Books, 2005.

Cohen, Adam, and Elizabeth Taylor. *American Pharaoh: Mayor Richard J. Daley—His Battle for Chicago and the Nation.* Boston: Little, Brown, 2000.

Delsohn, Steve. *Da Bears! How the 1985 Monsters of the Midway Became the Greatest Team in NFL History.* New York: Crown, 2010.

Dent, Jim. *Monster of the Midway: Bronko Nagurski, the 1943 Chicago Bears, and the Greatest Comeback Ever.* New York: St. Martin's Press, 2003.

Dent, Richard, with Fred Mitchell. *Blood, Sweat, and Bears: Putting a Dent in the Game I Love.* Olathe, KS: Ascend Books, 2012.

Ditka, Mike, with Don Pierson. *Ditka: An Autobiography.* Chicago: Bonus Books, 1986.

Ditka, Mike, with Rick Telander. *In Life, First You Kick Ass.* New York: Sports Publishing, 2005.

Finks, Jim, et al. *It's Been a Pleasure: The Jim Finks Story, One Man's Pro Football Journey.* Newport Beach, CA: AMO Productions, 2003.

———. *The '85 Bears: We Were the Greatest.* Chicago: Triumph Books, 2010.

Fleder, Rob, ed. *Great Football Writing, Sports Illustrated, 1954–2006.* New York: Sports Illustrated Books, 2006.

Foer, Franklin, and Marc Tracy, eds. *Jewish Jocks: An Unorthodox Hall of Fame.* New York: Twelve, 2012.

Freedman, Lew. *Chicago Bears: The Complete Illustrated History*. Minneapolis: MBI Publishing, 2008.

Gent, Peter. *North Dallas Forty*. New York: William Morrow, 1973.

Gorn, Elliott, and Warren Goldstein. *A Brief History of American Sports*. New York: Hill and Wang, 1993.

Greenberg, Murray. *Passing Game: Benny Friedman and the Transformation of Football*. New York: PublicAffairs, 2008.

Grossman, James R., Ann Durkin Keating, and Janice L. Reiff, eds. *The Encyclopedia of Chicago*. Chicago: University of Chicago Press, 2004.

Halas, George, with Gwen Morgan and Arthur Veysey. *Halas by Halas: The Autobiography of George Halas*. New York: McGraw-Hill, 1979.

Harris, David. *The Genius: How Bill Walsh Reinvented Football and Created an NFL Dynasty*. New York: Random House, 2008.

Jaworski, Ron, with Greg Cosell and David Plaut. *The Games That Changed the Game: The Evolution of the NFL in Seven Sundays*. New York: ESPN Books, 2010.

Jiggetts, Dan, with Fred Mitchell. *"Then Ditka Said to Payton . . ." The Best Chicago Bears Stories Ever Told*. Chicago: Triumph Books, 2008.

Kriegel, Mark. *Namath: A Biography*. New York: Penguin, 2005.

Landry, Tom, with Gregg Lewis. *Tom Landry: An Autobiography*. Grand Rapids, MI: Zondervan, 1990.

Layden, Tim. *Blood, Sweat, and Chalk: The Ultimate Football Playbook*. New York: Sports Illustrated Books, 2011.

Lazenby, Roland. *Johnny Unitas: The Best There Ever Was*. Chicago: Triumph Books, 2002.

Lewis, Michael. *The Blind Side: Evolution of a Game*. New York: Norton, 2006.

Luckman, Sid. *Luckman at Quarterback: Football as a Sport and a Career*. Chicago: Ziff-Davis, 1949.

Maraniss, David. *When Pride Still Mattered: Lombardi*. New York: Simon & Schuster, 1999.

McCaskey, Michael B. *The Executive Challenge: Managing Change and Ambiguity*. New York: HarperCollins, 1982.

McCaskey, Patrick, with Mike Sandrolini. *Bear With Me: A Family History of George Halas and the Chicago Bears*. Chicago: Triumph Books, 2009.

McMahon, Jim, with Bob Verdi. *McMahon! The Bare Truth About Chicago's Brashest Bear*. New York: Warner Books, 1986.

McMichael, Steve, with Phil Arvia. *Steve McMichael's Tales from the Chicago Bears Sideline*. Champaign, IL: Sports Publishing, 2004.

Meggyesy, Dave. *Out of Their League*. Lincoln: University of Nebraska Press, 2005.

Miller, John J. *The Big Scrum: How Teddy Roosevelt Saved Football*. New York: HarperCollins, 2011.

Mullin, John. *The Rise and Self-Destruction of the Greatest Football Team in History: The Chicago Bears and Super Bowl XX*. Chicago: Triumph Books, 2005.

Namath, Joe, with Bob Oates Jr. *A Matter of Style*. Boston: Little, Brown, 1973.

Namath, Joe, with Dick Schaap. *I Can't Wait Until Tomorrow . . . 'Cause I Get Better-Looking Every Day*. New York: Random House, 1969.

Neft, David S., Richard M. Cohen, and Richard Korch. *The Football Encyclopedia: The Complete History of Professional Football from 1892 to the Present*. New York: St. Martin's Press, 1994.

Nowinski, Christopher. *Head Games: Football's Concussion Crisis from the NFL to Youth Leagues*. East Bridgewater, MA: Drummond Publishing, 2007.

Pacyga, Dominic A. *Chicago: A Biography*. Chicago: University of Chicago Press, 2009.

Paolantonio, Sal. *How Football Explains America*. Chicago: Triumph Books, 2005.

Parrish, Bernie. *They Call It a Game*. New York: Dial Press, 1971.

Payton, Eddie, with Paul T. Brown. *Walter & Me: Standing in the Shadow of Sweetness*. Chicago: Triumph Books, 2012.

Payton, Walter, with Don Yaeger. *Never Die Easy: The Autobiography of Walter Payton*. New York: Villard, 2000.

Pearlman, Jeff. *Sweetness: The Enigmatic Life of Walter Payton*. New York: Gotham Books, 2011.

Peterson, Robert W. *Pigskin: The Early Years of Pro Football*. New York: Oxford University Press, 1997.

Plimpton, George. *Paper Lion: Confessions of a Last-String Quarterback*. Guilford, CT: Lyons Press, 2006.

Poole, Gary Andrew. *The Galloping Ghost: Red Grange, an American Football Legend*. Boston: Houghton Mifflin, 2008.

Rice, Grantland. *The Tumult and the Shouting: My Life in Sport*. New York: A. S. Barnes, 1954.

Royko, Mike. *Boss: Richard J. Daley of Chicago*. New York: Dutton, 1971.

———. *One More Time: The Best of Mike Royko*. Chicago: University of Chicago Press, 1999.

Ryan, Rex. *Play It Like You Mean It: Passion, Laughs, and Leadership in the World's Most Beautiful Game*. New York: Doubleday, 2011.

Sayers, Gale, with Al Silverman. *I Am Third*. New York: Viking, 1970.

Sayers, Gale, with Fred Mitchell. *My Life and Times*. Chicago: Triumph Books, 2007.

Shea, Stuart, with George Castle. *Wrigley Field: The Unauthorized Biography*. Washington, DC: Brassey's, 2004.

Singletary, Mike, with Armen Keteyian. *Calling the Shots*. Chicago: Contemporary Books, 1986.

Smith, Thomas G. *Showdown: JFK and the Integration of the Washington Redskins*. Boston: Beacon Press, 2011.

Snyder, Donnie, with Ken Horton. *Tom Landry: Man of Character*. Grand Island, NE: Cross Training Publishing, 2009.

Stump, Al. *Cobb: A Biography*. Chapel Hill, NC: Algonquin Books, 1994.

Taylor, Lawrence, with David Falkner. *LT: Living on the Edge*. New York: Times Books, 1987.

Telander, Rick. *Like a Rose: A Celebration of Football*. Champaign, IL: Sports Publishing, 2004.

Wheeler, Robert W. *Jim Thorpe: World's Greatest Athlete*. Norman: University of Oklahoma Press, 1979.

Whittingham, Richard. *What a Game They Played: An Inside Look at the Golden Era of Pro Football*. Lincoln: University of Nebraska Press, 2001.

Wind, Herbert Warren, ed. *The Realm of Sport*. New York: Simon & Schuster, 1966.

ACKNOWLEDGMENTS

I'm going to thank everyone who helped with this book, then take a nap.

First, my father, who watched all those games with me in the 1970s and '80s; the same goes for the friends who were by my side at Soldier Field and on the couch in the family room, as well as the girlfriends who either cared or pretended to. Thanks to Brian McCaskey, who told me his stories and showed me around and, as they say in the mob, treated me real cordial. Thanks to Doug Plank, who, I mean, DOUG PLANK! His stories opened my eyes. Thanks to all the players and coaches I interviewed, with special emphasis on those with the old zipperoo—Baschnagel, Fencik, Wilson, Ditka, McMahon. Thanks to Jean Brown, who transcribed all the interviews and served as a first audience. Thanks to Julie Tate at *The Washington Post*, who fact-checked many of the chapters. Thanks to the editors who helped me along the way: Graydon Carter and Dana Brown at *Vanity Fair*; Scott Stossel and Chris Orr at *The Atlantic*; and Franklin Foer and Isaac Chotiner at *The New Republic*, who published an essay on my drive to Canton. Thanks to Ian Frazier, who helped with the first draft and played every position on the Sandy Frazier Dream Team. Thanks to Alec Wilkinson, Jerry Weintraub, David Lipsky, Mark Varouxakis, Denis Cohn, and Matt Lederer, wherever you are. Thanks to Pete Wilson and Sid Holt, whose editorial skill and passion for the Windy City arcana I tapped like a well. Special thanks to Roger Bennett, perhaps the only Englishman to fully grasp the magnitude and importance of the Bears. Thanks to Mark Bazer for his great interview with Steve McMichael, as well as his support. Ditto Jake Tapper, Neil Steinberg, Josh Karp, and Mark Kilroy. Thanks to Seth Davis—don't leave! All the trees are going to die! Thanks to my brother, Steven, and his wife, Lisa Melmed. Thanks to my sister, Sharon Levin, and her husband, my brother-in-law Bill. Thanks to Matt Levin, who helped with the research and is never anything but fantastic to be around. Thanks to my mother—gosh, I love my mom! Thanks to my brother a second time, and he knows why. Thanks to the Medoffs: Dorothy, Jeremy, and Stephanie. A different, more intimate kind of thanks to my wife, Jessica Medoff, who, when we were engaged, I used to introduce as the future Mrs. Jessica Medoff. She was as involved with this book as any person other than the writer can be—reading, editing, rereading, fact-checking, reading again.

Thanks to my agent, Jennifer Rudolph Walsh, at William Morris Endeavor, as well as to Anna Deroy, Erin Conroy, and Margaret Riley. Thanks to everyone at FSG, especially my editor, Jonathan Galassi, whom I intend to take to a Bears game this fall. A special thanks to Miranda Popkey at FSG, who has been my partner in all this gridiron madness. I mean it, Miranda. Thank you! Also at FSG: Debra Helfand, who among other wonderful things diagrammed all the formations but one and wrote up the team roster in the way I might have if my teachers had not forced me to write with my right hand. You will soon receive a bottle of Ditka's Kick Ass Red. Thanks to Jeff Seroy, Sarita Varma, and Kathy Daneman. Thanks to the people of Chicago—the greatest city on earth. Thanks to Glencoe, Big Al's, Soldier Field, Gilson Beach, Lake Shore Drive, Ming Lee, Cycle Hills, Todd Johnston, Duffy, the Mizz, Mike Dorn, and the Nerf football company. And of course thank you, Francis Albert Sinatra.

INDEX

Page numbers in *italics* refer to illustrations.

ILLUSTRATION CREDITS